Creating Preschool Television

Also by Jeanette Steemers

CHANGING CHANNELS: The Prospects for Television in a Digital World (ed., 1998)

SELLING BRITISH TELEVISION: British Television in the Global Marketplace (2004)

EUROPEAN TELEVISION INDUSTRIES (with Petros Iosifidis and Mark Wheeler, 2005)

Creating Preschool Television

A Story of Commerce, Creativity and Curriculum

Jeanette Steemers

palgrave
macmillan

First published 2010 by
PALGRAVE MACMILLAN

Palgrave Macmillan in the UK is an imprint of Macmillan Publishers Limited, registered in England, company number 785998, of Houndmills, Basingstoke, Hampshire RG21 6XS.

Palgrave Macmillan in the US is a division of St Martin's Press LLC, 175 Fifth Avenue, New York, NY 10010.

Palgrave Macmillan is the global academic imprint of the above companies and has companies and representatives throughout the world.

Palgrave® and Macmillan® are registered trademarks in the United States, the United Kingdom, Europe and other countries.

ISBN-13: 978–0–230–57440–3 hardback

This book is printed on paper suitable for recycling and made from fully managed and sustained forest sources. Logging, pulping and manufacturing processes are expected to conform to the environmental regulations of the country of origin.

A catalogue record for this book is available from the British Library.

Library of Congress Cataloging-in-Publication Data
Steemers, Jeanette.
   Creating preschool television : a story of commerce, creativity and curriculum / Jeanette Steemers.
      p.   cm.
   Summary: "Around the world small children are captivated by programmes produced especially for them – from stalwarts like Sesame Street to recent arrivals such as Teletubbies. Focusing on the UK and US, this book shows how the pre-school television sector has shifted from a small localised industry to a complex, commercially-driven global business"—Provided by publisher.
   Includes bibliographical references and index.
   ISBN 978–0–230–57440–3 (hardback)
   1. Preschool children.   2. Children's television programs.   3. Television and children.   4. Educational television programs.   I. Title.
   HQ774.5.S68 2010
   791.45083′3—dc22   2009047547

10   9   8   7   6   5   4   3   2   1
19   18   17   16   15   14   13   12   11   10

Printed and bound in Great Britain by
CPI Antony Rowe, Chippenham and Eastbourne

Contents

List of Illustrations and Tables

Illustrations

Tables

Acknowledgements

This book would not have been completed without the assistance of several organisations and numerous individuals. First my thanks goes to the Arts and Humanities Research Council (AHRC) whose provision of a Research Grant (119149) from September 2006 to September 2008 funded the research underpinning this project, including interviews with over 100 individuals and observations within a range of production environments and industry settings. I am also indebted to the AHRC's Research Leave Scheme (AH/G003572/1), which gave me the time to complete this book between September 2008 and May 2009.

Above all this project would not have been possible without the support of numerous members of the children's television community. It is not possible here to name everyone who participated in the project for reasons of space but also to respect anonymity, but I am especially indebted to Jocelyn Stevenson (TT Animation), Josh Selig and Dr Laura Brown (Little Airplane Productions), Chloe van den Berg (Entertainment Rights//Boomerang Media), Mellie Buse (Adastra Creative), Greg Childs (Save Kids TV) and Frank Klasen (SuperRTL, Germany) whose advice and help throughout the project have proved invaluable.

At this point I should also declare an interest, which stems from the time I spent working at HIT Entertainment between 1990 and 1993. I am therefore also extremely grateful to the late Peter Orton, the founder of HIT Entertainment, who was always encouraging and helpful when I was first thinking about this project in 2005. At Palgrave Macmillan I would like to thank Jill Lake who commissioned this book and Christabel Scaife who has guided it to completion. The research benefited enormously from the assistance and input of James Walters and Alessandro D'Arma, the AHRC project's post-doctoral researchers and Andrea Medrado, the project's research assistant. All three were always full of ideas, and their contributions have been insightful and indispensable. Alessandro is co-author of Chapter 10 and James is lead author of Chapter 11.

A substantial proportion of the research for this book is based on interviews with producers, broadcasters, regulators and marketing personnel. I am grateful to them for sparing the time in their busy schedules to talk about their work. In particular I extend my thanks to the many freelancers we spoke to and also to individuals in the following organisations:

UK: 3Line Media, Abbey Home Media, Adastra Creative, Apollo Television (Boomerang), Astley Baker Davies, BBC Scotland, BBC Wales, BBC Worldwide, The Canning Factory, CBeebies, Collingwood O'Hare, Contender Entertainment Group, Disney, Five (Milkshake!), Entertainment Rights, Foundation TV (RDF), Granada Ventures, HIT Entertainment, Illuminated Films, ITV Kids, Kids Industries, Kindle Entertainment, Nickelodeon, Ofcom, Open Mind Productions, Ragdoll Productions, S4C, Save Kids TV, Sianco Cyf, TT Animation, Tattiemoon, Tiger Aspect Productions, Turner Broadcasting, Wish Films.

US: Classic Media, Little Airplane Productions, Mad Duck Consulting, Nick Junior US, Sesame Workshop.

Europe: KiKa, Nickelodeon, SuperRTL, ZDF, (Germany), NOS/Z@ppelin, Nickelodeon (The Netherlands), Tiji, TFI (France).

I would like to thank my former colleagues at De Montfort University, Sue Thomas and Paul Smith, particularly for their contributions to two industry/academic conferences, we held at the University of Westminster in January 2007 and September 2008. I also thank my colleagues at the University of Westminster, particularly Peter Goodwin, Annette Hill and David Gauntlett for their support, advice and encouragement. Finally I owe the greatest debt of gratitude to my family – Koen, Kai, Finn and Bonzo.

1
Understanding Preschool Television as a Production Ecology

Around the world small children are regularly captivated by television programmes produced especially for them by adults who inhabit a distinctive production community. Alongside long-running series such as *Sesame Street*, more recent arrivals such as *Bob the Builder, Teletubbies* and *Dora the Explorer* have become enduring favourites with children and their parents. The international presence of these series alone underlines the phenomenal changes experienced by preschool television in recent years with the emergence of globally branded channels and blocks and the discovery of young children as a valuable target audience.

However, while there is a longstanding and rich seam of research devoted to the impact of television on young children, especially in terms of their cognitive development and educational achievement (see Berry and Asamen, 1993; Pecora et al., 2007), we know rather less about the professionals behind these productions or even the changing institutional and economic circumstances of children's television production in general. This stands in marked contrast to the vast literature on the effects of television on children, some of which has been critical of television's impact on children's attention, imagination and intellect (see Christakis et al., 2004; Kline, 1993; Postman, 1982; Winn, 1977).

We do know a great deal about the production of some preschool programmes. For example the history and development of US series *Sesame Street* has been widely documented since the late 1960s, because when it began it was unique in integrating educational content and research into production in ways that could be tested and publicised (see Fisch and Truglio, 2001; Lesser, 1975; Morrow, 2006). Similarly more recent productions like US series *Blue's Clues* have attracted attention because they incorporate different ways of addressing children and enhancing learning (Anderson, 2004). Yet we know much less about the production circumstances behind many other preschool shows and also about the assumptions that those who produce, broadcast and market preschool television make about their audiences. This is particularly the case for British shows, which, unlike *Sesame Street*, have often been driven less by pedagogical goals as by a desire to entertain children or simply to generate revenues for a series' investors.

Industry accounts of children's television tend to emphasise the special care taken by the industry in the best interests of children over and above any financial gain to themselves with claims about the educational and other benefits of their productions (see Laybourne, 1993). Anna Home, for example, former Head of BBC Children's, writes, 'Throughout the world it is apparent that the people who work in children's television do not do so for money or glory or power' (1993: 166). This may well have been true in the years of broadcast scarcity when most British children's television producers worked in the small self-contained world of BBC in-house production, which had its own programme-making philosophy and its own sense of continuity (ibid.). It may also have been true until the mid-1990s when the non-profit Public Broadcasting Service (PBS) dominated preschool broadcasting in the United States. Yet it is far less true of today's more disintegrated and globalised production environment where many production companies and freelancers exist alongside the in-house production units of large broadcasters and multimedia corporations, competing for scarce commissions and even scarcer funding in a highly competitive marketplace where the dynamics of production have changed considerably.

This in itself opens up some interesting questions about the broader institutional settings of production and the tensions that exist between creativity and commerce, between artistry and industry, between innovation and convention, between structure (organisational constraints) and agency (creative autonomy) (see for example Becker, 1982; Corner, 1999; Davis and Scase, 2000; Hesmondhalgh, 2007; Messenger Davies, 2006; Tunstall, 1993; Turow, 1984). Of course preschool television is not particularly different in this respect from other forms of television or cultural production which also have to cope with the institutional constraints of corporate intentions and conventions, limited resources and time and the inherent risks of production (Corner, 1999: 70; Kubey, 2004: 4). Like all productions preschool television is not simply 'producer-driven' (Tunstall, 1993), but subject to negotiation and compromise at all levels because it usually involves collective authorship and collaboration (see Becker, 1982: 24–5) around shared conventions, and increasingly diverse ownership and funding arrangements, which curtail individual creative autonomy to a considerable degree (Corner, 1999: 77; Cottle, 1995: 160–1). What makes children's television, including preschool television, different is the identification of children as 'a special audience with distinctive characteristics and needs' (Buckingham, 2005: 468), who require protection from commercial exploitation and 'from the consequences of their own vulnerability and ignorance' (Davies et al., 2004: 479). This suggests that different priorities, relating to commercial, creative or audience considerations may prevail at any one time.

Bearing these considerations in mind, and drawing primarily on interviews and observations from Britain combined with further evidence from US experience, this book constitutes an attempt to provide systematic analysis of one small part of children's television, preschool television, a section of the children's market that has changed radically since the mid-1990s, and is arguably quite distinctive from other forms of children's television in respect of how its audience is conceived, its economic underpinning and aesthetics. The book draws heavily on British examples, because the research underpinning it was funded by an Arts and Humanities Research Council (AHRC) Grant. However, preschool is also an area of content creation where Britain has a long tradition, and where it enjoys a strong international reputation (Steemers, 2004). It is also an area where US production has grown since the mid-1990s, reinforcing America's position as both a key exporter of and key destination for preschool brands. Focusing on these two countries as major originators of preschool content, this book considers the range of forces that shape the development and production of contemporary preschool television by examining how those involved in its creation and distribution negotiate the wider commercial, creative and cultural forces that impact production. It focuses on how programmes are made and why they are made in particular ways, revealing how a combination of external forces and internal strategies inform and shape the nature of what is produced.

What do we mean by preschool television?

If children are indeed a special audience, and preschoolers constitute one small section of this special audience, what exactly do we mean by preschool television, a constructed term, much like the definition of childhood itself (Ariès, 1962; Buckingham, 2000: 6; Kline, 1993: 47–8). What distinguishes it from television targeted at older children and where exactly are boundaries drawn, if at all?

First, it clearly relates to an 'age and stage-related organisation of television' (Messenger Davies, 2001a: 79) rather than a genre-specific classification, although the two are often conflated in official reports (see Atwal et al., 2003; Blumler, 1992: 37; Messenger Davies and Corbett, 1997; Ofcom, 2007a), with preschool television output analysed along-side children's factual, drama, animation and entertainment program-ming when preschool television contains these same sub-categories of genre and form. Indeed preschool programming encompasses a very diverse range of genres including storytelling, music, entertainment, drama and a wide range of factual content (make and do, science, nat-ural history, cookery) and hybrid forms. Programmes can be animated or live action or a mixture of both. As a form animation can range from complex 3D stop-frame model animation, 3D CGI, motion capture and digital puppetry as well as simpler 2D flash and CelAction techniques (Wells, 2006, 2007). Live action programmes sometimes do not contain any humans at all, consisting almost entirely of costumed characters and/or puppets.

However, in terms of age it is not always clear where preschool tele-vision begins and where it ends. Most channels and blocks (CBeebies, Nick Jr., Playhouse Disney) target children under six, with the upper end of the age-range (4–6) already having started formal schooling. Indeed CBeebies is labelled not as a service for preschoolers but as a service for 'the BBC's youngest audience' under six (BBC, 2008a: 28), and some practitioners prefer to use the term 'early years' rather than preschool because it prioritises children's 'own specific needs, interests and amuse-ments' rather than school-readiness (see CPBF, 2007). In Scandinavia, preschool extends to the under-sevens, because children start school later (Cederborg, 2002). Where preschool programming was once hardly differentiated at all, nowadays within the two-to-six age-range, pro-gramming may be targeted at younger (2–3) or older children (4–6), but the majority of programming targets three- to five-year-olds. Most mainstream broadcast outlets do not commission programming for the under-twos. This is because the market is assumed to be too small to be economically viable, but also because of concerns about infant viewing (Carrington, 2007a; Klasen, 2008; Skala, 2007) including a recommen-dation by the American Academy of Paediatrics Committee on Public Education (1999) that advises no screen time before the age of two, because it might negatively impact infant development.

These concerns have not prevented the more recent arrival of chan-nels targeting infants under two and their parents (BabyFirst, BabyTV) and a range of DVDs (*Baby Einstein, Brainy Baby, Baby Genius*) that encourage beliefs in infant learning in spite of little evidence to support this (Anderson and Pempek, 2005; Garrison and Christakis, 2005; Kirkorian and Anderson, 2008: 192–3). For the purposes of this study emphasis has been placed on programming commissioned by broadcasters for channels or slots that are targeted at young children between the ages of two and six, because most productions are created for this age group.

In terms of the market, preschoolers, even more so than older children whose own viewing boundaries have become increasingly blurred with adult viewing (Kapur, 1999: 124), are identifiable as a market niche with their own age-specific programmes. They may of course watch a variety of shows, often in the company of older children, and including those not specifically targeted at them such as *Teenage Mutant Ninja Turtles* (Kinder, 1991: 125). However, programmes designed specifically for a preschool audience are usually of little interest to adults, except as cult viewing (see Buckingham, 2002: 56). Like all niches linked to consumption the segment is a marketing construction which allows some form of categorisation of an otherwise un-categorisable group in terms of pricing, demand and audience availability (Buckingham, 2007a: 19–20; Kapur, 1999: 126; Pecora, 1998: 98).

Yet as a marketing category preschoolers are not consumers in the same way as older children. They do not usually receive pocket money, and their ability to pester their parents for products linked to television programmes is more limited. They are not just emotionally and financially dependent on parents, but also much more dependent on parents for choosing what they watch, eat, wear or do. As a consequence producers, broadcasters and those interested in extending preschool brands into other product areas are also targeting parents, who exercise considerable control over their children's media consumption at this age, and are much more likely to accept shows that meet their parental expectations. Parental approval is therefore an important aspect of preschool television (Eryl-Jones, 2003) marking it out from programming aimed at older children, where parental approval is often not an objective at all (see Banet-Weiser, 2007).

Away from market categorisations, there is a different concept of preschool television based on children's emotional and cognitive development, drawn largely from psychology (see Buckingham, 2005: 472–3). As a group perceived to 'lack experience and thus need to be gently introduced to basic information about the world' (Messenger Davies, 2001b: 102), there is recognition that programming for preschoolers should meet their developmental needs and cognitive abilities by being age-appropriate in respect of pacing, language, storytelling, sound, editing and visual representations. Many producers of preschool television therefore invariably 'see it as part of their job to be thoroughly well-informed about their audience' (Messenger Davies, 1995: 16) and many, yet not all, are specialists in making programming for young children.

This acknowledgement of preschoolers' lack of life experience underpins the underlying educational slant of much preschool programming which in turn is closely linked to an ethos of public service – that this is content that should not be entirely driven by commercial imperatives (see Messenger-Davies, 1995: 18). For example CBeebies in the United Kingdom has a service licence which requires it to promote education and learning with 'a very high level of educational output' that supports the school and preschool curricula (BBC Trust, 2008a: 3), and in the United States most preschool shows, either on commercial or public channels, are expected to satisfy educational goals (Dudko, 2008a).

In summary, preschool television is defined by different perceptions of its audience. At one level it is clearly marked by programming designed to meet the developmental needs of this particular age group. However, as Pecora points out (1998: 98–9; also Linn, 2004: 24), the provision of age-specific programming in niches is also connected to commercial demand and corporate strategies, where the child audience is segmented in ways that appeal to commercial interests and advertisers.

Organisation and production in preschool television

So where does preschool television fit within the organisational contexts and production practices of television and children's television in general? To understand the decisions taken by preschool programme-makers we need to understand the contexts in which they work, the internal workings of organisations and the relationships that exist between individuals and organisations (Croteau and Hoynes, 2003: 23). Yet studies of media production, essentially 'research about people who make television programmes and how these people work' (Messenger Davies, 2006: 21) are rather rare (Caldwell, 1995: 74; Davis and Scase, 2000: 13), possibly because access can be difficult (Corner, 1999: 70). There are plenty of studies about the economic and institutional structures of the communications marketplace, including its global manifestations (Herman and McChesney, 1997; Schiller, 1989), and equally many that concern themselves with media representations, but not that many that deal with production processes (see Caldwell, 2008; Ettema and Whitney, 1982; Gitlin, 2000; Newcomb and Alley, 1983; Turow, 1984) and how market structures impact production practices at an everyday level (see Corner, 1999: 70; Hesmondhalgh, 2007: 36). While production studies are rather scant, studies that tackle issues connected with the production of children's programming (Bryant, 2007a; Buckingham et al., 1999; Hendershot, 2004; Palmer, 1987, 1988; Turow, 1981) are even rarer.

Nevertheless the growing commercialisation of children's television and the extent to which it is linked to the broader business of children's entertainment and consumer products do open up avenues for a wider-ranging analytical perspective of the context in which production takes place. Looking beyond the 'marketplace determinations' of political economy and 'the play of cultural discourses' represented by cultural studies, Cottle puts forward the case for exploring the 'relatively unexplored and under-theorised "middle ground" of organisational structures and workplace practices' and how media professionals manage the range of forces that enable or constrain what they do (Cottle, 2003a: 4–5; also Cunningham and Jacka, 1996: 22). Taking this further we can draw on Cottle's work on natural history programming, to demonstrate how the creation of preschool television takes place within a complex production ecology comprising 'competitive institutional relationships and co-operative dependencies' (2003b: 170), that shape the organisation, production practices and content of preschool television, extending beyond broadcasters and producers to include a number of other players.

The term ecology derives from Bourdieu's notion of a 'cultural field', a series of institutions, rules, rituals, conventions and categories that constitute the sites of cultural practice, interaction and conflict between different players over resources (Bourdieu, 1993; Webb et al., 2002: 21–2). According to Cottle, the concept is helpful for examining not just those dynamics which operate 'inside individual media organisations' but also the 'organisational relationships and dynamics that exist *within* a particular field of media production' (2003b: 170–1) such as internationalising markets, fragmenting audiences and the particular conventions that dominate production. By examining the broader field of production including institutional relationships, dependencies, key players and professional practices, we can gain a better understanding of how media outputs change and the internal and external factors that influence them. Essentially it is the idea that production functions like an eco-system involving relationships between individuals and organisations, so that a change somewhere in that eco-system will have an impact on everything else that inhabits the system, altering interactions in the process.

Focusing on the production ecology of preschool television therefore means looking beyond the immediate sphere of any one organisation such as the BBC or PBS or Nickelodeon. Nor is it just about examining the minutiae of the production process within one organisation. It extends to the development of initial ideas right through to the extension of a programme concept to other forms of media consumption. It means examining the wider economic, technological, regulatory, commercial and cultural dynamics of production and how these forces are 'managed and creatively negotiated' by broadcasters, producers, distributors, rights-owners, co-producers and others in the broader ecology (Cottle, 2003b: 172). It entails looking at how players co-exist, co-operate and compete in a complex changing field and the impact of their decisions and actions on what children are offered as media content (Cottle, 2004: 82). It also involves looking at how those in the broader production community balance creative and commercial considerations and how they manage risk in an unpredictable business, where success is never assured because of the unpredictability of the audience and the production process itself (Casey et al., 2002: 175; Hesmondhalgh, 2007: 18–19). It also suggests taking into consideration the constraints, which are specific to preschool television in respect of funding and the audience's perceived needs (Bryant, 2007b: 39).

For the production ecology of preschool television, the period since the mid-1990s is particularly interesting because it not only coincides with the international success of preschool series such as *Teletubbies* and *Blue's Clues* which marked the importance of global distribution and noticeably different funding models. It also coincides with the launch of several dedicated preschool blocks or channels including Nick Jr. and Playhouse Disney in both the United States and Britain and CBeebies in Britain. Preschool television therefore provides a good example of a production ecology governed by a rapidly changing and complex set of industry relationships and dependencies, focused on content, which needs to satisfy a wide range of domestic and international circumstances as well as public service and commercial prerogatives. In this sense preschool television, as one particular type of production ecology, provides a fascinating point of departure because it represents a microcosm of the broader changes in television – including the shift from scarcity to plenty to digital abundance (Ellis, 2000), and from local to global patterns of production, distribution and consumption. It is these complex and changing relationships between broadcasters, programme-makers, financiers and regulators that constitute the production ecology of preschool television.

Key players in the preschool television production ecology

Who then are the actors in this ecology? Preschool television involves a spectrum of players who may be pulling in the same or opposing directions according to their own shifting economic, ideological or creative priorities at any one time. This is a close-knit, but complex community comprising individuals and corporations with 'multiple intentions, corporate and individual' (Corner, 1999: 70), who are engaged both in business and creativity. Individual relationships and networks are crucially important, both locally and internationally. Individuals meet at the same conferences, international trade conventions and broadcaster presentations, and read the same trade publications and online bulletins. Focusing on these different players and their relationships allows us to examine their different levels of interaction, interdependence, co-operation and competition, and how they position themselves in relation to changing national and international circumstances and to each other. For the purposes of this study I use the concept of production ecology to reflect both the community of players involved and the different levels of analysis within preschool television (see 'Levels of analysis within the production process') which affect relationships within the ecology.

Concentrating on the US Bryant describes the children's television sector *as a whole* as a community, a system or network of different players or populations that has evolved over time, 'based on internal dynamics and external pressures' (2007b: 36). The 'internal dynamics' referred to in Bryant's account allude to the ways in which the different player populations within the community interact with each other and respond to external challenges, altering the make-up of the community over time. This definition has the advantage of explaining not just how children's television is created, broadcast and distributed by those directly involved, but also how production and relationships are impacted more broadly by regulatory, political, economic, technological and marketing considerations.

As a sub-set of children's television it is possible to identify a preschool production ecology with its own distinctive players and relationships. Sometimes these overlap with television production for children in general – as is the case with regulatory bodies, advocacy groups, professional bodies and those organisations that produce or broadcast for a range of ages. However, with the emergence of preschool channels and blocks, specialist preschool producers and merchandise licensing activities that focus on this age group, it is possible to distinguish a production ecology that characterises this particular field of cultural production.

Within this ecology the relationships are not all equal and some players have more influence or impact than others. Members may have different interests and goals, and at different times relationships may be mutually beneficial, predatory or competitive depending on the production climate (see Bryant, 2007b: 38). For example the relationship would be mutually beneficial in a co-production or when creative and commercial interests collaborate to build a preschool brand or if the community as a whole is co-ordinating a response in the face of some threat to its existence (see Chapter 10). It would be competitive during a pitch for a broadcast slot or predatory in battles for ownership and control of companies or properties.

In Britain and the United States the preschool production ecology comprises the following players involved in broadcasting, content creation, ancillary rights exploitation, regulation and advocacy. The categories are not exclusive or static. There is a certain amount of overlap and fluidity in the relationships with some players located in one or more categories, particularly if they form part of a vertically integrated organisation such as Disney or Viacom or the BBC, who are involved in different media and different aspects of production, distribution and marketing.

Broadcasters comprise mainly the broadcast and cable networks that transmit preschool television as commissioned content, as co-productions or acquisitions. In the United States the range of broadcasters includes the preschool block of the non-profit-making broadcast network, PBS, and its digital preschool co-venture with commercial partners, PBS Kids Sprout. It also encompasses commercial cable networks that transmit branded blocks of preschool programming (Nick Jr. on Nickelodeon, Playhouse Disney on Disney or the short-lived Tickle U block on Cartoon Network which was withdrawn in 2006 after launching in 2005) and Noggin, a preschool channel, owned by Nickelodeon, which was re-branded as Nick Jr. in 2009. With the exception of PBS, these are not just content programmers, but also significant creators of preschool content and brands, which are marketed globally through parent media conglomerates (Disney, Time Warner, Viacom) well versed in 'repurposing' content across borders and platforms (see Caldwell, 2008: 9).

In Britain broadcast outlets include CBeebies, the preschool brand of the BBC, a publicly funded non-profit-making public service institution, which is both a broadcaster and a significant content creator through the in-house production division of the BBC Children's department. The BBC is also an important co-funder and manager of preschool intellectual property (IP), including third party product, through BBC Worldwide, a separate commercial subsidiary, which operates independently of BBC Children's and CBeebies, channelling profits back to the BBC. Then there are the commercially funded public service generalist channels, ITV1 and Five, who function mainly as broadcasters, subject to limited public service obligations on the quality and range of their children's programming (Communications Act, 2003; Thickett, 2007a). Five's morning preschool block, *Milkshake!*, is a significant competitor to CBeebies. Finally there are commercial preschool channels that comprise the dedicated preschool channel offshoots and time-shifted services of US-owned brands Nick Jr. (1999), Playhouse Disney (2000), Cartoonito (2006, owned by Time Warner) and infant-focused channels BabyFirst! and BabyTV.

In terms of content creation Bryant writing about the United States draws a distinction between content creators who produce explicitly educational programmes and those who make programming that is 'primarily entertaining' (Bryant, 2007b: 41). Significantly the educational examples she cites – *Sesame Street, Mr Rogers' Neighborhood* and *Blue's Clues* produced by Sesame Workshop, Family Communications Inc and Nick Jr., respectively – are all preschool programmes, because little educational programming is made for older children. Bryant points out that there is some overlap between the two, but it is worth pointing out that for preschool programming, content creators in the United States nearly always pursue curricular objectives. In the United Kingdom this distinction between educational and entertaining preschool television is not normally made (see Chapter 6).

Further within content creation there are a range of different entities, which vary hugely in the size and scope of their activities. As mentioned, some broadcasters and cable networks are heavily involved in content creation through their own in-house production arms. Larger production companies may be involved in the creation, distribution and ancillary exploitation of their own shows as well as third-party properties, which they then use to build home entertainment, international sales and consumer product divisions. They include British companies, who have made the brand management of preschool content a key focus of their operations in recent years – including HIT Entertainment and Chorion (see Chapter 5). Some run their own production divisions; others confine their creative activities to development, outsourcing production to others. Some, wishing to secure broadcast access in key markets, particularly the United States, have become involved in programming/broadcasting. For example HIT Entertainment is a partner in the preschool cable network and on-demand service, PBS Kids Sprout in the United States as well as the international preschool channel, JimJam.

Within the hierarchy of content creation there are many smaller production entities, often creatively led and concentrated on one or two individuals with skills as preschool animators, writers, directors or producers, who are dependent on broadcasters and larger producer-distributors to fund their projects through pre-sales, commissions and ancillary exploitation because they lack the resources, skills, infrastructure or inclination to do this themselves. Broadcasters and larger producers in turn are dependent on smaller creative entities to take on some of the risks associated with creative development and to come up with the ideas that underpin and reinforce their status and credibility as a creative force, which they can then exploit commercially on a global scale (see Hesmondhalgh, 2007: 176). In the words of one US preschool producer,

> There's a belief that if they [broadcasters] could create this content themselves they would. They know that they can't. They know that they need independents because they have a fresh perspective. They're closer to the ground. They're not part of a very large corporation. They rely on companies like mine and others, to generate fresh new ideas [...] They do it because that's where the interesting works come from. (Interview, 2007)

Beyond broadcasting and the creation of content there are other players and activities within the preschool production ecology that impact content. Licensees such as toy companies create consumer products based on the characters and environments of preschool television programmes, which in turn are dependent on retail distribution. Licensing considerations have a considerable impact on the type of programmes made, because young children are now the primary market for toys, and licensing revenues constitute such an important part of preschool television programme funding (see Chapter 9). Bryant (2007b) identifies advertisers as a further player in US children's television, but their influence has always been less prominent in Britain, particularly since the advertising of HFSS (high in fat, sugar and salt) foods was banned in 2007 within and around programming targeted at the under-16s.

Legislative and regulatory bodies that enact regulations are also important members of this ecology. In terms of enforcing legislation and regulatory oversight this extends to the Federal Communications Commission (FCC) and Federal Trade Commission (FTC) in the United States and the Office of Communications (Ofcom) in Britain. Children's advocacy groups that campaign for the public interest responsibilities of children's television have a longer history in the United States because of a tradition of public activism over children's television-related issues, particularly those to do with violence, educational programming and advertising. Starting with Action for Children's Television (ACT) in the late 1960s and until 2003 the Center for Media Education, this campaign work has been continued by a host of other child and public health-focused groups (see Kunkel, 2007: 222–3; Montgomery, 2007). In Britain advocacy came later because for many years children's television was deemed well served by terrestrial broadcasters with public service obligations – foremost the BBC, but including commercially funded broadcaster, ITV. Advocacy for children's television, as we shall see in Chapter 10, has only emerged intermittently in Britain in response to perceived regulatory failings that threaten levels of home-grown transmissions and production.

Levels of analysis within the production process

Having identified the different players within the production ecology of preschool television, it is worth considering the system in which production is situated and organised. Different commentators, writing about media production in general (Cottle, 2003a; Davis and Scase, 2000; Goldsmiths Media Group, 2000; Williams, 2003: 97) or television production in particular (Alvarado and Buscombe, 1978; Corner, 1999) have identified different levels of analysis in the production process, which range from the broadest institutional, political and economic contexts to the most specific creative and business choices. In combination or individually these all have the potential to determine the shape and content of a production.

At the macro-level there are the general political, cultural, regulatory, technological and economic parameters within which television gets made, which can promote or constrain it, and which condition the decision-making process, According to Corner these constitute the 'historical contexts of production' (1999: 71). For example at this level one fundamental distinction between the United States and the British media is the greater emphasis placed in Britain on publicly funded public service media as opposed to the US system, where commercial media and profit-making have prevailed (Gitlin, 2000). However, within preschool television, this distinction between public service and commercial media is not nearly so clear-cut, with different historical and regulatory traditions translating into different expectations about the goals of preschool television. In the United States, preschool television since the late 1960s has become strongly focused on content that has explicit educational goals that now extend across public television to the programming of commercial outlets like Nick Jr. and Playhouse Disney. In Britain, there is a longer more sustained preschool television tradition dating back to the early 1950s, strongly influenced by the public service ethos of the licence-fee funded BBC, but educational goals have always been less formalised.

At the meso-level there are the institutional, financial and organisational contexts of production focused on what Cottle calls 'impinging organisational cultures, corporate strategy and editorial policies' that inform production choices at a strategic and planning level (2003a: 20). Activities here are focused largely on broadcasters, larger producers and large corporations whose 'creative managers' (Hesmondhalgh, 2007: 64) decide what actually gets made in keeping with an organisation's corporate objectives. Combining corporate goals with the creative aspirations of those involved in the day-to-day production of programmes constitutes one of the main challenges of content creation (Casey et al., 2002: 177; Davis and Scase, 2000: 4), requiring management and negotiation by individuals such as broadcast commissioners, executive producers or creative directors who act as 'brokers or mediators' (see Hesmondhalgh, 2007: 64–5) with creative practitioners. Within this organisational context, co-ordination and negotiation also extend to those involved in the marketing and promotion of shows, both to audiences (ibid.) and other commercial interests as part of an organisation's other strategic priorities (e.g. in consumer products).

Relationships at this meso-level are determined in large part by the institutional stance of an organisation. For example, CBeebies, the BBC's dedicated channel for preschoolers, has public service obligations and a publicly funded budget, in contrast with its commercial rival Nick Jr., which has commercial responsibilities, underpinned by commercial funding, and a corporate philosophy, which originates in the United States. The different organisational contexts of these broadcasters (stemming in part from history, policy and regulatory contexts at the macro-level) influence the type of content they are able or willing to support (see Chapters 3 and 4). Yet this is not the whole picture. The increasingly complicated funding structure of preschool television means that the institutional and corporate ambitions of several players may impinge on production choices – including those of overseas broadcasters, co-producers and those involved in ancillary exploitation (e.g. toy manufacturers). This is a fluid and variable process, where no two preschool projects are ever the same in terms of their funding, execution or the staff and resources employed.

At the micro-level where individuals are directly involved in the creation of preschool programmes, production can be viewed as 'an interlocking network of everyday working practices, artistic and other cultural demands, the beliefs and actions of individuals and social groups' (Alvarado and Buscombe, 1978: 3). This is where corporate and managerial intentions need to be balanced with creative considerations and where different sets of priorities may emerge in a process which Davis and Scase call 'mutual adjustment', where creative contributions and aesthetic criteria are tailored to the demands of the marketplace and each production's specific budgetary and time constraints (2000: 14–15). At this level Corner makes a distinction between production mentalities and production practices. Production mentalities comprise the different 'dispositions, values and working "practical consciousness"' of those involved in the production process, who may have different 'creative, craft, professional and corporate goals in mind' (1999: 71). Production practices consist of the actual skills and conventions involved in making a television programme (1999: 71). Production practices involve a greater variety of individuals – animators, musicians, editors and skin artists etcetera – but many of the key decisions have already been made by this stage during development with regard to scripts, characters, style and direction (see Chapter 6). In this sense there is a clear distinction between what Hesmondhalgh (2007: 64) calls 'primary creative personnel' (symbol creators) who have a creative role, and 'technical workers' whose importance rests on their craft skills rather than a creative contribution to the conception, interpretation or communication of ideas (also Davis and Scase, 2000: 52–3). For it is the production mentalities and assumptions about what works and what doesn't that inform the practicalities of audio-visual construction and performance.

At the micro-level individuals function within a hierarchy, where their decisions are guided by groups and individuals that exist above or below them, even if they have some degree of autonomy. This leads to co-dependence and co-operation. As well as being aware of what audiences and broadcasters want, preschool television producers for example, may also need to take account of what product licensees and retailers want, so that their programmes work as brands on shop shelves, and recoup production investment. Their 'practical consciousness' is therefore affected by other professional or financial priorities, which may influence the way a preschool television project is tackled. Creatives involved in the production of preschool television may have doubts about programming becoming too centred on such licensing considerations in respect of character development and settings (see Chapter 10). The resolution of these conflicting priorities involves negotiation between different players including producers, broadcasters, marketers, international distributors, writers and so on who each bring their own professional priorities to the table.

Methods and outline

This chapter has sought to contextualise the production of preschool television, positioning analysis within the analytical framework of production ecology in order to pinpoint how different players co-exist, co-operate and compete across different levels of activity, informing the nature of preschool programming in the process. In keeping with this approach the rest of the book comprises a mid-range analysis of preschool television production, designed to give greater insight into the different facets of production – facets that are determined by broader historical, structural, cultural, technological and regulatory circumstances, as well as activities and relationships within the ecology, which are managed and negotiated on a day-to-day basis. This mid-range approach is focused on how preschool television concepts are generated, developed, commissioned, produced and exploited to meet a complex set of creative, cultural, international and market priorities.

Evidence has largely been drawn from 88 face-to-face interviews between 2006 and 2008 with British players involved variously in aspects of broadcasting, production, international distribution, marketing, regulation and advocacy. This was supplemented by 20 interviews with US and European players involved in production, research, acquisitions, broadcasting and marketing.[1] Interviews were semi-structured to the extent that the same basic themes were introduced, but questions were left open-ended to allow respondents to develop their own line of thought. In addition to background information, information was sought on the commissioning and acquisition process, funding models, creative, educational and commercial considerations and the extent to which these are implemented, negotiated and managed by different players. The line of questioning was adapted in each interview to reflect the nature of involvement. Although this material is often coloured by personal experience, themes and ideas do emerge which can be followed up in other interviews and in documentary evidence. In order to pinpoint key stages in the production process, observations (14 in total) took place within a range of production environments (live action and animation; studio, location, post-production; focus group research) and at industry events, with each observation lasting variously from a day to a week. This has occurred alongside the examination of primary material (schedules, regulatory and policy documents, company reports, websites, insider accounts), secondary sources (trade publications) and the analysis of select samples of preschool television, produced and broadcast since 1995.

While this chapter has provided an analytical framework for examining preschool television production, Chapter 2 moves onto the historical origins of preschool television, examining how the public service rationale behind preschool television initiatives has been differently inflected in Britain and America. Chapter 3 considers the global dimension of preschool television and its transition from an essentially small localised industry to a more commercially and internationally oriented multiplatform enterprise. It examines the economics of production and provides an overview of international markets drawing on interviews with overseas buyers who function as gatekeepers. Particular attention is focused on the United States, the most important market for international exploitation. Using Britain as a case study, Chapter 4 focuses on the role of broadcasters and the nature and extent of their involvement in funding, scheduling, shaping and promoting programming. Having outlined the broader historical and institutional context of preschool television, Chapter 5 concentrates on those companies who have forged a business by focusing on the production and/or rights management of preschool television content including larger producer-distributors (HIT Entertainment, Entertainment Rights, Chorion) as well as smaller niche operators. Issues surrounding development and research are considered in Chapter 6, before moving to an examination of the assumptions and conventions that guide British programme-makers in Chapter 7. Chapter 8 starts by looking at changes in the organisational structures and forms of preschool television production before focusing on a case study, which illustrates different facets of the production process. Chapter 9 examines the crucial importance of licensed merchandise for the preschool market and how product licensing impacts production strategies. Chapter 10 moves to regulatory policy. Starting with a comparison of the situation in Britain and America, the United Kingdom is used as a case study to illustrate the role of regulation in ensuring diversity of content and supply. Looking beyond the policy and economic dimensions of preschool television, Chapter 11 examines the aesthetic qualities and motivations that underpin preschool production, qualities through which extraordinary works are recognised and valued. The final chapter provides an overview of the issues, concepts and arguments discussed throughout the book as well as assessing the future of preschool television in the light of technological change and the emergence of new media platforms.

Having outlined what this book is about, it is also useful to establish what it does not cover. Its primary focus is the production of preschool television programmes, and the external forces and internal production practices that inform their development. It is not about the experience of young viewers; nor is it about the effects of programmes on them, although the assumptions that the industry makes about this audience are clearly very important indeed in determining what is made and distributed (see Chapter 6 and 7). Nor does it provide an exhaustive inventory of preschool programmes, although key examples are highlighted to underscore significant features and steps in the production process. It concentrates primarily on programming targeting two- to six-year-olds, which achieves prominence through broadcast distribution. The circulation of content to children under two, including DVDs and infant channels, does raise important issues about the impact of programming and the further segmentation of the marketplace by commercial interests, but for reasons of time and space, lie outside the scope of this book. This study focuses on preschool programming originated for television, and on the ways that those who make and market programmes negotiate the wider commercial, cultural, regulatory and technological forces that impact production. As such it can be seen as a case study and analysis of the state of preschool television, which places the changing relationships and dependencies that constitute the ecology at the heart of the analysis.

Note

1. All quotations, unless otherwise indicated, are taken from personal interviews and production observations between 2006 and 2008, some of which have been anonymised.

2
Safe at Home: The Origins of Preschool Television as a Public Service Project

As Buckingham points out children's television is 'not produced *by* children but *for* them'. As such children's programmes are frequently more a manifestation of adult 'interests or fantasies or desires' and their construction of childhood rather than a reflection of what children want (1995a: 47). This is apparent in the history of children's television, where programming is nearly always incontrovertibly linked to the cultural and institutional context in which it was conceived, mirroring the concerns, trends and beliefs held by adults at the time (see Mitroff and Herr Stephenson, 2007). An analysis of what has been prescribed for young children in the past can therefore be illuminating because it tells us something about how this small audience was created and conceived to fit the institutional requirements of the time, as well as how these assumptions and institutional requirements have changed (see Wagg, 1992: 151).

Britain and America are currently significant producers of preschool content, competing for the attention of buyers, young audiences and parents. It is therefore useful to ascertain how they got to this position by delving into the origins of preschool television to explain similarities and differences that exist now. Initially the focus in both countries was almost entirely driven by domestic considerations, which shaped each ecology in distinctive ways, because the institutional basis of television was quite different – grounded on the supremacy of commercial broadcasting in the United States and the initial dominance of the publicly funded BBC public service monopoly in Britain. Yet as we shall see, in preschool television the difference between the two was not so much between public service and the market. After all in both countries preschool television provision originated predominantly from within a public service context – with the BBC in Britain and with PBS

(Public Broadcasting Service) in America. Where British and American approaches differed was in their different conceptions of the audience and in different ideas about what television should be doing for this age group.

This chapter provides the historical background of preschool television in Britain and America from the 1950s to the 1990s, how it was developed and promoted as separate from programming for older children, both in terms of content and the delineation of the audience's needs. Examining developments decade by decade, the chapter considers the degree to which early preschool television initiatives were the outcome of a particular social climate and institutional setting. Core to this analysis is the role of the BBC and the non-profit educational programme producer Children's Television Workshop (CTW, later Sesame Workshop), which worked with the nascent PBS in the 1960s to shape American educational preschool television. What was the rationale behind early preschool television initiatives and how were these differently inflected in both countries in terms of creative goals, educational objectives, commercial priorities and production practices?

Preschool television in the 1950s

Although television was reintroduced into the United States and Britain after the Second World War, programming produced specifically for young children did not become a regular feature until the early 1950s (Home, 1993; Pecora, 2007).

In Britain, according to Oswell, there was 'little sense of the child audience as a distinct and separate entity' (2002: 44) before 1945, with *Children's Hour* on BBC radio targeted more at family audiences. It was not until the resurrection of television in 1946, and the challenges that it presented in terms of serving the public in new ways, that the BBC began to address children as a differentiated audience with their own distinct interests and concerns (ibid.). However, while older children were recognised as a discernible part of the television audience from the start with *For the Children* on Sunday afternoons, the Corporation found it much harder to conceptualise the preschool audience (Oswell, 1995: 36, 2002: 24). For example *Muffin the Mule* (1946–57) a puppet programme, hosted by 'motherly' authority figure, Annette Mills, was not expressly targeted at preschoolers (1995: 40).

It was not until 1950 with the expansion of the children's television department that preschoolers became a focus of attention. Before 1950 the BBC had not catered for very young children because they simply 'didn't know how to *imagine* this audience' (Oswell, 1995: 37). According to Oswell the arrival of the marionette toddler *Andy Pandy* in July 1950, and the incorporation of the *Watch with Mother* preschool strand in 1953 as an umbrella for all preschool content effectively 'signifies the *invention* of this small audience *for broadcasters* and *within the institution of broadcasting* (1995: 37). Scheduled for 15 minutes at 3.45 p.m., separately from content for older children, *Watch with Mother* with its simple puppets (*Andy Pandy, The Flower Pot Men, The Woodentops, Rag, Tag and Bobtail*) and storytelling (*Picture Book*) was not only designed to fit the routines of young children and mothers, but was also conceived as a first step in children's television consumption.

Watch with Mother's preschool audience was, according to Oswell, 'created' largely as a response to the BBC's concern about whether television was actually appropriate for this age group, and whether mothers would simply let children watch unsupervised (1995: 37, 2002: 70). Wary of criticism the Corporation consulted educationalists and child psychologists before transmission and conducted surveys with mothers to address these uncertainties (Oswell, 1995: 37–8, 2002: 68–9). Mindful of external condemnation it sought to 'invent' preschool television as part of a broader public service initiative, which contributed to the public good by fitting 1950s notions of motherhood and family life. In this sense *Andy Pandy* became less about entertaining or even educating young children than about constructing a viewing situation, which fitted contemporary discourses about families and mothers. *Andy Pandy* was not only a programme which could be watched 'with mother', but integrated mother's voice through narration – directly addressing children at home (Oswell, 1995: 41–2), and reinforcing the notion that television was somewhere which was 'safe, maternal, and homely' (Oswell, 2002: 64).

Watch with Mother suggested a viewing situation, which became less relevant as mothers went out to work and more children attended nurseries or simply watched on their own (Home, 1993: 77). At the time it represented a particular response to fears about the potential harmful effects of television as the BBC began to build up in-house expertise in producing content for its youngest viewers. With the arrival of commercially funded ITV in 1955, the BBC had to contend with competition. It soon became apparent that a programming policy based on children's needs rather than their wants was no longer entirely sustainable, as children exercised their choice to watch ITV's more populist, family-oriented drama and entertainment (Buckingham et al., 1999: 21). One victim of competition in 1956 was the Toddlers' Truce, a period between

6 and 7 p.m. when television went off air to allow children to be put to bed. ITV did have a *Watch with Mother* equivalent, *Small Time*, but the main battleground was for the attention of older children and the family (Buckingham et al., 1999: 83; Home, 1993: 34–5). The BBC might have lost large swathes of older children to ITV, but it remained the main producer and broadcaster of limited amounts of preschool programming throughout the 1950s.

Emerging from within a publicly funded non-commercial broadcasting monopoly, the British approach was borne out of a public service tradition where broadcasting was conceived not simply as entertainment, but as an uplifting endeavour designed to create good citizens, who would be educated and informed through a range of developmentally appropriate programmes, constituting public service broadcasting 'in miniature' (Buckingham et al., 1999: 17). Yet it is also important to note that children's broadcasting, including preschool programming, was separate from school's broadcasting, and while education was an important part of the remit, children's television was never purposefully instructive or linked to a formal curriculum (Oswell, 2002: 32; Palmer, 1988: 58). Children's broadcasting was expected to inform and educate in the broadest sense. Indeed, according to Buckingham et al. (1999: 123–4), both the BBC and ITV were hostile to recommendations by a jointly convened committee (the O'Conor Report) in 1960, which proposed external involvement by educational advisors in production, insisting instead on their creative autonomy and internal codes of practice.

At this time the situation in the United States was less focused, with some 'paltry early preschooler offerings' (Kline, 1993: 121) on commercial radio and the least attractive network television slots (Turow, 1981: 29). Children and families had been targeted in the early days of television to get sets into the home (Melody, 1973: 36; Mitroff and Herr Stephenson, 2007: 10–11), but as the 1950s wore on children's content became more marginalised because the audience was not sufficiently valuable to advertisers (Palmer, 1988: 21–3; Schneider, 1987: 14). Just as the British commercial network ITV1 would withdraw from broadcasting children's programmes during weekdays in 2007 citing economic reasons, the three US Networks' (ABC, CBS, NBC) commitment to children's content fell inexorably from a peak of 48.75 hours a week in 1950–51 to 24.25 hours by 1958–59 (Turow, 1981: 23) as children's programming became largely confined to Saturday mornings (Alexander, 2001: 496). In the early 1950s puppetry and live action programming were still plentiful, but by the late 1950s cheaper partial animation techniques, pioneered by Hanna-Barbara, made animation less prohibitively expensive, resulting in the demise of puppetry and live action (Palmer, 1987: 8; Pecora, 2007: 9), forms that appealed to younger children in particular.

American children were avid viewers but had little money to spend on advertised goods, which meant children's programming attracted fewer sponsors and advertisers. Preschool children were even less attractive because they were not viewed as consumers in their own right at all. As a consequence there was little incentive to produce programmes exclusively for them (Palmer, 1988: 23). Examples of 1950s programming aimed at young children on the three US networks included puppet show *Howdy Doody* (1947–60, NBC), educational magazine *Ding Dong School* (1952–56, NBC) and the long-running daily mixture of entertainment and education that comprised the variety format *Captain Kangaroo* (1955–81, CBS) (Pecora, 2007: 9; Woolery, 1985). *Romper Room* (Claster TV Productions, 1953–94) a syndicated preschool magazine format with an educational focus was franchised to local US stations and also internationally (Woolery, 1985: 423–5). However, apart from some preschool programmes on non-commercial local educational television stations, commercial priorities prevailed, sometimes impinging directly on content. For instance *Ding Dong School*, although designed and hosted by an educational consultant, attracted criticism for encouraging children to bring parents to the television set to hear messages from the show's sponsors (Morrow, 2006: 20). Yet sponsorship was not enough to prevent cancellation and it was ousted from the NBC network in 1956 to be replaced by the more commercially rewarding game show *The Price is Right* (Woolery, 1985: 151).

Throughout the 1950s preschool provision in both countries was sparse, but fundamentally different. In Britain, the BBC promoted a particular 1950s vision of family life. Under-funded and under-resourced British preschool television was built not only on variety in form (puppetry, animation, live action), but also on protection of the young child and its relationship with mother. BBC producers had some notions about what their audience might need (songs, stories, a 'motherly' narrator, opportunities to view with mother), but there was less certainty about what their young audience wanted or even the impact of the programming they made (see Buckingham et al., 1999: 20). In the United States, provision was patchier. Without a public service model that conceived the child audience outside of commercial interests, the Americans would have to devise their own concept of public service, which resulted in the formulation of a very particular approach to preschool television.

The British had a head start in the 1950s. By the 1960s, however, forces within the United States would assert the specific needs of the preschool audience and a different philosophy.

Preschool television in the 1960s

America had to wait until 1969 for its 'preschool moment' (Morrow, 2006). Throughout the 1960s children's network television was relegated to Saturday mornings. Live action programmes disappeared to be replaced by cheaply produced, half-hour animation series which could be syndicated after network transmission on local stations in the afternoon, and which did not necessitate actor royalties for re-runs (see Franklin et al., 2001; Melody, 1973; Mittel, 2003; Turow, 1981). Children's television became predominantly a tool of entertainment, and producers were not expected to fulfil public service or educational goals (Cohen, 2001: 572). According to Cantor many producers considered themselves to be businessmen first and foremost, meeting the demands of the networks ahead of the audience (1975: 116–17). Concern about how commercial broadcasting was serving children was highlighted in 1961 when Newton Minow, the new Federal Communications Commission (FCC) Chairman, described television as a 'vast wasteland' (Minow and Lamay, 1995: 188) which served children particularly poorly with 'massive doses of cartoons, violence, and more violence' (p. 190). However, by the 1960s commercial broadcasting had become a powerful vested interest making it harder to instigate reform that benefited the public interest (Palmer, 1988: 30; Turow, 1981: 82). This commercial orientation was in marked contrast to Britain where a public service ethos applied to both the BBC and its commercially funded rival, ITV (see Palmer, 1988: 27–8).

The US 'preschool moment' occurred on 10 November 1969 with the first transmission of CTW's *Sesame Street* on PBS. With the creation of the Corporation for Public Broadcasting (CPB) in 1967 public broadcasting became a national entity. PBS was created as a network for sourcing programming nationally across disparate individual stations (Marcus, 2003: 56). Before PBS local non-profit educational stations had produced children's shows, which tended to be under-funded, poorly produced and dull (Palmer, 1988: 91; Simensky, 2007: 132). With the exception of *Mister Rogers' Neighborhood*, a presenter-led show focused on emotional development, which had started as a local programme in 1954, before launching nationally in 1968, there was little of note for preschoolers on public television and little that focused on developing their cognitive skills (Hendershot, 2002: 83). With the launch of *Sesame Street* preschool programming would become a key component of PBS' output and *Sesame Street*, according to Morrow, would become 'PBS' symbol and its best justification' (2006: 29).

However the real impetus for better preschool provision came not from PBS, but from the tenacity of educational television producer Joan Ganz Cooney and Lloyd Morrisett, vice president of the Carnegie Corporation, in raising the $8m necessary to produce *Sesame Street's* first season and in formulating a system which integrated child development research with production (Morrow, 2006: 62; Palmer, 1988: 92). Created to cater for and educate young children aged three to six, particularly those from deprived or minority groups, *Sesame Street* signalled a new way of reaching out to young children, making them better prepared for school. What made it different from British preschool programming was the integration of formal educational curriculum and entertainment in one programme as a hybrid (Palmer, 1988: 58). According to Palmer this was born out of necessity, because unlike Britain, there was no adequate commercial provision of either educational or entertaining content, leaving programmes like *Sesame Street* to work in both settings (ibid.).

As well as concern about the paucity of what commercial television was offering, the birth of *Sesame Street* was also connected to the prevailing US social climate, where education was increasingly seen as a means of enabling children from low-income backgrounds to escape poverty (Franklin et al., 2001: 510; Palmer and Fisch, 2001: 4–5). The approach adopted by CTW for *Sesame Street* comprised producers and writers working together with child development and subject specialists to inject curricular objectives and developmental insight into the creative process, in what became known as the 'CTW model'. Formative research, involving testing with children before and during production, was designed to inform content so that it could be revised to become more comprehensible, educationally effective, appealing and age-appropriate (Fisch and Bernstein, 2001: 41). Summative research by independent researchers after transmission evaluated the extent to which a programme's educational objectives were met (Palmer and Fisch, 2001: 9). Producers used fast-paced techniques employed in advertising and entertainment shows combined with animation, puppet skits, short films and repetition to catch children's awareness and teach cognitive skills associated with literacy, numeracy, geometric shapes, relational concepts and reasoning (Morrow, 2006: 88–9; Palmer, 1987: 21). Notwithstanding the limitations of testing practices, which did not always take account of the social and cultural context of television viewing and assumed that recall is the same as learning (see Hendershot, 1999: 153), the CTW Model did constitute a departure from previous practice where producers and broadcasters simply relied on ratings and past experience to gain an understanding of their audience (Morrow, 2006: 71).

Sesame Street soon became an American institution, but also highlighted the funding instability of US public television. As an intervention, designed to plug the deficits of commercial television, PBS' reliance on an ad hoc mixture of meagre federal funding and viewer pledges combined with corporate sponsorship and philanthropic donations for *particular* programmes meant that it never developed the institutional purpose or independent funding base to define television either generally or in children's television in particular (Marcus, 2003: 56; Palmer, 1988: 64). Unable to finance *Sesame Street* from its own coffers, PBS was reliant on CTW's ability to generate funding itself from sponsors and ancillary activities (Palmer, 1988: 74). The first series was funded by philanthropic organisations (the Carnegie, Ford and Markle Foundations) and federal bodies including the Office of Education (Polsky, 1974: 114). New funders had to be found for every series, and funding from organisations like the National Science Foundation was usually linked to meeting the backer's short-term educational goals, rather than any overriding interest in the sustained provision of high-quality preschool television (Palmer, 1988: 75–6).

The series was not without its critics who doubted its educational effectiveness (see Hendershot, 1999 and Morrow, 2006 for detailed accounts of these criticisms). They disapproved of its fast pace, cognitive overload, repetition, lack of narrative structure and use of commercial techniques to educate (see also Postman, 1982; Winn, 1977). Yet *Sesame Street* did make children's television more child-focused and representative of US society as a whole with its inner-city setting. It could not bridge the education gap between poor and middle-class children as originally intended (Lesser, 1974; Palmer and Fisch, 2001: 5) but there is some evidence of modest educational benefits in learning and literacy from programming that was crafted to match children's developmental capabilities (see Comstock and Scharrer, 2007: 139–41 for an overview; also Huston et al., 2001; Mielke, 2001; Wright et al., 2001). However, the wider commercial industry was reluctant to emulate a model, which involved costly research (Morrow, 2006: 132), and so for many years *Sesame Street* remained rather exceptional.

In Britain *Watch with Mother* continued throughout the 1960s with the addition of stop-frame animation programmes including *Camberwick Green* (1966), *Trumpton* (1967) and *Chigley* (1969) produced by Gordon Murray Puppets. These stories, which emphasised nostalgia, rural life, and industriousness in an orderly community were somewhat at variance with the social upheavals of the time, but were a step away from the domestic settings of *Andy Pandy* (Northam, 2005: 251–4) and even further removed from gag-laden US cartoons (Wells, 2001a: 105). Murray's productions were also representative of a growing cottage industry of home-grown animation producers, such as Smallfilms which produced for both the BBC (*Noggin the Nog*, *Pogle's Wood*) and ITV (*Dogwatch*, *Pingwings*, *Ivor the Engine*) and John Ryan Studios (*Mary, Mungo and Midge*). With British broadcasters rarely producing animation in-house, these small companies laid the foundations of later stop-frame success, and pre-dated the general shift towards independent television production in the 1980s.

Yet the real departure for British preschool television in the 1960s was the magazine show *Play School*. Launched in 1964 on new channel, BBC2, it immediately more than doubled BBC provision. Conceived, like *Sesame Street*, to be child-centred and socially representative, it was broadcast daily Monday to Friday in the morning on BBC2 and repeated in the early afternoon on BBC1. From a basic studio setting *Play School* featured a cast of pets, toys and two presenters, who were replaced every week by two others from a rotating team. Filmed inserts often featuring children engaged in everyday activities represented a departure from previous practice where 'real' children had barely featured at all. Like *Sesame Street*, *Play School* had pro-social goals informed by 'an explicit philosophy of caring and nurturing' which went beyond 'the standard broadcasting functions of informing, educating and entertaining' (Messenger Davies, 1995: 17). However, there were different conceptions of both the audience and the educational role of television. First *Play School* was not designed to remedy the educational deprivation of inner-city children, a key factor underpinning *Sesame Street's* funding support (Messenger Davies, 1995: 18). The *Play School* audience was addressed as 'one child in a room' (Cynthia Felgate, Executive Producer cited in Messenger Davies, 1995: 15) and conceptualised as 'an extended family' who viewed regularly and shared common experiences, something more difficult to achieve in America with its multiple time zones (ibid.: 22). Unlike *Sesame Street* there were no puppets or children in the studio. Unlike *Sesame Street* with its fast-paced and unpredictable mix of sketches and films, *Play School* had continuity and a recognisable format comprising an introductory sequence, story and film. With presenters often addressing children directly and inviting them to participate, *Play School* was certainly 'a new kind of programme' introduced at a time when there was debate about the poor quality of nursery education (Home, 1993: 68–9). However, there was no formal and explicit incorporation of educational objectives (Home, 1993: 75) or formative testing. Educational specialists were consulted, but the production team were 'relatively inexperienced', learning through practice and occasional home visits, intended to give them a better understanding of their audience (Buckingham et al., 1999: 36; Home, 1993: 69–71).

The differences between *Sesame Street* and *Play School* became apparent when the Head of the BBC Children's Department, Monica Sims, turned down an opportunity to produce a British version of *Sesame Street* in 1971. Argument focused on the difference between learning and teaching, with the British emphasis firmly placed on the connection between play and learning rather than the more purposeful educational goals promoted by CTW (see Buckingham et al., 1999: 159–60). These divergences were based on a different conception of the audience (deprived inner city children/all children), a different conception of education (literacy and numeracy/learning as play), differences in pace (fast/slow), style (unrelated programme segments/real-life situations presented in real time) and some disquiet within the BBC about the effects of the commercial techniques used in *Sesame Street* (see Home, 1993: 42–5; also Buckingham et al., 1999: 35). Sims' view was that young children should be offered television programmes that they recognised from their own cultural experience, helping them 'to integrate into the national "pattern of life"' (Sims, cit. in Buckingham et al., 1999: 35). In this sense the debate highlighted broader concerns about US dominance and the need for smaller countries to retain some sense of cultural autonomy.

Preschool television in the 1970s and 1980s

Where the 1950s and 1960s saw the establishment of preschool television, the 1970s and 1980s were a period of consolidation within a broadcasting landscape that was still dominated by a limited number of broadcasters. In Britain the 1970s saw a shift from the paternalistic approach embodied by *Watch with Mother*, which was dropped in 1980, to the more child-centred discourse, embodied by *Play School* which emphasised children's autonomy (Buckingham et al., 1999: 149) as 'playful learner[s]' (ibid.: 160), without yet incorporating the distractions of the marketplace and the positioning of the child as consumer, which would come to the fore later. Drawing on the educational backgrounds of producers versed in the progressive traditions of the time, this concept of learning as play provided, according to Buckingham 'a justification for programme-making for the under-fives' (ibid.: 160). However provision was largely limited to morning, lunchtime and early afternoon slots on BBC1 and ITV. The 1970s and 1980s may have been the 'golden age' of preschool programming on terrestrial television (BBC and ITV), with preschool accounting for up to one-fifth of children's transmissions (ibid.: 98), but the number of shows was still small with schedule stalwarts like *Play School* and its successor *Playdays* accounting for more than three-quarters of the 30–40 minutes dedicated to preschoolers on each channel on week days.

From the 1970s a number of small British animation companies made short series, usually 13 five-minute episodes, for younger children. They included FilmFair (*The Herbs*, 1967; *The Wombles*, 1973–75; *Paddington Bear*, 1975–83), Smallfilms (*Bagpuss*, 1974) and Woodland Animations (*Postman Pat*, 1981–82). Some productions were destined for *Watch with Mother* such as *Mr Benn* (Zephyr Films, 1970), *Bod* (Bodfilms, 1975) and *The Mister Men* (Mister Films, 1974–76). Others with cross-over appeal (*The Wombles, Paddington Bear*) filled a 5-minute pre-news slot at 5.35 p.m. on BBC1, encouraging a mixed audience of children and adults and a window of opportunity for those producers who had toys associated with their productions (Sheridan, 2004: 18–19).

However, the main change during this period was the replacement in 1988 of *Play School* with *Playdays*. Shown daily in 'real time' it not only represented a continuation of the mixed format, but also featured children and presenters together, as well as jokes, songs, rhymes and crafts, all linked by frequent encouragement to children to join in and help solve the puzzles and clues in each episode (Messenger Davies, 1995: 24–8) in much the same way as *Blue's Clues* in the United States almost a decade later. More didactic than *Play School*, *Playdays* was, according to Anna Home, an attempt to make preschool television more contemporary and multicultural (1993: 76).

In the 1960s ITV had not been a high-profile provider of preschool television and in 1962 it had been criticised by the government-appointed Pilkington Committee for its over-reliance on US imports (Pilkington Committee, 1962). Subjected thereafter to greater supervision by the regulator, the Independent Television Authority (ITA) and mandated to provide children's programming, including preschool programming, it began to develop a more varied children's schedule. Indeed until the 1990 Broadcasting Act the IBA (Independent Broadcasting Authority, the successor to the ITA) undertook an interventionist role on issues such as scheduling and programme range, and was represented on the ITV network's Children's Sub-Committee (Blumler, 1992: 30). However, ITV always suffered from the fragmented federal structure of the ITV network, with separate regional companies often more interested in competing with each other than in co-ordinating an effective children's schedule (Home, 1993: 45–6; Messenger Davies, 1995: 23). Its historical commitment to children's television and preschool television was never as strong as the BBC's, a weakness which became all too apparent from 2005 onwards when it sought to reduce its commitment to children's originations, which had became a burden in a more competitive environment (see Chapter 10). Nevertheless, in 1972 ITV started to show preschool programmes in a half-hour lunchtime slot, inspired by the success of *Sesame Street* (Sheridan, 2004: 202). Combining human presenters, puppets and costumed characters, with a more concerted attempt to integrate numeracy and literacy in preparation for school, in-house produced shows such as *Rainbow* (1972–95, Thames Television), *Pipkins* (1974–81, ATV), *Hickory House* (1973–77, Granada) and *Mr Trimble* (1973–76, Yorkshire TV) began to erode the BBC's dominance for the first time (McGown, ND). Like *Play School* these shows were embedded in British life with filmed inserts that reflected children's everyday experiences.

In America the 1970s and 1980s became, according to Seiter, a battleground of 'competing and contradictory positions' about the benefits or disadvantages of television by producers, advocacy groups and academics (1993: 30–1). This was a period of public advocacy, foremost by Action for Children's Television (ACT), which petitioned the FCC to adopt rules prohibiting sponsorship and advertising in and around children's programmes (see Hendershot, 1998: 62ff; Palmer, 1987: 31–4). Responding to public pressure the FCC underlined broadcasters' obligations to children in 1974, recommending better compliance with the industry's own advertising standards and more varied and better scheduled children's output (FCC, 1974; Palmer, 1988: 41). However, essentially the commercial television industry was left to self-regulate, and had no real incentive to substantially change its practices (Kunkel and Watkins, 1987: 375). Indeed by the early 1980s under the deregulatory Reagan administration, the FCC 'ratified its indifference to children's interests' (Palmer, 1988: 43) by rescinding all its previous guidelines on children's content and advertising (FCC, 1984a, b).

Saturday morning animation continued to rule on the US commercial networks (ABC, CBS, NBC) with syndicated repeats on local stations on weekday afternoons. Cable was beginning to make an impact in the 1980s, but there were no changes in the economics of children's television, which persisted in favouring mass audiences, animation and commercial interests over the public interest (Allen, 2001: 482; Turow, 1981: 120). Preschool programming was largely confined to PBS with *Sesame Street* (39 hours) and *Mister Rogers' Neighborhood* (7.5 hours) accounting for 53 per cent of new children's programme hours broadcast by PBS in 1984–85 (Palmer, 1988: 10). In the meantime a whole raft of studies began to appear on children's age-related attention to and comprehension of television, drawing on psychological models of child development (see e.g. Bryant and Anderson, 1983; Dorr, 1986), reinforcing the view that programming needed to recognise age variation and the constraints which younger children's development places on their understanding and ability to learn. This emphasis on educational content within preschool provision served to justify PBS' continued existence (Hendershot, 2002: 83). According to Palmer, when PBS faced financial and deregulatory threats in the 1980s, commercial broadcasters supported it because they feared that PBS' demise would signal the burden of unprofitable educational preschool programming which 'had been steadily swept clean over the years' (1987: 65). This view would change in the 1990s.

Where the United States differed from the United Kingdom at this time was in the targeting of children with programmes designed to function as 30-minute commercials for toys and games (see Engelhardt, 1986), a development encouraged by the FCC's removal of limited advertising restrictions in 1984. Animated series such as *Care Bears*, *Transformers* and *He-Man*, which appealed to preschoolers as well as school-age children, were created and funded by toy manufacturers with stories and characters shaped by the commercial priorities of the toy companies (Engelhardt, 1986; Hendershot, 1998). Children's television in the United States thus became a victim of ineffective regulation and government disinterest as the business in licensed characters boomed. In the words of one commentator the children's television business in the 1980s was based on three principles: 'keep the audience up, the costs down and the regulators out' (Schneider, 1987: 5).

In some ways the 1970s and 1980s were preschool highpoints for the BBC and PBS, but there was little competition for this audience. This began to change in the 1980s with the emergence of cable, allowing more channels, including niche channels. What set Britain and America apart at this point was the distinction between institution and product. The BBC's preschool output came largely from one institution that had its own corporate ethos and 'shared references with its audience', which were about 'enculturate'[ing] the child viewer into becoming' part of the 'grown-up world' of British public service broadcasting (Messenger Davies, 1995: 23). Within the 'cosy duopoly' that constituted public service across both the BBC and ITV, there was less concern about educational efficacy because children's television was already underpinned by a public service ethos, which assumed an underlying educational rationale, even if this was not expressly articulated. The British approach was something that PBS and *Sesame Street* or *Mr Rogers' Neighborhood* as specific programmes, could not emulate because there were insufficient resources to experiment with alternative preschool formats or to use preschool as a springboard for programming targeting older children, which could compete with commercial television's entertainment offerings.

Preschool television in the 1990s

By the 1990s both countries were part of a multi-channel landscape and initially it looked as if children's provision might decline as generalist channels fought to secure their share of the adult audience. By 1996 BBC1 had more than halved its preschool provision from 490 minutes in 1991 to less than 200 minutes (Messenger Davies and Corbett, 1997: 233) in order to free up daytime schedules for adult programming. At the same time, however, preschool programming on BBC2 grew from less than 100 to more than 700 minutes a year (ibid.). ITV also reduced its preschool provision, dropping its lunchtime slots, and broadcasting 338 minutes in 1996 down from 435 minutes in 1991 (ibid.). In 1991 Channel 4 had briefly become the largest purveyor of preschool programming among terrestrial broadcasters (1225 minutes), because of daily transmissions of *Sesame Street*, but provision virtually disappeared from 1992 onwards (ibid.: 234). In 1992 a report commissioned by the Broadcasting Standards Council identified preschool programming, among others, as a programming form under threat because of a surge in animation (accounting for 28 per cent of children's programming on BBC1 and 20 per cent on ITV in 1991) (Blumler, 1992: 4, 39), a concern that was repeated in a follow-up report in 1997 (Messenger Davies and Corbett, 1997:74). However it should be noted that preschool provision is underestimated to some degree because the BARB data used by both studies tend to classify preschool animation (*Fireman Sam, Postman Pat, Oakie Doke, Adventures of Spot*) and even some live action shows (*Brum,*

Bananas in Pyjamas, Barney, Eureeka's Castle) as animation (see Messenger Davies and Corbett, 1997: 14, 179ff).

Palmer (1988: 27–30) identified the regulated public service ethos underpinning the BBC-ITV duopoly as a model of quality children's programming, because of its ability to sustain high levels of original production across a range of genres and ages. By the 1990s this model was under deregulatory strain. The forces of commerce, technology, deregulation and global markets brought new players in the form of US-owned children's channels including Nickelodeon (1993), Cartoon Network (1993) and Disney (1995). What had been a small world of producers with similar backgrounds and programme-making philosophies employed either by the BBC or individual ITV companies, was further altered by the 1990 Broadcasting Act, which required ITV and the BBC to source 25 per cent of qualifying originations from independent producers. ITV was still mandated under the 1990 Broadcasting Act to broadcast a range of children's programmes (set at 10 hours a week) and obliged by the Independent Television Commission (ITC) to invest in originations, including 70 hours of preschool programming annually. Yet mindful of its commercial competitiveness, it is doubtful whether ITV, without its regulatory obligations, would have maintained this commitment to programme range in children's television (see Vanessa Chapman, Controller of Children's, ITV, cited in Messenger Davies, 2001a: 27). The economics of the market place were also changing in other ways. Whereas most British productions had been fully funded by broadcasters, this became more difficult in the 1990s as audiences and revenues fragmented, forcing programme-makers to locate additional funding in overseas and ancillary (home entertainment, consumer products) markets.

Teletubbies produced by Ragdoll Productions for the BBC in 1997 exemplified these new challenges, particularly in balancing public service, educational, international and commercial priorities in a more commercialised global marketplace. As a replacement for the BBC's *Playdays*, its bright costumed characters and surreal settings, looked and sounded very different to anything that had preceded it, prompting widespread controversy about 'dumbing down' because of its use of 'baby talk' and lack of traditional instructional content (see Buckingham, 2002 for an account), particularly from those who saw it as a cynical attempt to target the under-twos with what were seen as spurious educational claims (Linn, 2004: 55–9). As a joint venture with the BBC Schools Department the series was underpinned by a broad educational logic and it was targeted at a younger narrower age group

(2- to 3-year olds) than previous BBC programmes. What marked it out as a product for the international market was the involvement of the corporation's commercial subsidiary, BBC Worldwide, which clearly saw early potential from overseas sales and ancillary rights exploitation, and whose involvement was crucial in funding the series' many episodes. This placed the BBC precariously on the boundary of public service and commercial activities, a dilemma, which as we shall see was also beginning to confront PBS in the United States.

In America in the meantime concerted attempts were underway to regulate children's television. The 1990 Children's Television Act demanded that US broadcasters provide educational and informational programming. However, because the definition of educational programming was so liberally interpreted, it remained largely ineffective until the passage of an amendment in 1996, which requires broadcasters to transmit 3 hours of identifiable educational programming a week in specific timeslots (FCC, 1996; Kunkel, 2007). This led to broadcasters and producers engaging educational experts and consultants in order to meet the demands of the Act and legitimise the educational value of their programming, even if a show's educational value might have been quite limited (see Cohen, 2001: 577; Hendershot, 2002: 81; Oswell, 2002: 161–2). Yet the effectiveness of these rules has became less important as cable channels (particularly Nickelodeon), which are not subject to the 3-hour stipulation, began to dominate children's viewing of children's programming from the mid-1990s (Pecora, 2004: 35–7). With decreasing incentives to fund and programme children's content, the networks began to lease their Saturday morning blocks to external programme suppliers or programme providers within the parent company (Grant, 2008a; Mitroff and Herr Stephenson, 2007: 21). For example ABC, which was acquired by Disney in 1995, airs Disney shows on its Saturday morning block.

In preschool television, PBS remained unchallenged until the mid-1990s as the main purveyor of educational preschool programming with stalwarts such as *Mister Rogers' Neighborhood* and *Sesame Street* and new arrivals including *Barney and Friends*. Yet it was challenged on two fronts in the 1990s. First the commercial success of *Sesame Street* products and also of programmes produced for PBS by private companies such as the Lyon Group's *Barney* began to constitute a political threat, opening PBS up to criticism that it was wasting public funding and enriching producers who benefited from PBS exposure (for particularly stinging criticisms of PBS see Jarvik, 1998: 47–51). In attempts to cut federal funding the Republicans, unsuccessfully campaigned for the privatisation of the

Corporation for Public Broadcasting, even suggesting that merchandise income generated by shows such as *Sesame Street* and *Barney* be used to fund public broadcasting (Carter, 1992; Molotsky, 1997; Morrow, 2006: 165–7). Of course this argument neglected to show that government funding or direct contributions from PBS and CPB constituted only a small proportion of funding for these shows, and that licensing revenues, which were often exaggerated in press reports, were needed by the production companies to make the programmes in the first place, because PBS did not have the resources to fully fund content (Franklin et al., 2001: 517). PBS did participate in the ancillary revenues of *Barney*, which launched in 1992, but these were limited because PBS did not anticipate the success of the show (Pecora, 1998: 108). Privatisation of PBS had been resisted, but there is no doubt that that the use of programming from privately owned profit-making companies had blurred the boundaries between public and commercial interests during this period, as PBS became a platform for commercial interests (see Pecora, 1998: 109–10), undermining its claims to be a pure, educational alternative to commercial provision.

Second by the mid-1990s commercial cable channels had also discovered the preschool audience, and the commercial merits of 'edutainment' (Pecora, 2004: 30). Although cable had emerged as the dominant player within the children's market overall in the 1980s, cable channels would not turn their attention to preschool with any vigour until the 1990s when the global revenue potential of licensed merchandise was finally recognised. Attracted by the commercial success of shows like *Barney and Friends* which incorporated softer pro-social educational goals rather than the more didactic content of *Sesame Street*, Nickelodeon launched its preschool Nick Jr. block in 1994, announcing plans to invest $30m in programming over 3 years (Carter, 1994). Up until that point preschool programming had, according to Nickelodeon President, Geraldine Laybourne, not always been 'an easy sell to advertisers' (cited in Pecora, 1998: 99), but as advertisers began to recognise the ' "extraordinary" influence that preschoolers can have on their parents' (ibid.), it became a more promising commercial prospect.

This was soon demonstrated with the commercial success of Nick Jr.'s *Blues Clues* from 1996. Based on a simple animated puppy, Blue, who assists the human presenter Steve in problem-solving, the show stood out because of its interactivity, inviting children at home to participate. Like PBS shows, and in a break with Nickelodeon tradition, which had encouraged 'a kids only environment', it was based on a written curriculum and formative testing, applied by educational advisors (Anderson,

2004). In this respect *Sesame Street* and the CTW model did have a legacy as a 'gold standard' for commercial rivals (Herb Scannell, cited in Beatty, 2002), who in the absence of regulatory pressure, saw educational content and testing as a means of achieving both parental approval as well as their wider commercial goals in areas like tie-in merchandise (see Sandler, 2004).

Conclusion

Since the 1950s when the preschool audience could hardly be imagined by most broadcasters, young children can now access a wide range of preschool content across many outlets. Starting in the 1950s through to the 1970s preschoolers were recognised as an audience in their own right with their own developmental needs and interests, but programming was largely guided by non-profit, public service goals. In the 1980s and 1990s, however, preschoolers and their parents became an attractive audience for a wide range of shows that combined public service/educational and commercial priorities. As we shall see in Chapter 3, it was this ability of preschool shows to exist beyond broadcast transmission in international sales and licensed merchandise, that would sustain the industry and allow it to expand beyond the child-centred confines of public broadcasting to commercial producers, whose interest in preschool television is not solely driven by the desire to produce popular and educative programming. In this sense British and American preschool production cultures, which were so different in the 1950s have converged on what Mitroff and Stephenson call the 'constant negotiation between the desire to shape children's programming around children's educational, informational and socioemotional needs and the perpetuation of television as a business' (2007: 4).

The origins of preschool television in Britain and America were based on different conceptions of the audience and different institutional contexts. In Britain the public service ethos of the BBC assumed a shared national culture which was inclusive and sought, often paternalistically, to educate children as viewers in the broadest sense, raising their tastes, so that watching *Play School* would inevitably lead to the enjoyment of more stretching plays and serials as adults (see Buckingham et al., 1999: 37). This assumed that all television was potentially 'educational'. The fact that public service broadcasting preceded commercial broadcasting in Britain was also important, because it later influenced the practices of commercially funded public service broadcaster, ITV and later Five, who were required to serve children with a range of diverse programming including preschool content as part of specific licence requirements.

In contrast the United States took a more 'laissez-faire approach' prioritising 'free enterprise' over 'government regulation' (Palmer, 1988: 30). PBS emerged within this environment as a stopgap solution for the failings of commercial television. Chronically under-funded it had little influence on the wider broadcasting landscape, but did acquire kudos for a small number of flagship educational preschool shows, whose success was really based on the energy and foresight of individual producers rather than a strong institutional ethos within PBS. With external funding from sponsors and government linked to individual programmes, there were fewer options to develop a strategy that allowed PBS to use preschool programming as a way of leading young viewers to other PBS programming. In terms of legacy, however, what PBS and *Sesame Street* did achieve was the incorporation of educational goals and research into US preschool production as a whole, validating the efforts of Nickelodeon and Disney with parents and experts, but also supporting their broader commercial ambitions in licensed products and cross-media applications.

3
Growing Up: The Rise of the Global Market in Preschool Programming

> The international market is a big piece of the success story for shows that can travel. It's really key to the survival of any production company. And any production company who thinks they're going to just make local shows and have budgets that are any good, is living a dream. (US Producer, 2007)

Preschool television is often cited as the most exportable and commercially exploitable form of children's television content (Cassy, 2000; Ofcom, 2007a). Like all children's programming, there is a new audience every 2 years as the old one grows up and moves on. Where many preschool series differ, however, is in their longer shelf life with some animation and costumed character shows exhibiting a timeless 'classic' quality, which means that they date less quickly than other forms of children's media such as drama for older children. If they are not too culturally specific they can be marketed overseas, where they can be endlessly repeated and adapted for a variety of revenue-generating ancillary products including toys and clothing (see Chapter 9). With their simple language and often non-human characters they are well suited to commercial exploitation on a global scale because they can be more easily and cheaply dubbed than live action. These factors contribute to the global success of *some* preschool series, an aspect reinforced by technological advances, which allow content to be globally distributed.

This chapter examines the transition of preschool television from an essentially local endeavour to a more global enterprise. It will chart how it evolved from prioritising public service objectives (Chapter 2) towards a more commercially competitive system, shaped by technological change, global distribution networks and the liberalisation of television markets (Cunningham and Jacka, 1996; Sinclair et al., 1996). The previous chapter contextualised preschool television in respect of its historical background, grounding in public service principles, specific national origins and underlying educational ethos. This chapter considers how audience fragmentation has affected the economics of preschool television with a shift away from full funding by domestic broadcasters towards greater reliance on multiple sources of finance from overseas sales, co-production finance and ancillary revenues. Having outlined and evaluated the increasingly global dimensions and economics of making television programmes for young children, the chapter will then consider how these programmes are marketed and sold, and the cultural specificities of overseas sales and marketing. Drawing on interviews with executives in Britain, America, Germany, France and the Netherlands, the chapter will focus on buyers' gatekeeper role and their views about the suitability of preschool programming. How are programmes acquired, what is the role of programme buyers and what influences their decisions?

From monopoly to multichannel – From local to global

The international children's television landscape is mimicking adult network expansion. Local culture is intertwined with global culture, whereby children from around the world share the same interests, watch the same programming, play the same games, and share in the media preferences available in their living room, creating a space for the process of glocalization to occur as local and global influences collide. (Moran, 2006: 288)

Moran suggests that children's like adult television has become both more uniform with the greater global circulation of content and yet also 'glocal' (Robertson, 1994, 1995) as young audiences experience and interpret programmes from within their own culture. For some, these developments raise concerns about standardised content, conceived, controlled and distributed by a small number of transnational media conglomerates, based predominantly in the United States, whose corporate and cultural concerns represent globalisation and control from above, and which may be at variance with both local interests and children's rights (Hamelink, 2002; Herman and McChesney, 1997; McChesney, 2002; Zanker, 2002).

However, as we established in Chapter 2 historically preschoolers were not a major industry priority, and the first *significant* preschool endeavours in the United States (*Sesame Street*) and Britain (*Watch with Mother*) emerged from concerns about children's development and well-being rather than their international potential as a market niche. Animation for older children may have been internationally lucrative, but little preschool programming was produced or traded internationally with the notable exceptions of the 1960s US format *Romper Room* (Woolery, 1985: 424), *Play School* and especially *Sesame Street*, whose format has been adapted in over 20 countries (Cole et al., 2001).

This perception of preschool as an enterprise for a small audience, guided by public service goals, but with little commercial value changed from the mid-1990s because of the interplay and confluence of two factors. First, the arrival of multi-channel cable and satellite television (and later digital television) combined with deregulatory pressures that facilitated the opening of markets, resulted in airtime expansion, which permitted broadcasters to target children, including preschoolers, through dedicated channels or blocks, allowing the shift from 'scarcity' to 'plenty' to 'abundance' (Ellis, 2000). Second, the industry began to recognise the value of separating preschoolers from older children, not just in terms of audience needs, but also in terms of market segmentation and 'distinct brand identities' (Eryl-Jones, 2003: 3) that could be promoted and exploited across territorial borders and platforms (Cahn et al., 2008: 32; Pecora, 1998). This falling away of technological barriers and the growth in outlets at home and abroad reinforced the shift away from domestic public service priorities towards a more market-oriented global perspective.

Nickelodeon's establishment of its Nick Jr. block in 1994, now available in over 96m US homes (Rusak, 2008a), followed by the introduction of the Playhouse Disney block in 1997 signalled the 'discovery' of preschool beyond PBS (Public Broadcasting Service), and the beginnings of an international network of branded preschool blocks and channels across Asia, Europe, South America and the Middle East, as Viacom/Nickelodeon and Disney built on the network of dedicated channels for older children that they had established earlier in the decade (Westcott, 2002). Where America led, others followed with their own channels and blocks, particularly among public service broadcasters whose markets were being targeted by US transnationals. Public service initiatives have included dedicated preschool channels CBeebies in Britain and RaiSat YoYo in Italy as well as significant preschool blocks on European children's channels in Germany (KiKa), Spain (Clan TVE), the Netherlands (Z@ppelin), Norway (NRK Super) and Sweden (Barnkanalen).

The surge in dedicated channels and slots fuelled demand, forcing broadcasters to look beyond America for cost-effective acquisitions, especially as Disney and Nickelodeon were reserving their own productions for their own international outlets. This provided opportunities for non-US suppliers, foremost in Canada and Britain, whose preschool producers exploited what was then an undersupplied niche (Steemers, 2004: 134; Westcott, 2002: 74–5). In the United States a small number of British players developed relationships with Nick Jr. and PBS Kids to ensure the television access necessary to create an ancillary business in the lucrative US market (Steemers, 2004: 134–5). Starting with the sale to PBS of *Thomas the Tank Engine* (formatted within *Shining Time Station*) and *Tots TV* (Ragdoll) in the early to mid-1990s, other sales included *Teletubbies* (Ragdoll) and *Noddy in Toyland* (BBC Worldwide) to PBS in 1998 and HIT Entertainment's *Bob the Builder* to Nick Jr. in 2001.

Since then Nick Jr. and Playhouse Disney have filled their US preschool blocks largely with their own long-running shows, allowing both to profit from the benefits of a large domestic US marketplace to kick-start their own international expansion (Grant, 2009a; Steemers, 2004: 41). These players, with the addition of Time Warner (Cartoon Network), were estimated in 2001 to own or part-own 60 per cent of the estimated 100 dedicated children's channels worldwide (Jeremy, 2002). Rather than selling shows to potential competitors overseas, Nickelodeon and Disney, who are estimated to create and/or own 70–80 per cent of their output (Grant, 2009a; Ofcom, 2007b: 58; Westcott, 2002: 72) have used their own productions to feed their overseas channels and blocks. This allows them to exploit their brands in a co-ordinated way, consolidating revenue streams and capitalising on the synergies created by their position within vertically integrated corporations, involved in production, broadcasting, home entertainment and consumer products (Hamelink, 2002: 36; Segal, 2002: 14; Westcott, 2002). In the words of one US producer, these companies are focused on 'creating billion dollar franchises'. This also appears to be the strategy of the BBC's commercial subsidiary, BBC Worldwide, which has been establishing its own overseas network of dedicated children's and preschool channels (see Chapter 5) as a platform for other business interests.

In spite of the consolidated nature of the US market (Holt, 2003), focused on three children's players (Disney, Nickelodeon/Viacom, Cartoon Network/Time Warner), the United States remains the most important children's market internationally, accounting for two-thirds of the licensed goods business worldwide (Grant, 2009a; Westcott, 2002: 69), making it the most important market for exporters. However, with reduced access to Playhouse Disney, Nick Jr. and to Nickelodeon-owned channel, Noggin, (renamed Nick Jr. since September 2009) British and Canadian preschool players have taken stakes in alternative outlets available on TV, on demand and online. These include PBS Kids Sprout, a commercial joint venture launched in 2005 by Comcast, PBS, Sesame Workshop and HIT Entertainment; Qubo, a joint venture between NBC Universal, Ion Media Networks, Scholastic, Corus Entertainment and Entertainment Rights/Classic Media; and Kabillion Jr, a joint venture between Taffy Entertainment, Moonscoop, Remix Entertainment and EM Entertainment. PBS Kids Sprout (40m) has a lower reach than Nick Jr. (96m), but does provide an alternative outlet for content producers, who can not always access Nick Jr. to drive their ancillary rights business, reinforcing the view that mainstream distribution and promotion remain key parts of the value chain (Hofman and Schmid, 2002). Next in importance after the United States, particularly in terms of presales and co-production opportunities are the Western European territories of Britain, France and Germany, as well as Canada, Australia and Japan.

With a raft of new players (see Chapter 5) from the mid-1990s as opportunities expanded, the international preschool market soon became crowded (Fry, 2002). The sector flowered briefly but saturation and audience fragmentation pushed broadcast licence fees down (Lees, 2005a). Combined with the recent recession and a downturn in retail revenues from licensed products, producers of all types of children's programmes have had to think about different funding models.

The economics of preschool television

> Every show we've made has been financed in a different way [...] Financing the shows has become the most creative bit now. (UK Producer, 2007)

> We feel it's wiser to have a variety of programmes out there in different forms with different deal structures and the cumulative effect is that the company does well. (US Producer, 2007)

Like all television programmes, preschool television is distinguished by three attributes, which mark it out from other products and affect its global distribution (Hoskins, McFadyen, Finn, 1997: 4). First the enjoyment of a programme does not reduce its enjoyment by others. Although initial production costs are high (and may not be covered by the primary broadcast licence), duplication costs for other markets are low, allowing programmes to be sold into secondary and overseas markets below production cost, making acquisitions attractive (Wildman and Siwek, 1987: 3–4). For example it cost $65,000 to produce a 10-minute episode of *Bob the Builder*, but half an hour of animation can be acquired for a little as $4,000 in the major territories (Steemers, 2004: 34). Second acquisitions are affected by what Hoskins and Mirus call 'cultural discount' (1988: 500). This is where programming 'rooted in one culture' is less appealing elsewhere if viewers cannot identify with the style, values and beliefs of the material (ibid.). Preschool programming often exhibits lower cultural discount than other programmes because simple narratives comprising animation and/or puppets and costumed characters can be easily dubbed, and because shows are specifically designed to appeal to younger children regardless of their cultural origins. However cultural discount is higher for presenter-led live action programmes, which are more rooted in specific cultures in terms of pacing, dress, the foreign 'look' of the casts, body language, settings and unfamiliar forms of storytelling. Third, Hoskins, McFadyen and Finn refer to the 'external benefits' of television. This means that rather than purchasing programming cheaply from overseas, countries will invest in originations for cultural, political or industrial reasons, a factor underpinned by the existence of subsidies and quotas, aimed at encouraging domestic production or stemming imports (Hoskins, Mirus and Rozeboom, 1989: 71–2). For example in children's production Australia, Canada and France use broadcast output and production quotas as well as a range of other interventions including direct funding, co-production treaties and tax benefits to support local production and/or wider cultural goals (Cahn et al., 2008; TBI, 2006a). In France public subsidies are estimated to account for a fifth of animation production funding (Ofcom, 2007b: 25). In Canada tax credits and direct funding account for a third of spending on children's programming (ibid: 10).

Funding models for preschool programming reflect the diversity of content and national circumstances. In Britain, which has traditionally been bereft of tax breaks, a modest computer-animated 2D cel-action animation show might cost anything between £100,000 and £200,000 per half-hour, but more complex 3D CGI or stop-frame animation could cost anything between £200,000 and £300,000. For example Chapman Entertainment's stop-frame series *Fifi and the Flowertots* cost £3.5m for 52 eleven-minute episodes – about £200,000 per half-hour (Wood, 2004: 25). In the United States a show might cost anything between US$100,000 and US$400,000 per episode (Cahn et al., 2008: 34; Selig, 2009). Live action shows can cost as little as £30,000 per half-hour in Britain, but Ragdoll's complex live action costumed character show *In the Night Garden* is reputed to have cost £14m for 100 half-hour episodes (£140,000 per half-hour) (Lane, 2007).

In Britain cheaper studio-based live action programmes (factual, drama, entertainment, educational) that fulfil a public service remit but have little commercial or international value are often fully funded by the broadcaster (Oliver and Ohlbaum, 2007: 5). This is not the case for animation and preschool content with international potential. For example CBeebies fully funds about 50 per cent of its in-house productions and those that are 'purely public service', but programmes 'with a really tangible international feel' (Carrington, 2007a) need to be part-funded from other sources including the BBC's commercial subsidiary BBC Worldwide, an arrangement which has not found favour with commercial rivals, who believe that BBC Worldwide's investment in independently produced hits like *In the Night Garden* and *Charlie and Lola*, distorts the marketplace in CBeebies' favour in the battle for the best programming (ITV, 2004; Litton, 2007).

A pre-sale to a domestic broadcaster (primary commission), particularly in the larger territories, is now often regarded more as a platform for generating overseas sales and ancillary revenue streams. In Britain after commitment from a broadcaster, a producer might be looking for a further 75–90 per cent of funding for animation or any project with international potential (DCMS, 1999: 25; Oliver and Ohlbaum, 2007: 5). For live action the deficit might be smaller at 10–20 per cent. For a sale to PBS in the United States the primary commission may be nominal (Cahn, 2008: 35; Curtis, 2006a; Fry, 2002), with some independent producers bemoaning those 'who will still give things away for virtually nothing just to get them on air' in the hope of fuelling consumer product revenues. In America, Nickelodeon and Disney are still capable of funding programming in full on rare occasions, securing all rights in the process (see Allen, 2001: 479). Although producers might lose ownership they retain a backend share of net profits after the network has recouped its investment, and there are advantages in having the backing of a major corporation. As Brown Johnson, President of Nickelodeon Preschool, points out,

> If you have your show on a network like Nick Jr., then we'll play it every day. We'll promote it. What we provide is basically millions of dollars' worth of on-air promotion and support, because it goes on our dotcom, it goes in our magazine. (Johnson, 2001)

Without full funding producers must secure finance from other sources – from broadcaster presales/licences, co-production, distribution and merchandise advances (Cahn et al., 2008: 38) and in some cases stock market launches. To bridge or deficit finance these funding gaps smaller producers, without the expertise, time, inclination or resources to market their own shows may choose to sell an ownership stake in a property to a distributor or other investor. This has the benefit of allowing production to proceed, but also dilutes creative control and future revenue streams. Distributors may also advance against international and DVD revenues to secure distribution rights and sometimes a backend share of ancillary revenues, to be recouped from gross sales, but such advances have become rarer (Fry, 2002).

Broadcasters may also expect to participate in revenues from licensing and home entertainment in order to make a preschool slot with limited advertising potential economically worthwhile. For example, SuperRTL the leading commercial children's broadcaster in Germany operates its own licensing division and acts as an agent in the German marketplace, allowing it to take both a commission and a share of ancillary revenues in Germany. The prospect of ancillary revenues was persuasive in its decision to commit to preschool block, Toggolino, in 1999, allowing it to both acquire programming at low cost and make the slot profitable (Fry, 2002; Klasen, 2008; Schosser, 2002). This can be beneficial if it encourages a broadcaster to promote and schedule a show in a good slot, but according to some buyers, it works against shows that might do well in the ratings but exhibit only limited licensing potential.

In the past broadcast sales were an important part of the funding mix with international distributors expecting to secure up to three-quarters of a budget against a domestic sale, overseas pre-sales in North America and Europe and co-production finance before approving production (Fry, 2002). By 2007 distributors felt fortunate if they could secure 50 per cent of funding from presales and co-production before green-lighting a project (Schreiber, 2006; Skala, 2007). Moreover with a glut of product in the marketplace, buyers no longer feel the need to pre-buy at a premium, often waiting until a show is completed before committing.

With budgetary pressures, co-production financing has become more important, even impacting the US market. According to Michael Carrington, Controller of CBeebies:

The US wouldn't touch us with a bargepole for hundreds of years. Then suddenly in the last five to six years they're all on our doorstep saying 'Come and co-produce with us.' Now they wouldn't have done that six years ago [...] Well, they've got no revenue. Advertising revenues have plummeted in the US. Broadcasters therefore don't have the production budgets they used to have. So 100% at $300,000 an episode is now $230,000 an episode, but production costs have gone up. (2007a)

Preschool television co-productions are of course not new. *Sesame Street* has been produced with local partners overseas since the early 1970s, with co-productions numbering about 20 by 2005 (Cole et al., 2001; Moran, 2006). However in this case the primary motivation appears to have been about producing culturally appropriate, advertising-free, localised programming that satisfies educational criteria approved by local experts (Cole et al., 2001; Messenger Davies, 1995: 26–7; Moran, 2006: 291). Contemporary co-productions are usually much more about overcoming budget shortfalls and in contrast to *Sesame Street's* format model, which allows varying degrees of localisation the standard co-production model usually results in the same programme for each market.

Most co-productions involve collaboration between a project-initiating company with a funding and/or facilities partner. They can range from co-financing involving extensive editorial input and creative approvals to full co-productions where partners contribute production resources and share the division of labour. The advantages include risk reduction for all participants. For smaller countries, co-production represents an answer to a lack of scale and funding, particularly where the skills base is dispersed, allowing producers to compete more effectively with better-resourced competitors in North America (Cole, 2007). Beyond pooling finance and resources, other advantages include better access to partners' markets and editorial input which may benefit the production by reducing cultural discount (Hoskins et al., 1995: 240). The main drawbacks include the increased costs associated with co-ordinating a project and the need to compromise creatively resulting in less cultural specificity and more opportunities for dispute (ibid., 1995). Different partners may have different perceptions of what is appropriate for preschoolers especially when dealing with emotions like anger, fear, envy or loss (Brogan, 2008). According to one UK producer:

In an ideal world you would have a conversation with partners on major shows early on to see if you can […] get them to buy in at a development stage. Traditionally we've not done that, partly because the more people you have with a finger in the pie in the development and programming stage, the more compromises you would have forced on you […] Overseas there's an expectation on co-productions

[...] which usually is the animation model, of everybody having a say. And the risk is, of course, you create a show that's OK everywhere but not really hitting the spot in any market. (Interview, 2007)

Also for those interested in controlling rights to a core brand any dilution of ownership may be at odds with long term corporate strategies focused on building assets.

Increasingly such co-production initiatives are linked to securing tax credits and government subsidies in countries like Canada, France, Ireland and Australia. Access to the Canadian Film or Video Production Tax Credit (CPTC) or Film or Video Production Services Tax Credit (PSTC) is contingent on a minimum level of Canadian creative/and or managerial involvement and the use of Canada as a location (Cahn et al., 2008: 39–40; Canadian Heritage, 2009; Ofcom, 2007b: 17). Combined with co-production treaties these have made Canada an important partner in preschool television co-productions with American and European partners, accounting for up to 50 per cent of production budgets in some cases (Wood, 2004: 25). Funding is also available from the European Union's MEDIA programme for development, distribution and promotion.

Another piece in the funding jigsaw is the exploitation of programme-related goods such as DVDs and licensed merchandise. However only a small number of programmes have any value in ancillary markets. Before a licensed merchandise campaign can be launched, broadcast sales need to be in place to raise awareness (see Chapter 9), and there is always a risk that a property may not be successful on television. Declining children's DVD sales worldwide, from €1.2bn in 2002 to €911m in 2006 (Screen Digest cited in Reeve-Crook, 2007a), hit by the free availability of preschool programming on television, have encouraged some producers to look at alternative revenue sources in the online and on-demand domain. However, these new platforms have yet to prove profitable enterprises for content producers (see Chapter 12), suggesting that the skills of locating and co-ordinating funding from a variety of sources will continue to be crucial.

How are programmes traded?

The markets

I remember going to MIP and I was really shocked, at the way people were buying and selling programming. It felt like they were almost buying it by the yard to fit their schedules. They were saying 'What's the length of your show?' And you say 'Hang on don't you want to know about it?' (British Producer, 2007)

Programmes are usually launched at markets which are 'chaotic, unruly and unpredictable' and where no one knows, 'why certain programs sell one year and do not move off the shelves the next' (Cantor and Cantor, 1986: 514). The key television programming markets are MIP-TV and MIPCOM, which take place in March/April and October respectively in Cannes, France attracting over 10,000 participants (Steemers, 2004: 27). However, detailed negotiations usually take place away from this 'chaotic' environment at specialist European gatherings including the Annecy Animation Festival, Cartoon Forum, Showcomotion, Prix Jeunesse and MIP Junior. KidScreen is a key event in America. These gatherings are less concerned with programme sales and more about locating funding for new projects. According to Cole (2007: 6–7), they function both as business and social places where participants learn about trends, meet new people, share ideas, negotiate and piece together production funding in formal and informal settings.

The role of buyers and sellers

You have to understand the market and be absolutely in tune with what's going on so that you find a gap in it. It's not just what's going to work for children. Because to be honest a lot of ideas work for children but they're not necessarily the ones that get made [...] Preschoolers will pretty much sit in front of most things on television and enjoy them. [...] You have to understand the mentality of the buyers, understand the mentality of the toy companies, get to learn their language. So when I'm selling a show I'm using that terminology and making it work not just for somebody who's buying a TV show but somebody who's buying the concept. (UK Producer, 2007)

The key relationship for those wishing to sell programmes is with the television buyer or commissioning executive, a relationship dependent on frequent personal contact with executives in Europe, North America and Australasia. Sellers are 'very reliant on key individuals in powerful positions' within television stations who 'understand the power they have in their territories, especially when they know that you've got a particularly strong merchandising property' (UK Sales Executive, 2007). Brochures, the trade press, show reels and web sites inform buyers about particular programmes, but it is a sales executive's job to nurture these relationships through regular contact and information about new projects. For sellers it is more important to understand buyer rather than audience preferences. In the most important markets children's channels, preschool blocks and DVD sales are the main focus of attention, with the size, wealth and competitive situation in each territory determining prices and agreements (Doyle, 2002: 84; Steemers, 2004: 36). For example animation might sell for $1500 per half-hour in a rich, competitive market like the Netherlands but only $750 per half-hour in a larger, but less competitive market like China.

Within broadcasting organisations running mixed channels, children's departments often have a peripheral status, because broadcasters are more concerned with mainstream adult programming. In the United States and Germany sales to dedicated children's channels are now more important than sales to generalist channels, because they dominate children's viewing (Ofcom, 2007b: 1), a trend that is being replicated across other territories. On presales and co-productions buyers risk financial commitment without seeing the final product and without knowing how the programme has performed. In these cases decisions are made on trust, assessments of scripts and treatments, producer reputations, whether there has been a domestic sale, and pilots if these are available (Poussier, 2002; Van Kollenburg, 2008). Yet most international preschool sales are of finished programmes with buyers relying on trusted suppliers from America, Britain, Canada and France for animation, with European public service buyers sourcing live action shows from Scandinavia as well.

Most choices come down to a buyer's experience and intuition, 'a special feeling', and with the exception of the United States, acquisitions are rarely pre-tested with audiences either for appeal or educational appropriateness (Coolman, 2008; Klasen, 2008). Few buyers have a background in child psychology or education. Havens, however, argues that their choices *are* informed by a Western 'universal cognitive model of childhood development and tastes', which allows market segmentation of the audience. In this vein preschool buyers are apparently looking for 'simple storylines, recognizable characters, and non-violent educational programs' in contrast to the 'more complex stories and less educational content' preferred by older children (2007: 9). Buyers are clearly guided by developmental considerations in assessing the suitability of programming. This is apparent in the comments of the buyer for Dutch public service channel, NOS, who does have a background in education:

> There is such a variety of ages and development stages under the umbrella of preschool. We acquire early learning programmes, and

programmes for children a little bit older who can start to talk and can recognise elemental storytelling. And then there is a kind of a crossover age group between let's say 5, 6, 7, who are tending to step over to the Zapp programming [a block for older children]. Then there's a more developed type of storytelling, which involves more characters and more fiction in it and more human characters and less animals. What we try to do is to follow children in all the different developmental stages and to adjust the type of programming in the schedule. (Van Kollenburg, 2008)

These assessments form the basis of what sellers perceive as buyer preferences in individual markets. Programmes have to appeal to buyers in their role as gatekeepers, making decisions based variously on assumptions about what preschool children and their parents want, their own perceptions of quality, their experience of what has worked before, the priorities of their channel or block, their assessment of competing networks, the similarity of programming to other programmes, the target audience, and gender balance. Decisions are also affected by the amount of programming already in stock and how an acquisition relates to other programmes in the schedule. A key factor for preschool programming is that parents must be able to 'trust it perfectly' (Tenret, 2008), enough to be able to let their children watch alone.

For commercially funded television channels, these are often hard-nosed commercial choices related to the need to buy content that will deliver audience share at a competitive price or generate ancillary revenues (Klasen, 2008). For some public service networks, particularly those not supported by advertising (e.g. KiKa, Z@ppelin, CBeebies, PBS) preferences for quality, experimentation and variety may take precedence over ratings, resulting in choices being made from a greater range of programming types (live action and puppetry) and geographic sources (Steemers, 2004: 31;Van Kollenburg, 2008). In this case acquisitions may be mixed with in-house productions, often presenter–led, in order to 'balance the whole availability for children a little bit more, to make it more local and more European' (Van Kollenburg, 2008).

The adaptation and appeal of preschool programming

Broadcasters import or co-produce what they cannot make by themselves, and as children's programming is not usually a high production priority, it constitutes a fair proportion of the overall volume of global trade. Children's programming, consisting largely of animation, comprised 13 per cent of global TV programme trade by volume in

1996–97 (DCMS, 1999: 35). The United States was estimated to have a 60 per cent share of this trade ahead of Japan (6 per cent), Canada (5 per cent) and Britain (4 per cent) (ibid.: 34). In Britain preschool (*Bob the Builder, Fifi and the Flowertots, Little Princess, Make Way for Noddy, Peppa Pig, Teletubbies, Tweenies*) rather than older children's properties regularly feature in lists of Britain's top exports (BTDA, 2005: 15; Pact, 2007).

International trade in preschool programming tends to be dominated by a small number of properties from America, Britain and Canada. Among buyers there is a preference for animation and longer series (at least 26 episodes) to allow stripped scheduling. However, programme lengths can vary from short 5-minute episodes to longer 11-minute episodes that can be run back-to-back in a half-hour slot. Shorter episodes are sometimes preferred if advertising breaks are not allowed within programmes. Animation, either 2D or 3D, is the preferred form, with studio-based live action formats produced locally, if at all, because according to one French buyer, 'we noticed that children don't really want to see adults or to see live persons on air.' In one recent survey of the international children's television market animation constituted 68 per cent of blocks and 82 per cent of dedicated channel schedules (TBI, 2006b).

Producers focused on international preschool success will try to minimise anything that stands in the way of international sales, particularly to the United States. For overseas audiences it makes sense, for example, not to put written words on screen and the same applies to puns or language dependent jokes. The inclusion of songs is often unpopular with buyers, because these necessitate expensive re-versioning. British producers will even avoid words like 'biscuit' (cookie) or 'holiday' (vacation) when targeting the United States because, according to one British producer, 'you want to be as close to their children as possible. You don't want to have any barrier between your show and them.' Sometimes particular references or language are not acceptable. In the Middle East there is some discomfort with shows that refer to magic or 'hocus pocus stuff'. In America it is not acceptable for a character to tell another to 'shut up', call them an 'idiot' or express 'toiletty' humour because programming is expected to model appropriate behaviour (Copley, 2007; Dudko, 2008a; Johnson, 2001).

British programme-makers suggest that US buyers do not like programmes with too much cutting or narration, an assertion confirmed by Brown Johnson at Nick Jr., who justifies this by referring to young children's developmental capabilities,

When you make stop-frame animation you have to cut every eight seconds because there's only so long you can shoot a single scene. With our audience it's too hard for them to figure out the jump between the cuts. Little tiny kids are very literal in how they watch TV so if you watch the shows that we make in-house, there may be ten cuts in a half hour whereas with stop-frame they cut every eight seconds. (2001)

Yet preferences do change and Nick Jr. United States did acquire British stop-motion series *Bob the Builder* in 2001, because according to Johnson 'he speaks himself and the vehicles all speak' rather than relying on 'ponderous, old-fashioned narration' (2001). This connects with what one US executive has called the importance of 'kid relatability' where 'the kid has to identify with all the characters in the show' (Schwalbe, 2008). For instance Johnson's decision to screen *Bob the Builder* was influenced by what she perceived as the show's sensitivity to young children's concerns,

My philosophy is that you start with the audience. I try and think what our audience would be the most interested in seeing. What stories and characters would be the most compelling and what kinds of shows would add variety to our air. So when we were considering *Bob the Builder* there were lots of stop motion programmes that were available. There was *Thomas the Tank Engine, Jay Jay the Jet Plane, Bob the Builder* [...] I thought that Bob looked a little bit fresher than any of those other ones. And it was the least cutesy pie. I mean Bob is cute, don't get me wrong. But it wasn't twee, Bob's a real guy, and his machines feel real, and they have real kid problems (2001).

A key requirement in the United States is that preschool programming should be educational, that 'it has to be teaching them something' (Fowler, 2007). In the case of PBS, programmes should be curriculum-based and supportive of local Ready to Learn outreach initiatives (Dudko, 2008b; Schwalbe, 2008; Simensky, 2007: 139), a difficult proposition for non-US producers. One producer suggested that comments like 'It's not educational enough' or 'Where's the curriculum?' sometimes served as an excuse to reject programming for other reasons. According to Anne Wood of Ragdoll Productions, a sale of *In the Night Garden* (2007–) to the United States had not been possible because it was not considered sufficiently 'educational' (cited in Hayes, 2008: 215), although this had not been an impediment to its predecessor *Teletubbies* launched on PBS a decade earlier. According to one US producer:

> It's not that the US is discriminating against those markets. It's that US shows need to make sure that they're not modelling behaviour that they find inappropriate for *their* viewers. So unless you can meet a basic bar in terms of your writing and research, no matter how beautiful your show is, it's not going to get sold here. And I can give you examples of shows out of the UK where you have characters with large needles chasing characters with balloons and everybody is laughing except the US broadcaster. (2007)

For some non-US producers US insistence on curriculum is both creatively restrictive and over-protective, revealing discrepancies in both production culture and what is deemed appropriate for this age group. The perception that US executives are more cautious in their approach was highlighted by one British producer,

> I think one of the things that the Americans tend to do now with preschool is they don't want conflict. They seem scared of putting a child in a situation that shows conflict. So they try and round up all the edges of any spiky story towards a nice soft bouncy ball so that nobody could possibly be traumatised by any moment of the film. Of course, story comes from conflict [...] But you *can't* tell those kind of stories if you've got some child psychologist at the beginning who's coming at it, not from the story angle. (2007)

Sometimes differences can be overcome through negotiation. An episode entitled 'Dead Pet' in the British animation series *Charlie and Lola* did go ahead, because the producers wanted 'to deal with issues that upset kids' but only after discussions with co-producers, Disney and the BBC, about how to minimise any potential upset, including a debate on what type of pet it should be (they settled on a mouse) (Lloyd, 2007). Yet many non US-producers do adapt their content to make it more educationally appealing and age-appropriate for the United States, employing US educational specialists during development or even 'retro-fitting' existing shows to highlight socio-emotional benefits like teamwork and co-operation (Dudko, 2008a). For example, following HIT Entertainment's purchase of Gullane in 2002, the train series *Thomas and Friends* was rejuvenated with the assistance of a US educational advisor away from its original 1940s setting in Britain to become more multicultural with a wider range of engine and human characters, stories that satisfied broader educational objectives, and the inclusion of puzzles and activities that promote learning and interactivity (Spencer, 2007).

European buyers are less concerned with formal curriculum than their US counterparts. Public broadcasters refer to 'a slight curriculum' (Debertin, 2008) and 'elemental values' (van Kollenburg, 2008) that stress socio-emotional rather than curricular goals. In the words of one Dutch executive in charge of acquisitions for NOS' preschool block, Z@ppelin,

> It's important for young children to be stimulated by elemental colours. So as a result, for early learning programmes you should have these primary colours that are recognisable to young children. It's also important that they learn to work together with other children in problem solving. This is one of the values that are important for our channel [...] We think that children should solve their problems by working together and by interacting with friends, teachers and parents and not by fighting or forcing anything. The whole aspect of the battle against evil forces, that's not something that we would like to emphasise in our animation because we do not think that's the way that children should be educated. (Van Kollenburg, 2008)

Although there may be no formal evaluation of educational value, age-appropriateness and the idea that children should be able to identify with the stories and characters are just as important as in the United States. According to one French buyer,

> It's a bit subjective of course, but we need to have real stories. It's either 30 minutes or 26 minutes – real stories with child characters, with rhythm, dynamism and colour. We are looking for protagonists, which help the child to identify. So it means that for example on Rupert the Bear [Entertainment Rights], Rupert is a little boy who lives adventures. Or for example *Berenstain Bears*, it's a family and they go to the dentist and the first time at the dentist is a bit frightening. It has to be the same as life. (Tenret, 2008)

Among European public service broadcasters especially there is a keenness for European content where 'it's easy for young children to identify and to share to a certain extent the same values.' (Van Kollenburg, 2008). Referring to British preschool programming in particular, one German public service buyer explained,

A lot of UK kids programming does work. Probably also because the UK kids programming seems to be close to German kids' lives. Our audience can relate to the European feeling of the content of the programmes and the cheekiness of the UK kids programming appeals to them too. (Debertin, 2008)

However, not all programmes are perceived to be universally appealing. For example *Postman Pat* proved popular on Dutch Nick Jr., because it was felt that parents had grown up with the show (Coolman, 2008). In Germany it worked on commercial channel SuperRTL even though the character does not even look like a German postman (Klasen, 2007). However reception has been mixed among other overseas buyers, because the character was less well-known and thought to be too British (also Grant, 2008b).

The European offshoots of US brands Nick Jr. and Playhouse Disney acquire or commission only small amounts of programming from third parties, with up to 75 per cent of programming sourced from wholly owned US productions (Sandler, 2004: 65; Westcott, 2002: 73). On overseas versions of Nick Jr., *Dora the Explorer*, *The Wonder Pets!*, *Go, Diego, Go* and *The Backyardigans* form the backbone of what is on offer, with other programming occupying a more peripheral position, amounting to perhaps one or two acquisitions a year. However where there is strong local competition, there are greater efforts to impart a more local flavour in keeping with local needs and tastes. For example Nick Jr. in the Netherlands acquired Dutch animation series *Pim and Pom* in 2008 based on a popular Dutch book series by Mies Bouhuys and illustrator Fiep Westendorp (Coolman, 2008; Delphis Films, 2008). In the competitive British market Nick Jr. has also invested in local production to distinguish itself from rival, CBeebies (see Chapter 4). Buyers in these overseas outposts look for programming that meets the 'Play to Learn' aspect of the Nick Jr. brand, but apart from being 'a little educational, but in a soft way', the educational aspect tends to be largely inherited from the United States with occasional adjustments. For example in Germany *Dora the Explorer* teaches English rather than Spanish.

Conclusion

The production and dissemination of preschool television has certainly become more of a global enterprise. On the one hand there are the transnational giants, Disney and Nickelodeon, who have long recognised the preschool sector as a lucrative business. Supported by the synergies of vertical integration they can afford to take a long-term, multiplatform, international view, emphasising brands, characters and stories designed to attract a global audience, fuelling ancillary revenue streams in the process. The growth in overseas markets has also encouraged a small number of producer-distributors to take advantage of multiple sources of funding to produce ambitious shows with international value. In this sense preschool television can sometimes be phenomenally successful, but there are also costs. In many countries preschool provision was traditionally the preserve of state-owned or public service broadcasters. The introduction of competition may have enhanced provision, forcing domestic broadcasters to improve their offerings. Some like the BBC or ARD and ZDF in Germany are large and sufficiently well-resourced to compete with US players, recognising the importance of engaging domestic audiences at an early age if they are to attract them as adults. However, this is not the case in all territories, where resources may be more limited. Herein lies the potential disadvantage of a global marketplace, if global brands and tastes come to dominate the sector at the expense of programming that reflects local culture. The predominance of animation, which can be endlessly repeated represents a major challenge, particularly to indigenous programmes that have more limited international potential. Moreover even if programming is built around international appeal, this is often targeted at the priorities of the US market, which may be at variance with local preferences and educational concerns. The demand in some European countries from public service broadcasters for European content that reflects European tastes represents a degree of resistance to these developments and a concern to preserve European sensibilities and plurality of supply.

4
Broadcaster Perspectives on Preschool Production

Chapter 3 stressed the international and economic dimensions of preschool programme production. In doing so it highlighted the significance of the United States both as the major market for preschool programming, and as a source of channel brands and productions. This chapter moves on to consider the broadcast environment within a specific national context – Britain – underlining the role of broadcast distribution as a key component of the value chain, and highlighting Britain as a useful case study in a global market, where broadcasters were reputed to have invested Euros 1 billion in children's programming in 2006 (Reeve-Crook, 2007a). The emphasis here is on British preschool players including publicly funded providers (CBeebies/BBC, S4C), commercially funded channels with public service obligations (Five, ITV1) and commercial channels dedicated to preschool television, namely US offshoots, Nick Jr., Playhouse Disney and Cartoonito (part of Cartoon Network). Focusing initially on the market, output, scheduling and expenditure, the chapter then examines the commissioning process and production from a broadcaster's perspective, using interviews to establish the extent of their involvement in determining what type of programmes get made.

However, before focusing on Britain it is useful to outline the US market, because insight into American circumstances provides a useful point of comparison with Britain, where US players are also active. The United States is the largest preschool television market with blocks like Nick Jr. available in 96m homes. However, opportunities for new preschool productions are, as we established in Chapter 2 and 3, largely limited to three players – Disney (Playhouse Disney), Nickelodeon (Nick Jr. and Noggin) and PBS (PBS Kids), who produce about two new series each every year, relying on past successes to fill their schedules (Rusak,

2008a; Simensky, 2007: 139). In February 2009 Nickelodeon announced that it would be consolidating its US preschool interests on one dedicated channel, re-branding the Noggin channel as Nick Jr. (Steinberg, 2009; Umstead, 2009). This re-branding took place at the end of September 2009. However, aside from Noggin (now Nick Jr.), US cable channel commitment to preschool had been mainly confined to preschool blocks. In the case of the Playhouse Disney block (6–12 noon) and both the Nick Jr. (9–2 p.m. Eastern time) block and channel, schedules are largely occupied by wholly owned productions.

In the week beginning 23 February 2009 US Nick Jr.'s weekly block schedule comprised ten slots a day and nine properties, stripped across the week. Transmissions included wholly owned shows (*Go, Diego, Go; Dora the Explorer; Ni Hao Kai-Lan; The Wonderpets!*), often shown twice a day and co-productions (*The Backyardigans; Olivia; Max and Ruby*). With the exception of one single transmission of costumed character live action acquisition, *Yo Gabba Gabba*, all shows were animated. Similarly US Playhouse Disney's schedule is built largely around stripped wholly owned animation (*Handy Manny, Mickey Mouse Clubhouse, Little Einsteins, My Friends Tigger and Pooh*), and an occasional co-production (*Charlie and Lola*) or live action show (*Imagination Movers; The Wiggles*). Noggin's 24-hour schedule comprises in the main animation and the occasional live action-hybrid (*Blue's Clues, Lazytown, Yo Gabba Gabba, The Upside Down Show*), often broadcast previously on Nick Jr. PBS' point of difference is its more emphatic educational thrust. While Nick Jr. and Playhouse Disney focus mainly on properties that highlight socio-emotional skills or basic foreign language acquisition (*Dora, Diego, Ni Hao Kai-Lan*), the *PBS Kids* block (as distinct from *PBS Kids Go!* for children aged 5–9), in line with its remit and the demands of its funders, concentrates more on programmes that encourage school readiness with literacy (*Word World, Super Why!*), numeracy or science-based shows (*Sid the Science Kid*) (Rusak, 2008a; Simensky, 2007). Apart from *Sesame Street* and *Barney and Friends* animation had come to dominate the block by 2009. Without the resources, distribution and exploitation possibilities of its vertically integrated commercial rivals, PBS is at a competitive disadvantage (Sandler, 2004: 64), a situation reinforced by the fact that it is not a producer, simply licensing programming for small sums without retaining an ownership stake. As a largely consolidated commercial market with a limited public service presence and few broadcast slots, the United States is therefore a difficult market for third-party producers to access.

The British broadcast and cable sector by contrast represents a rather different picture with US players forced to compete with formidable domestic players, foremost public service broadcaster BBC's preschool brand, CBeebies. Preschool children's channels comprised almost one-third (eight) of the 25 dedicated children's channels (including time-shifted channels) available in Britain in 2007 (Ofcom, 2007a: 23) alongside preschool blocks on mixed genre channels BBC1, BBC2 (CBeebies), Five (Milkshake!) and S4C Digidol (Cyw). Unlike America, preschool channels – CBeebies, Nick Jr. (1 & 2), Playhouse Disney (1 & 2), Cartoonito – rather than blocks are pre-eminent, offering more slots and possibilities. Most target the two-to-six age bracket although recent arrivals BabyTV (launched in Britain in 2005) and BabyFirst! (2007) focus on the under-twos and their parents. This chapter concentrates on those channels that target children over two.

Market overview

CBeebies, the BBC's tri-media brand available across television (CBeebies, BBC2), radio (BBC Radio 7) and online (www.bbc.co.uk/cbeebies/) was the market leader in 2008, fuelled by its availability in 63 per cent of homes accessing the Freeview digital terrestrial platform, rising to 87 per cent in cable and satellite homes (Ofcom, 2008a: 10). Established in 2002, CBeebies was the tenth most popular channel in multichannel homes in 2007 (p. 227). Meeting parental preferences for a channel without advertising that emphasises educational value and British content (BBC, 2001; Steemers, 2010a; Thomson, 2001), CBeebies has been praised as 'a triumph, an exemplary PSB service' (DCMS, 2004: 37) that contributes to the BBC's public purposes of promoting learning, creativity, diversity and emerging communication (BBC Trust, 2009: 23). Competitors regard this public service heritage as an important 'mark of distinction,

> I think CBeebies' advantage isn't necessarily the lack of advertising, although that's a plus for them. Their advantage is that they're the BBC. They are the most accepted thing you can ever get in this area in the UK. Anything they do is always highly regarded. Any show is successful by default because it's the BBC. (Commissioning Editor, UK, 2007)

These public service credentials are reinforced by a service licence and annual statements of programme policy, which specify that 80 per cent of CBeebies' channel content be dedicated to original productions (including repeats, in-house and independent commissions), and a general requirement to provide a mixed schedule that encourages 'learning through play' (DCMS, 2001; BBC, 2008a: 28–9; BBC Trust, 2008a). Traditionally the channel had a younger age profile than commercial rivals. In 2007 the target age range was extended from 2–5 to 2–6 to include children in their first year of school. This was done because it was felt that older children, particularly boys, were growing out of CBeebies at four, migrating to commercial channels and not necessarily transferring to CBBC for older children at six (Carrington, 2007a).

The launch of CBeebies boosted commissioning as the Corporation sought to fill a 6 a.m.–7 p.m. schedule with home-grown product such as the 250-episode live action preschool 'soap', *Balamory* (BBC Scotland). Unlike its competitors, BBC Children's, the department in which CBeebies resides, is a significant in-house producer. Of the 100 hours originated by CBeebies in 2009, about 50 per cent were produced in-house, 45 per cent by independents and 5 per cent by international partners (Carrington, 2009).

Commercially funded terrestrial rival Five established its preschool morning block, Milkshake! in 1997 before the arrival of preschool channels. Mandated to provide children's content as a public service obligation, Director of Children's Programming, Nick Wilson, identified a market gap, which could be filled with low-cost acquisitions which could not be accommodated at that time by terrestrial broadcasters (Wilson, 2006). Since then Five's focus has shifted from acquisitions to animation commissions and co-productions (about two-thirds of output) (Five, 2008a: 17), often in collaboration with Nick Jr. (*Peppa Pig, Fifi and the Flowertots, Roary the Racing Car*). Scheduling 22 hours a week, Five was an important commissioner by 2008, providing exposure for British programmes, but small commissioning fees (Ofcom, 2007a: 142).

Having been a major player in both children's and preschool production, ITV sought to withdraw from what was perceived as a costly public service commitment on generalist channel ITV1 (see Chapter 10). In 2003 and 2004 ITV1 was commissioning about two preschool series a year including *Boohbahs* (Ragdoll), *Pocoyo* (Zinkia/ITV Kids), *Jim Jam and Sunny* (Wish Films) and *Engie Benjy* (Cosgrove Hall), accounting for about 20 per cent of children's transmissions on ITV1 (Hughes, 2007). In December 2005 ITV stopped commissioning new children's programming, removing an estimated £25m a year of investment (Andrews, 2006; Oliver and Ohlbaum, 2007: 25). ITV launched digital children's channel CiTV in February 2006, but CiTV's £3.5m programming budget in 2008 (McMahon, 2008) falls well short of ITV's previous expenditure. In the summer of 2006 ITV announced the closure of in-house production unit, ITV Kids. From January 2007 it effectively ceased transmitting children's programmes on weekday afternoons on ITV1, because these programmes no longer attracted sufficient advertising revenue (ITV, 2007). CiTV, with preschool slots in the early morning and afternoons, now constitutes ITV's main engagement with children's television. ITV resumed commissioning of new series in 2008 but at much reduced levels (Rushton, 2008a).

S4C, the publicly funded Welsh language broadcaster, re-launched its previous preschool offering, *Planed Plant Bach*, as *Cyw* in June 2008 with a six-and-a-half-hour weekday block on digital service, S4C Digidol, and a 1-hour lunchtime block on its analogue service.

Ranged against terrestrial providers and the BBC are commercial children's channels available on cable and satellite platforms. Nickelodeon and Disney established Nick Jr. and Playhouse Disney in 1999 and 2000, respectively. Nick Jr. is 40 per cent owned by BSkyB and 60 per cent by MTV Networks, part of Viacom. Cartoonito, part of Cartoon Network, became a full channel in May 2007, having launched as a block in September 2006 on Cartoon Network 2. Unlike Nick Jr. and Playhouse Disney, Cartoonito only exists in Britain.

Broadcaster transmissions and range

In 2006 a phenomenal 15,428 hours were devoted to preschool, 13.7 per cent of all UK children's transmissions and a ten-fold increase on the 1,592 hours broadcast in 1998 (Ofcom, 2007a: 35). Seventy per cent were attributable to commercial children's channels, twenty per cent to CBeebies and the remainder to terrestrial channels (p. 42). However schedule analysis suggests substantial variations in range and form. According to Ofcom, CBeebies offered factual (91 hours), drama (153), light entertainment (271) and preschool programming (3189) in 2006 and only small amounts of cartoons (about 5 per cent of output) (Ofcom, 2007a: 38–41; Ofcom, 2007c). The figures need to be treated with some caution however, as Ofcom classifies animation for preschoolers (*Go, Diego, Go!*, *Dora the Explorer*) as preschool programming, confusing form and genre. Nevertheless drama, factual programming and entertainment were not identified by Ofcom as genres transmitted by either Nick Jr. or Playhouse Disney, whose output is classified predominantly as preschool (about 70 per cent in the case of Nick Jr.), followed by animation (Ofcom, 2007c).

Five's weekday Milkshake! schedule, beginning 24 February 2009, was dominated by animation with the exception of 10-minute preschool documentary *Big School*. Nick Jr.'s schedule that same week also comprised mainly animation with the exception of *Lazytown* (shown three times a day) and the live action animation hybrids *Blue's Clues* (shown once) and *What's Your News?* (shown twice), which accounted for about 20 per cent of the schedule. Playhouse Disney transmitted some live action shows (*Bear in the Big Blue House, Happy Monsters Band, Imagination Movers*), but output is also predominantly focused on animation. By contrast CBeebies broadcasts less animation and more presenter-led, costumed character and puppet shows, involving a broad mix of storytelling, movement and make and do which feature much less on rival schedules. In the same week animation accounted for just under a third of CBeebies' output, more or less confirming the BBC Trust's claims that while rivals devote 70 per cent of airtime to animation, CBeebies devotes 76 per cent of airtime to non-animation (BBC Trust, 2009: 23). Ofcom expressed concerns about the future range of preschool programming if reliance on globally attractive animation increases at the expense of live action and presenter-led shows (Ofcom, 2007a: 198). These concerns seem to be borne out by schedule analysis, which shows a prevalence of animation on many outlets.

Scheduling and promotion

With so much availability channels need to differentiate themselves so that each one represents a 'recognizable place within the domestic broadcasting landscape' (Lury, 2002: 35). Five and CBeebies rely on presenters talking directly to the audience from a studio setting. This creates a sense of identity and continuity, reinforcing, according to Messenger Davies, commenting about CBeebies, the sense of the channel as 'a real "place", a place with history' (Messenger Davies, 2004: 17) rather than a virtual space. Nick Jr., by contrast, is more graphic with no human presenters. In the morning, programmes are presented by the Early Worm puppets, Arnie and Barnie, who are replaced after 9.30 by Piper-O-Possum, a 3D CG-generated character, re-voiced and imported from Nick Jr. US. This is interspersed with animated channel or network 'idents' between shows, based around different depictions of the Nick Jr. orange and blue logo, and short-form live action interstitials (2–3 minutes) featuring British children involved in various activities between scheduled programming.

Alongside these logos, promotional trailers and mini-sequences, distinctiveness is also achieved through scheduling. Writing in 2002 Lury suggested that niche channel scheduling practices were eroding 'the traditional way in which time is structured by the television schedule and its relationship to the domestic routines of the child viewer' (Lury,

2002: 15, 2005: 100–1). Traditionally mixed-genre schedules were constructed according to age and availability to view. The BBC and ITV1 would schedule preschool programming in the morning or at lunchtime when older children were at school, and start their afternoon blocks with content for younger children, before moving to shows for older children. The emergence of children's channels seemed to make such age-and-stage-related scheduling and references to domestic routines largely redundant.

However, while channels for older children may have been divorced from children's domestic routines, this is not entirely true of channels for younger children (Calder, 2008a). For a start programmers need to appeal to an age-range (two to six) with huge developmental differences, and during the day older children are at school or nursery. To maximise audiences the mornings (7–8 a.m.) before school and afternoons (4–6 p.m.) after school are built around the availability of older children (aged 4–6), with programmes for younger children (aged 2–3) scheduled in between. Executives talk about schedules designed to fit children's 'rhythm', 'day patterns' and 'mood'. According to an executive at Cartoonito, 'It's gentle as they wake up. Then we become more active. Then we start to probe them and get them thinking. And then they have their lunch and, again lots of activity. As we get to the end of the day we slow down again' (Barlow, 2007).

Schedules are built around repetition and regular daily transmissions of landmark shows, which draw audiences in such as *Dora the Explorer* (Nick Jr.) or *In the Night Garden* (CBeebies). Repeats, totalling 95 per cent of output on CBeebies, for example (Ofcom, 2008a: 204), occur either short-term with the same programme repeated on the same day (CBeebies) or long-term over a period of time. Notwithstanding cost savings, repeats and regularity are, according to Howard Litton Managing Director of Nickelodeon UK, beneficial because parents and children do not want 'massive choice'. They 'want programming regularly scheduled at the times of the day when they need to be there' because 'in the preschool arena mums and dads have got this real habit and the day's very structured. You mess with it at your peril' (Litton, 2007). On a typical Nick Jr. day 18 different shows might be scheduled across approximately 40 slots with key shows (*Lazytown, Dora the Explorer, The Wonder Pets!, The Backyardigans*) occupying at least two slots. At Five's Milkshake! efforts are made not to alienate viewers between 7.00 and 8.30 a.m. by broadcasting family–friendly shows that appeal to older children before school (*Roary the Racing Car; Fifi and the Flowertots*) or have nostalgic appeal for parents (*Make Way for Noddy*) (Fanthome, 2006: 310; Wilson, 2006).

Attempts to recognise the rhythm of a child's day are exemplified by CBeebies. In March 2007 CBeebies introduced viewing zones targeting particular age groups, acknowledging children's connection with real time. Here schedules and notions of availability still matter. *Get Set Go!* (6–9 a.m.) targets 4- to 6-year olds with content that fits their morning rituals before nursery or school. *Discover and Do* (9 a.m.–3 p.m.) is aimed at the under-fours with an emphasis on storytelling, exploring, making and doing. *Big Fun Time* (3–6 p.m.) provides entertainment of appeal to an older post-school audience aged four to six, with *Bedtime* (6–7 p.m.) providing gentler slower-paced content as CBeebies approaches closedown. However, zoning programming according to age, and stripping the same programme everyday at the same time, tends to work against programming that does not comprise multiple episodes. Talking about CBeebies' *Springwatch* and *Autumnwatch* natural history magazines, a CBeebies producer, explained how it had become harder to accommodate this sort of event programming in a more competitive environment, even one so connected to public service purposes:

> Everybody knows the value of the programmes and the quality of the programmes. But the fact is that *Springwatch* and *Autumnwatch* are programmes made to a period of time, and it's not really repeatable without unstringing it and slightly repackaging it. So schedulers are not thrilled with them, because they get one showing, they're not cheap to make [...] Three weeks and it's off the air. You have to work harder and harder to justify it. Now I think the perception of the programmes and the feedback that one gets, and the knowledge of the value of having it across all channels, is a strong argument. But, it's getting harder and harder to justify it. And there's a phrase they love which is 'It's got to work harder for the channel' which means it's got more of a life. And you hear that all the time. And so nobody would say it shouldn't be there. They all know the value of it, but when the money gets tighter and tighter, and every fiver needs to go somewhere that's justifiable, there are strong arguments for saying that under the current scheme of things, we can't keep funding it like we have been. (2007)

Commissioning levels and expenditure

High levels of preschool transmissions contrast with low levels of commissions and investment across all UK outlets. Broadcasters do not feel compelled to commission large amounts of new programming every year, because they can rely on repeats in excess of 85 per cent. This is not necessarily bad for all producers as repeats increase exposure sustaining awareness for consumer products and home entertainment.

Of the 1,388 hours of first-run original British children's programmes aired in 2006 (excluding off-the-shelf acquisitions and repeats) (Ofcom, 2007a: 27) about 132 hours were preschool programming (p. 30) commissioned by public service broadcasters (mainly CBeebies, Five, ITV1). This represented a decline from 403 hours in 2002 when CBeebies was launched and even down from the 220 hours produced in 1998 (p. 30). CBeebies, the largest commissioner, was originating about 100 hours annually in 2008–09 (Carrington, 2009). Numbers of preschool hours for commercial children's channels are harder to determine, but if we know that commercial children's channels originated 135 hours of children's programmes in 2006 (p. 28), one might assume that preschool originations might account for at least 10–15 per cent of these hours. The domestic market in preschool production had clearly boomed briefly in 2002 with over 400 hours before contracting as the market became saturated with product, and the wider economic problems of the television industry began to hit the children's sector.

Low levels of commissioning are matched by low levels of broadcaster investment in the expectation that producers will locate up to 75 per cent of funding for the most internationally attractive shows from international pre-sales, co-production finance, master toy licences and equity investment (see Chapter 3). For animation British broadcasters will only invest a maximum of 30 per cent for a commission, dropping to less than 10 per cent for a pre-sale, although the differences between the two appear to have blurred with the decline in broadcaster investment (Oliver and Ohlbaum, 2007; Ofcom, 2007a: 68). A useful illustration of broadcaster funding is provided by Five (Five, 2008b: 16). In 2007 Five paid £2.5m for the virtual full funding of nine low-cost UK commissions. It also contributed £2.5m to 9 co-productions, which raised £19.2m from other sources. Five's co-production contributions therefore amounted to about 11–12 per cent of funding for co-produced shows.

Although broadcasters only invest small amounts in originations, support from a domestic broadcaster like CBeebies or Five is crucial if a property is to attract overseas buyers and consumer product licensees (See Chapter 9). This explains why the withdrawal of ITV1 from commissioning and transmitting children's programmes was so devastating for the UK children's production sector, depriving it of a key competitor to CBeebies. The UK producers lost an important showcase, but they also lost a generous source of support, because the ITV network funded commissions with contributions of up to 50 per cent in some cases, without taking an ownership position, because of network commissioning arrangements that prohibited this (Hughes, 2007).

Of the £109m spent in 2006 on original children's programming by all UK broadcasters (Ofcom, 2007a: 47), Ofcom estimated that only £11m was spent on first-run original preschool programmes, falling from a peak of £22m in 2002 (pp. 61–2). Of course the wider economic value of animation and preschool programming is much greater with 90 per cent of the £69m generated by UK children's television producers from programme sales (£35m), home entertainment (£11m) and consumer products (£23m) in 2006 estimated to derive from animation and preschool content (Oliver and Ohlbaum, 2007: 32). International licensing revenues might add a further £70m (ibid.: 33). The small amounts invested by broadcasters bear comparison with costs, where even modest 2D animation series can cost from £100,000 per half-hour, and the £14m spent on Ragdoll's *In the Night Garden* far exceeds the £11.5m budget for all CBeebies television content in 2006–07 (BBC Trust, 2009: 49). Of the £11m spent by all British channels on preschool first-run originations in 2006, Ofcom calculated that approximately £9m was spent by broadcasters with public service obligations (CBeebies, ITV1, Five, and S4C) (p. 64), suggesting that commercial children's channels, primarily Nick Jr. and Playhouse Disney, spent approximately £2m in 2006.

According to Ofcom, CBeebies contributed the most in terms of originations (£5.9m) in 2006 with commercial PSBs (mainly ITV and Five) accounting for £1.8m of investment (Ofcom, 2007a: 62; Oliver and Ohlbaum, 2007: 26). Other estimates vary. According to Five, the BBC spent £11m a year on 120 hours of preschool originations (including £5.5m on independent commissions) in 2007 (Five, 2008b: 7; also BBC Trust, 2009: 49). This compares with Five's £5m expenditure (excluding acquisitions and repeats) on 130 originated hours (Five, 2008b: 7) split between 9 commissions (£2.5m) and 9 co-productions (£2.5m) (p. 16). These figures underscore the BBC's dominance as a funder. In short the ongoing withdrawal of ITV from children's television has reinforced the BBC's position as the key supporter of and outlet for home-grown children's content, including preschool content, raising concerns about the plurality and quality of supply, and whether the market will become 'dangerously unbalanced' (Bennett,

2007) if domestic suppliers become largely reliant on the BBC (also Ofcom, 2007a).

The commissioning and acquisition process

Although broadcasters commission and spend little, linear broadcasting remains the bedrock of the preschool market, underpinning the power of broadcasters to determine what gets commissioned. Access to a small number of commissioning executives often depends on relationships that recognise previous success, providing commissioners with confidence that additional funding can be raised to complete a project (Litton, 2007; also Cottle, 1997: 137). The most important commissioners of first-run originations in Britain are CBeebies, Five and Nick Jr.

Commissions and co-productions, unlike acquisitions, are purpose-made for a network, so there is usually creative involvement from the broadcaster, especially during development and pre-production. Commissioners have clear ideas of what sort of originations are most likely to work for their channel and brand. According to Michael Carrington in determining what CBeebies needs:

> We look at the schedule. We look at our programming portfolio. We talk to kids. We talk to our scheduling team. We talk to the online response team. We look at the international market. And with all of those elements we start to build up a picture for what may be gaps in our existing schedule. There might be gaps adjoined to a particular genre, for example drama. They might be attached to a duration, for example short interstitials. They might be attached to a technique, like animation. (2007a)

All commissioners want shows that make them stand out from the competition, but as Carrington indicates requirements do change. At certain times there may be more demand for boy-led over girl-led shows, or shows for older children, or drama or music-based shows. Some programmes are deemed important because they tap into key issues. For example Nick Jr. was prepared to share transmission rights with CBeebies on the Icelandic live action series *Lazytown* that promotes exercise and healthy living, because 'kids' health and kids' obesity are bigger issues than a corporate battle between us and the BBC' (Litton, 2007).

CBeebies provides commissioning briefs for about 100 original hours a year that indicate which slots are open solely to independent producers

(25 per cent), to in-house producers (50 per cent) or to competition from both under the Window of Creative Competition (WoCC, 25 per cent), an initiative introduced in 2006 (CBeebies, 2009). In 2007 CBeebies was looking to fill two animation slots for 4- to 6-year olds, a comedy drama for 4- to 6-year olds, and a 'landmark preschool series' for the under fours (CBeebies, 2007). A rise in the upper-end of CBeebies' target age group from 5 to 6 years necessitated commissions for older children that bridged the gap between CBeebies and CBBC. In this vein CBeebies Controller, Michael Carrington was seeking 'slapstick' and 'personality driven' comedy drama, comparable to shows (*Basil Brush, Chucklevision*) shown on CBBC (Carrington, 2007a; CBeebies, 2007), but appealing to a younger audience.

Age is a key criterion of selection with most channels targeting the 2- to 6-year age bracket. Aware of concerns about targeting children under two, no channels (except BabyTV, Baby First!) target the under-twos, although some programming (*Teletubbies, In the Night Garden*) does appeal to infants. Within the two-to-six age range, broadcasters will target younger (2–4) and older children (4–6).

Another important criterion is that programming should not alienate parents and carers. Nick Jr., for example, cannot be 'crazy and mad and funny and wacky' like Nickelodeon for older children (Litton, 2007). Nickelodeon's Managing Director Howard Litton elaborates further,

> You have to have those building blocks around safety. Mum and dad have to feel secure with it. There's a big conservative element in preschool [...] There's still ABC, 123, colours, shapes. All that stuff is really important to mums and dads and quite rightly. And language. (2007)

Educational considerations and testing play less of a role among British broadcasters than they do in the United States where most preschool programming follows a written curriculum and is tested for appeal and comprehension (see Chapter 6). Some broadcasters are openly hostile to curriculum. Nick Wilson, Director of Programming for Five's Milkshake! has commented,

> Just don't make them too long or too full of curriculum. I hate that. If your first line in the pitch talks about the curriculum at all, I'm not reading any further. (Cited in Rusak, 2008b)

CBeebies is the most didactic of the preschool channels and the promotion of education and learning forms part of its public service purposes (BBC, 2008; BBC Trust, 2008a). CBeebies content is supposed to be linked to official preschool and school curricula, and developed and produced using 'pre-school specialists' (BBC Trust, 2008a), although the nature and provenance of this specialist advice is not set out in detail. In practice educational objectives are approached pragmatically with all programming perceived to have 'implicit learning value' (Carrington, 2007a, b). Educational and child-development experts are often consulted for specific projects, but educational objectives are rarely overt or tested. According to CBeebies Controller, Carrington:

> We are an entertainment network, don't get me wrong. But everything we do we think about the effect on the child. And whether it's through personal development or whether it's actually teaching them something like maths through *NumberJacks*, we'll do it. We just won't say we're doing it because [that's'] the last thing the audience wants to hear. (2007a)

This pragmatism is reflected in commissioning briefs, which contain little educational detail: 'Although any concept should have strong underlying learning values, as with all CBeebies output, the storytelling is "key" ' (CBeebies, 2009). However, educational underpinning within the BBC is seen as an increasingly important adjunct to its production activities in the light of criticism (see e.g. Sigman, 2007) that television is harmful to children (Stewart, 2007). Other channels make a point of distinguishing themselves from CBeebies by being less 'overtly educational'. Nick Jr. UK does not undertake the same level of formative testing for its UK originations as US Nick Jr., preferring to be 'educational with a small "e" ' because 'mostly it's about entertainment' (Litton, 2007). Newcomer Cartoonito consulted French language experts in the course of developing the *Cartoonitos*, French-speaking cartoon characters that are used as interstitials between scheduled programming. However, the emphasis remains firmly on 'entertaining and laughter' (Persson, 2007) rather than education.

All those who commission programmes are fairly consistent about what inspires them with well-defined stories, good scripts and characters which children can 'connect with' high in their list of priorities. For example, for Michael Carrington, Bob in *Bob the Builder* appealed because he was a real character, and 'if you didn't have Bob, and you just had the animated vehicles, I suspect that it would do less well on

CBeebies' because 'you can't just rely on inanimated objects animated' (Carrington, 2007a). However, just like their overseas counterparts (see Chapter 3), final decisions are often accredited to 'gut instinct' or something that 'just touches you somewhere inside your head or your heart immediately you see it' (Litton, 2007). Certainly other constraints – the availability of resources, space in the schedule, how a commission relates to other programmes – also play a role. For commercial channels looking to make a preschool slot pay, opportunities to benefit from a programme financially, in the form of a share of ancillary revenues from consumer products and home entertainment may also be decisive (Litton, 2007; Wilson, 2006).

Different channels, of course, have different priorities. Nick Wilson at Five's Milkshake! has been keen on 3D animation for a schedule dominated by British animation series. Although 2D series such as *Peppa Pig* and *Little Princess* are important, Milkshake! had by 2008 built a reputation on high profile 3D CGI or stop-frame animation including *Make Way for Noddy* (Chorion), *Fifi and the Flowertots* (Chapman Entertainment) and *Rupert Bear* (Entertainment Rights, ER) which according to Wilson are 'very typical Milkshake programmes' because 'you feel you could put your hands into the screen and hold the characters' (Wilson, 2006). In 2009 there was no demand for presenter-led or studio-based half-hour shows, but there was a call for drama for 4- to 7-year olds (Five, 2009). Although it only had an annual programming budget of £6m in 2008, Five has made small but strategic investments (5–50 percent) in highly commercial British programmes, often in collaboration with Nick Jr. (*Peppa Pig, Roary the Racing Car, Fifi and the Flowertots*) which also allow it to benefit from backend revenues, making the slot more profitable than programming for children older than seven (Wilson, 2006), which was dropped in 2007, only to be resurrected at weekends in September 2009. Full funding is available for cheaper 2D animation and a small number of mini-documentaries (*Animal Antics, Insect Antics, When I Grow Up, Big School*), which benefit smaller producers (Five, 2008b: 11) but more costly series can only be partially funded. According to Wilson, 'Co-production is the absolute key to being able to maintain the schedule that we do' (Wilson, 2006).

In line with its service licence CBeebies looks at a broader programme range than the narrative-led animation that forms the core of output on rival broadcasters. Live action shows with humans and puppets (e.g. *Tikkabilla, Boogie Beebies, Space Pirates, Storytellers*) are often produced and fully funded in-house, because they have less value internationally. A case in point is provided by *Something Special* a programme for and featuring children with special needs, that also attracts a wider audience, or *Nina and the Neurons*, a science show from BBC Scotland. It is notable that while independent producers were invited in 2009 to pitch for a 22-minute 'Discover and Do' slot that drew inspiration mainly from internationally successful animation and costume character shows (*In the Night Garden, Charlie and Lola*), in-house producers were asked to draw inspiration predominantly from cheaper live action formats with humans and puppets (*Get Squiggling, Come Outside, Tikkabilla*) (CBeebies, 2009). Consistent with the strategy of 'fewer, bigger, better' (BBC, 2008b; CBeebies, 2006), which involves prioritising resources on fewer titles which can be viewed more than once, there are few openings for new programmes, raising concerns from the BBC Trust about more repeats and reduced range in children's provision generally (BBC Trust, 2009: 13), particularly if commissioning decisions become more closely aligned to co-production funding (see Chapter 5).

Welsh-language public service broadcaster, S4C, pursues a different strategy linked to its goal of promoting Welsh language and culture among a growing community of young Welsh speakers (41 per cent in 2001, Ofcom, 2007a: 33; S4C, 2006). In stark contrast to the aspirations of global giants, its ambitions, sustained by government grant and advertising revenues, are decidedly focused on local culture with preschool regarded as a key part of this thrust. According to Merion Davis (2008), S4C's Head of Content,

> Preschool was the obvious place to invest because it's a transient community of viewers. They are only there for a certain amount of time. But if you catch them young and if you inspire them and make them feel that they are important, they have got a life-long loyalty then.

Having prioritising children's television to promote Welsh culture, S4C has since become Britain's second largest broadcast funder of children's content, spending £9.7m on originations in 2006 (Ofcom, 2007a: 66). In June 2008 it launched Cyw, a six-and-a-half-hour preschool block on digital channel, S4C Digidol. Cyw builds on a core of co-produced animation programmes with 'iconic status' (Davis, 2008) such as *Holi Hana* (Hana's Helpline/Calon) and *Sam Tân* (Fireman Sam/HIT Entertainment), costume character series *Meees* (Baaas, co-produced with Ceidiog and Al Jazeera), dubbed acquisitions (*Fifi and the Flowertots,*

Peppa Pig) and locally produced Welsh-language commissions (*Triongl, Pentre Bach*).

As in other territories, Nick Jr. and Playhouse Disney rely on programming from their US parents 'with amazing writers, amazing creatives, the best animation money can buy' (Litton, 2007). One could argue that commissioning shows from third parties undermines the commercial potential of wholly owned properties. Yet according to Nickelodeon's, Howard Litton, this is not always the case,

> If you think it's amazing but you won't buy it because it doesn't have commercial potential off screen or it has huge commercial potential but it might compete with something else, somehow you've just got to make it work. My thing is to grab it, stick it on, promote it brilliantly and all the rest of it. All that running channels is about is picking all the most gorgeous objects in the shop and having them all for yourself and stopping anyone else having them. And that's the way forward. You've just got to have the best things. (2007)

Access to a whole channel as opposed to just a block (as in the United States) does offer more flexibility to commission local content, a strategy pursued by Nick Jr. UK in efforts to reinforce its 'Britishness' against CBeebies in particular. Most US shows (but not *Dora the Explorer*) are revoiced, replacing words like 'cookie' with 'biscuit' because 'kids under five are learning how to speak, and their opinions are being formed, and it's so important that we're relevant to their lives' (Debbie MacDonald cited in Calder, 2008b). Nick Jr. UK has also invested in British productions through co-production or acquisition, and operates a pilot scheme, investing US$180,000 into two preschool pilots in 2005 (Jenkins, 2005). Approximately 50 per cent of the schedule was sourced from Britain in 2009. Commissions have included *Peppa Pig* (Astley Baker Davies) *Fifi and the Flower Tots* and *Roary the Racing Car* (both Chapman Entertainment), all co-funded with Five, and representing 10 per cent of investment in original content in 2006 and 15 per cent in 2007 (Ofcom, 2007a: 187). These investments have taken place independently of its US parent, suggesting some degree of autonomy from the United States. However, with more competition and out of a desire to retain exclusivity, Nick Jr. is increasingly less prepared to share rights, and has started to invest exclusively in British programmes such as *Ben and Holly's Little Kingdom* (Astley Baker Davies), *Humpf* (Contender) and *What's Your*

News? (TT Animation). Nick Jr. has sought to raise its profile as a channel with British sensibilities, but interestingly this is not programming which will necessarily air on Nick Jr. in the United States.

By contrast Playhouse Disney is more keyed into the global strategy of its parent. Playhouse Disney's British schedule is built much more around US shows (*Mickey Mouse Clubhouse, Handy Manny, Little Einsteins, My Friends Tigger and Pooh*) with few British or European-originated series (*Harry and his Bucketful of Dinosaurs; 64 Zoo Lane*). There is some reversioning and locally produced interstitials to reinforce a British 'feel' and reflect local culture, a strategy confirmed by Rich Ross, Disney Channel Worldwide President,

> It's vital to me and our entire Disney Channel team that kids see themselves, their friends, their families and their culture when they tune into our programming. (Cited in Webdale, 2007)

Disney has also made London a European production hub, but preschool commissions are clearly targeted primarily at the international marketplace, a point reinforced by the management of these productions from the United States. In 2007 Disney commissioned British producers, Baker Coogan and Spiffy Pictures to produce *Bunnytown* (26 × 30′) a slapstick comedy sketch show with puppets and music, its first international production from the London hub. The show was commissioned out of the United States to feed Disney's global network and although the UK channel team commented on scripts and the pilot, they had no overall creative control. The difference with Nickelodeon UK's strategy is that productions like *Bunnytown* and the CGI series *Jungle Junction* (Spider Eye) (Reeve-Crook, 2008) are designed to feed back to the States, capitalising on British creative talent among scriptwriters and puppeteers rather than focusing specifically on British audiences. Again this is confirmed by Ross who argues, 'We're not just interested in exporting US content around the world. We're also fully committed to producing local content that we can leverage globally' (cited in Webdale, 2007).

As the last entrant from the conglomerates, Cartoonito, part of Cartoon Network, is still largely reliant on acquisitions (*Hi-5, Barney, Pororo*) and archive material (*Baby Looney Tunes; A Pup Named Scooby Doo*). With a limited budget and a relatively small audience (see barb. co.uk), it has only limited resources for origination, but has sought to underpin its distinctiveness with animated interstitials, the Cartoonitos, between programming that teach children basic French, and short live action commissions that show children in everyday situations (*Go and Be a Grown Up*).

Once a programme has been commissioned broadcasters are not particularly interventionist. They do take an interest during development in treatments, scripts, designs, voices for animation and casting for live action. The ritual of 'giving notes' during development and scripting underlines their proprietary interest in a show (see Caldwell, 2008: 216), even though they may only be funding a project with small amounts. As a 'fresh pair of eyes' (Hughes, 2007), they may point out aspects that would be problematic internationally, for example the use of a red cross on an ambulance, or inappropriate for the age group in respect of language, health and safety (not wearing bicycle helmets) or similarities to other properties. Interventions also extend to the fundamentals of story structure:

> First of all I'd look at the narrative and make sure that the story is being told properly. I'd make sure that it was coming together as a decent programme [...] That there's nothing wrong with the actual construction of it. Then further on down the line whether it's appropriate for its age group, that what's in it is OK, that what they say is OK, and that it's true to its original brief really. And they go back as notes to a producer who will deal with the writers. (Stewart, 2007)

Broadcaster interventions will vary depending on how much they are investing and the producers' track record. Broadly, speaking if a broadcaster is investing 10 per cent or more for UK broadcast rights they would expect to see scripts and make comments on these (Wilson, 2006). For co-productions or commissions involving greater investment of up to 30 per cent they would expect more creative input including approvals as part of 'a much more collaborative event' (Carrington, 2007a). Once the terms of collaboration have been negotiated both financially and creatively, broadcaster involvement is light touch. The hardest part of the whole procedure is actually securing a commission and getting funded in the first place.

Conclusion

Although broadcasters often provide only small amounts of production funding they still occupy a powerful place in the value chain, as the main gateway to the audience, determining and shaping what gets made. Without this access there is no ancillary business, the largest revenue-generator for preschool programming (see Chapter 9). Deregulation and commercial pressures may have reduced the hold of some broadcasters, but for producers the 'big' decisions' are still taken by broadcasting executives who deal with the fundamental questions of whether to commission or not, and issues relating to scheduling and promotion. Preschoolers do now have access to more broadcast content than ever before. Much of this is recycled, and originations are low, but the variety available still probably exceeds what was available before the mid-1990s. However, as we shall see in Chapter 5, the emergence of a small core of producer-distributors has injected new dynamics into the process, with some companies increasingly discounting television programme sales in favour of ancillary revenues.

5
Players in Rights Management and Production

The previous two chapters illustrated the importance of primary broadcasters as a showcase for content and a key force in determining what gets made. They also highlighted the significant position of horizontally and vertically integrated US transnational corporations, Disney and Viacom (Nickelodeon), who since the 1990s have become active across all parts of the preschool television value chain (production, broadcast, distribution), both domestically and internationally. Yet children's television (including preschool) only constitutes one small part of the media conglomerates' activities, and it is difficult to produce financial data that relate specifically to their preschool activities. We do know that infant and preschool properties (*Handy Manny, Little Einsteins, Mickey Mouse Clubhouse* and *My Friends Tigger and Pooh*), together with other children's properties, represent an important segment of Disney's $2.9bn consumer products business, which in turn contributed to $37.8bn in revenues in 2008 (Disney, 2008: 28). Similarly *The Backyardigans* and *Dora the Explorer* are important contributors to Viacom's $1.67bn in ancillary revenues, part of $14.6bn in revenues generated in 2008 (Viacom, 2008). The approach by the US conglomerates is exemplified by Disney's integrated production and distribution strategy, which, in its own words, is,

> focused on reaching as many kids and families as possible around the world. The goal is to use this expanded reach to support the Disney brand, build existing franchises and launch new TV-based franchises that the entire company can leverage. (p. 38)

However, alongside the conglomerates, a further crucial component of preschool expansion since the 1990s has been the emergence of independent production and distribution entities, either specialising in content for younger children, or devoting a large proportion of their activities to satisfying this sector of the marketplace. What is also noticeable is how recent this expansion has been, with few companies involved before the mid-1990s because the preschool market was perceived to be 'too narrow and too geographically limited' (Dunfield, 2000) to offer any prospect of international success (Cahn et al., 2008: 32). The proliferation of preschool blocks and channels, the rise in co-production and international sales, the acceptance by US channels of some non-US shows and growing sales of television-related consumer products and toys, all worked to attract new players, including players from outside the United States.

Within this preschool niche it is possible to segment the market into larger and smaller players, variously motivated by 'commerce, education and creativity' (Cahn et al., 2008: 34). A small number of larger children's specialists (HIT Entertainment, Entertainment Rights, Chorion, DHX Media) have focused their attention on funding, owning and managing rights to preschool brands as a means of engaging children and parents across television, home entertainment (DVD), character merchandise (toys, publishing etc.), stage shows and increasingly digital rights, generating global revenues and satisfying shareholders – in much the same way as Disney or Viacom. Other specialists, particularly in the United States, but most famously Sesame Workshop, have focused their attention on using screen-based media as an educative tool. Between these two extremes there are many other smaller, less vertically integrated companies who regard preschool television as a means of 'exploring their art and creativity' (Cahn et al., 2008: 34) as well as generating sufficient funds to make a living and sustain future projects, or even of attracting potential ownership interest from larger production companies (see Faulkner et al., 2009). This chapter focuses on the background and strategies of a variety of players involved in the production and rights management of preschool content.

Rights-owning producer-distributors

Rights-owning producer-distributors are (with the exception of Nickelodeon and Disney) the giants of the preschool arena. In Britain, for example, BBC Worldwide, Chorion, Entertainment Rights and HIT Entertainment generated an estimated £350m in revenues in 2007 from children's properties, dwarfing the revenues of smaller British producers, whose turnover rarely exceeds single figures (Broadcast, 2009). Some of the larger players run their own production divisions; others confine their creative activities to development, outsourcing production to others. What distinguishes them from other producers is the emphasis on international exploitation and the management of preschool brands across revenue-generating opportunities, not just television.

HIT Entertainment

In many ways HIT Entertainment serves as a prototype for other rights-owning producer-distributors, because it was the first company outside North America to establish a business clearly based on the ownership and exploitation of all rights in enduring character-based preschool properties across territories and different media.

Established in 1989 as a distributor of third-party children's programming, HIT's management soon realised that sales of programmes owned by others, offered only limited growth potential as broadcast acquisition fees declined. Instead the company decided to shift its focus to the ownership and brand management of preschool properties (Caminada, 2001), funding and developing its own productions (*Bob the Builder, Angelina Ballerina*) as well as acquiring established properties (*Barney and Friends, Thomas and Friends, Pingu*) with global licensing potential. In 2009 it was listed as Britain's sixth largest independent company by turnover (£136.3m) and second largest producer of children's hours (45.5 hours) (Broadcast, 2009). As part of Sunshine Holdings, HIT had a turnover of $274m in 2008 (Table 5.1).

Preschool entertainment has been used as a platform for developing an ancillary rights business that now outperforms television programme sales. While television sales accounted for two-thirds of £20.6m generated in 2000 (HIT, 2001: 30), by 2008 they accounted for only 5 per cent of revenues, with the majority attributable to consumer products (64 per cent) and home entertainment (24 per cent) (Table 5.1). Television sales are simply the motor that drives profits in other areas.

The transformation of the company began in 1996 with a launch on the Alternative Investment Market (AIM), which raised £2.7m (HIT, 1996). A full stock market listing in 1997 and two further rights issues raised a further £30m (HIT, 1997, 1998, 1999). This allowed the company to fully fund its own productions and establish home entertainment and consumer products divisions, as well as an animation facility, HOT Animation, in Manchester in 1997, for the production of stop-frame animation series *Bob the Builder*.

Table 5.1 HIT Entertainment – Turnover by class of business, destination and origin ($m)

	2007	%	2008	%
Turnover	263.4	100.0	273.8	100.0
Pre–tax profits/(losses)	(41.8)	–	(16.1)	–
Turnover by class of business				
Home entertainment	86.9	33.0	65.9	24.1
Consumer products	147.0	55.8	175.5	64.1
Television	13.2	5.0	14.5	5.3
Stage show	16.3	6.2	17.9	6.5
Turnover by destination				
USA	142.6	54.1	129.4	47.4
UK	60.9	23.1	67.4	24.5
Rest of the world	38.0	14.5	51.4	18.8
Europe	21.9	8.3	25.6	9.3
Turnover by origin				
USA	139.9	53.1	127.4	46.5
UK	118.6	45.0	126.8	46.4
Rest of the world	4.9	1.9	19.6	7.1

Source: Sunshine Holdings 3 Limited (Y/E 31 July 2008), <http://www.hitentertainment.com/corporate/companymanagement.html>.

The risk is that properties funded by stock market money may not always fulfil expectations, particularly in a market that became flooded in the late 1990s with preschool content that was chasing too few television slots and too little shelf space for merchandise. However, the potential benefits from rare hits like *Bob the Builder* are substantial as HIT demonstrated when it launched *Bob* on US Nick Jr. in 2001 (the show moved to PBS (Public Broadcasting Service) in 2005). To fulfil market expectations, HIT needed to demonstrate that its success rested on more than *Bob the Builder*. In 2001 it acquired the US Lyrick Corporation for £189m (HIT, 2001: 2), producers of *Barney*, an enduringly successful live action show about a purple dinosaur, screened on PBS since 1992. This not only added US production facilities, but also allowed HIT to benefit from Lyrick's relationships with US retailers (ibid. 4). The incorporation of Lyrick fundamentally changed the company. US revenues began to dominate, growing from 27 per cent of turnover by destination in 2000 to 61 per cent in 2001 (Steemers, 2004: 97). In 2008 the United States accounted for just under half of turnover by destination. Further acquisitions followed. In 2001 HIT bought all rights to the animation series

Pingu for £15.9m, followed in 2002 by the acquisition of British rival, Gullane Entertainment, owner of preschool property *Thomas the Tank Engine*, for £137m. After an £11m fall in profits in 2004, because of a reduction in home entertainment retail space in the United States, combined with a break in US television exposure for *Bob the Builder* (HIT, 2004: 10), HIT was de-listed from the London Stock Exchange in 2005 and acquired by private equity investment group, Apax Partners, for £490m.

The key to HIT's growth has been the ownership and development of brands with long-term value that are driven by television exposure and work across different markets in home entertainment and consumer products. Recognising that broadcast exposure is 'the key to launching and maintaining a successful long-term cross-media property' and that 'correspondingly loss of broadcast is a key risk' (Sunshine Holdings, 2008: 2), HIT has tried to reduce this risk by investing in broadcast outlets, transforming itself 'into a vertically-integrated content owner/broadcaster' (HIT, 2004: 7). In 2004, it took a one-third stake in a US joint venture with PBS, Sesame Workshop and cable company, Comcast Corporation to run PBS Kids Sprout, a digital cable, video-on-demand and online service for preschoolers. With a potential television audience of 40m households in 2008 (HIT, N.D), the company described the initiative as a 'transforming deal that gives HIT direct input on the scheduling and transmission of our high quality content portfolio, as well as allowing participation in growing subscription, sponsorship and advertising revenue' (HIT, 2004: 7). In 2007 it entered into another joint venture with Chello Zone, a division of US group Liberty Global, to launch an international preschool channel (excluding the crowded British market). JimJam, reaching 6m homes in 2008 (HIT, N.D), has since been rolled out across cable and satellite platforms in Europe, North Africa and the Middle East.

Since 2007 the company's strategy has been to update its core brands. In 2008 it decided to outsource new CGI versions of stop-frame shows *Bob the Builder* and *Fireman Sam*, live action model property *Thomas and Friends* and 2D animation series *Angelina Ballerina* to North America and China (Buxton, 2008; Schreiber, 2008), substantially reducing production operations at its British-based HOT studio where *Bob the Builder* had been made since 1997 (Brooks, 2007). The decision was partly economic, fuelled by the then strong pound and high costs of producing stop-frame, but was also driven by tests that seemed to show that young audiences preferred 3D CGI (see Chapter 8). Seen in recent years more as an 'acquisitor' of properties than as a developer of new content, the company signalled its intention in 2008 of investing more in development and of undertaking more third-party representation (Christie, 2008a) in order to strengthen its portfolio.

Other players

A number of other companies, particularly in Britain, have sought to emulate the HIT model, but with varying levels of success.

Of these **Chorion** had become the most prominent by 2008 with ambitions to become a $2bn company by 2012 (Alli, cited in Christie, 2008b). Formed from a demerger in 2002, Chorion has focused on branded preschool animation, but with much more emphasis on acquiring classic, book-based properties, which it perceives as 'underperforming', 'creatively re-inventing [ing] them for today's child' (Chorion, 2004: 5).

Chorion's first foray into this type of transformation was Enid Blyton's classic children's property *Noddy*. Having acquired the Enid Blyton catalogue of children's stories, Chorion commissioned Los Angeles-based animation studio SD Entertainment in 2000 to produce a new television adaptation of Noddy. In defining a strategy for the £10m CGI production of *Make Way for Noddy* (100 × 10') (Broadcast, 2004a) the company was careful to outline a combination of educational and commercial possibilities to maximise the show's appeal among children, parents and commercial interests:

> During the DNA identification and development process for the new Noddy we focused on the various different brand extensions that suit the Noddy brand. We included the educational opportunities, such as language learning suitability for the early learning curriculum and developed a strong new visual appeal that could be used to create a range of compelling toys. (Chorion, 2004: 5)

Targeted at children aged three to five the series launched in Britain on Five's Milkshake! in 2002, debuting on PBS Kids in 2005. By 2009 *Noddy* had generated over 100 international television sales, over 200 licensees and 1,000 products (http://www.chorion.co.uk). A new series *Noddy in Toyland* (52 × 11'), produced by Irish company Brown Bag Films, was set to air in 2009.

This strategy of updating 'classic' publishing properties continued with subsequent acquisitions. In 2004 Chorion acquired The Hargreaves Organisation and Mister Films for £28m (Chorion, 2004: 15), the companies behind Roger Hargreaves' *Mr Men* and *Little Miss* books. The next step was the development of a new animated sketch comedy series, *The Mr Men Show* (52 × 11′) based on the original concept, but substantially different from the single character shows that aired in the 1970s and 1980s. Animated by Californian studio Renegade Animation at a cost of US$8–9m (Grant, 2008c), *The Mr Men Show* debuted with co-production broadcast partners, Five in Britain and Cartoon Network in the United States in 2008.

In November 2007 Chorion acquired British licensing firm The Copyrights Group, a specialist in managing third-party children's brands including Beatrix Potter and Paddington Bear. A US presence was secured in 2005 through the acquisition of New York-based Silver Lining Productions, who owned television, film and merchandising rights to children's books *The Very Hungry Caterpillar* (by Eric Carle) and *Max and Ruby* (by Rosemary Wells). One of these properties, *Olivia*, about a small pig, written by Ian Falconer has become Chorion's largest production to-date. Co-produced with Nick Jr. in the United States and produced by Brown Bag Films, the CG $15m series (52 × 11′) launched on Nick Jr. US in January 2009.

Chorion was de-listed from the AIM market in London in 2006 when it was taken into private ownership in a £111m buyout led by the management team under executive chair Lord Waheed Alli, backed by venture capital firm, 3i. This was done to provide the time and space to develop the company's existing brands, at a cost of £22m (Garside, 2008; Grant, 2008c). In 2007 the group generated turnover of £37.6m, but pre-tax losses totalled almost £21m because of interest on borrowings (Garside, 2008; Table 5.2). By 2009, the new properties appeared to be paying off. It was reported that Chorion had generated turnover of £46m with gross profits of £28.4m (Waller, 2009). Revenue from children's content accounted for 56 per cent (£26m) of turnover. Seventy-eight per cent of this came from licensed merchandise and over half from outside Britain (ibid.). Chorion has secured access for its properties on key US outlets – Nick Jr., PBS and Cartoon Network – a first step in recouping not inconsiderable investment. However, unlike HIT, the United States only accounts for 13 per cent of revenues (ibid.), suggesting it still has some way to go if it wishes to capitalise on ancillary rights in the world's largest market. In April 2009 it entered negotiations to sell its literary estates arm (Agatha Christie, Raymond Chandler), suggesting an even stronger focus on the children's business in future.

Founded in 1999 UK-based **Entertainment Rights** (ER) charted a path similar to HIT, establishing itself as a specialist in the rights management of wholly owned (*Rupert Bear, Postman Pat*) and third party children's

Table 5.2   Chorion Turnover by class of business and destination (£m)

	2003	%	2004	%	2006*	%	2007	%
Turnover	18.6	100.0	23.9	100.0	23.6	100.0	37.6	100.0
Pre-tax profits/ (losses)	3.2	–	4.3	–	(7.7)	–	(20.7)	–
Turnover by revenue stream								
Publishing/ audio/ magazine/ partworks	5.3	28.4	5.7	24.0	6.0	25.4	9.4	25.0
Television/ video/ films	11.2	60.3	14.3	59.7	9.6	40.7	14.2	37.8
Merchandising	1.6	8.4	3.3	14.0	7.2	30.5	12.3	32.7
Other	0.6	3.0	0.5	2.3	0.8	3.4	1.7	4.5
Turnover by destination								
The United Kingdom	11.1	59.9	14.8	61.8	12.7	53.8	17.7	47.1
Other European Community	4.4	23.7	5.9	24.6	6.8	28.8	10.0	26.6
Americas	2.1	11.3	2.1	8.8	1.8	7.6	4.7	12.5
Asia and Australia	0.8	4.4	1.1	4.5	1.9	8.1	4.6	12.2
Other	0.1	0.6	0.1	0.3	0.4	1.7	0.6	1.6

Source: Planet Acquisitions Holdings Ltd (Y/E 31 December 2007) and Chorion PLC Reports.
*17 months to 31 December 2006
Note: Turnover by revenue stream does not distinguish between the company's two portfolios – Children's and Crime.

properties (including Mattel's *Barbie* and Hasbro's *Transformers*). Unlike HIT or Chorion, ER's porfolio was more broadly based including live action (*Basil Brush*) and animation for older children.

Like HIT growth was driven by acquisitions. In March 2001 ER bought Link Licensing for £15m, increasing its library to 770 hours (Broadcast, 2001a). This was followed that same year by the £5.1m purchase of UK-based Woodland Animations, producer of the 1980s stop-frame perennial *Postman Pat* (Broadcast, 2001b). This became the launch pad for a new series, produced by Cosgrove Hall, which aired on CBeebies in 2004, followed by a further series, *Postman Pat: Special Delivery Service* in September 2008. The acquisition of the character brand *Rupert Bear* from the UK's Express Newspapers for £6m in 2005 expanded ER's brand

Table 5.3   Entertainment Rights –Turnover by destination (£m)

	2002	2003	2004	2005	2006	2007
Turnover	24.1	29.5	25.5	30.7	29.7	68.1
Pre-tax profits (losses)	−1.1	−0.4	2.2	6.0	7.8	7.9
UK	17.2	21.7	12.3	18.0	12.7	9.8
Rest of Europe	2.9	4.5	7.4	7.9	4.4	6.5
Americas	0.2	2.0	3.0	2.6	11.9	48.7
Rest of the world	3.8	1.3	2.8	2.3	0.7	3.1

Source: Entertainment Rights Annual reports and accounts.

portfolio further. This was transformed into a new preschool animation series, *Rupert Bear – Follow the Magic* (52 × 10′), produced by Cosgrove Hall, which launched on Five's Milkshake! in November 2006.

In 2004 ER bought US animation library Filmation from Hallmark Entertainment for £11m, adding 500 hours to its library including action–adventure animation produced in the 1980s (*He-Man and Masters of the Universe* and *She-Ra*) (Broadcast, 2004b: 6). That same year it acquired British producer, Tell-Tale Productions, creator of the live action costumed character series *The Tweenies* for £3.1m (Broadcast, 2004c), a purchase which management saw as strengthening its position as 'a creative force in children's programming' (Rod Bransgrove, Chairman, cited in Jenkinson, 2005). With the acquisition in January 2007 of Classic Media for £156m (ER, 2007: 15) – a US-based rights owner of 3,500 hours, including brands for older children (*Casper the Friendly Ghost, George of the Jungle, Lassie*), ER more than doubled its turnover from £30m in 2006 to £68m in 2007 (Table 5.3).

The acquisition of Classic Media was meant to strengthen ER's US presence, effecting a similar transformation to that achieved by HIT following its acquisition of Lyrick. However, by the end of 2007 ER was experiencing the downside of its expansion drive, as it sought to manage the considerable debt (£108m) it had incurred to finance its acquisitions, combined with home entertainment distribution problems (ER, 2007: 2–3). Management was replaced, redundancies announced and attempts made to sell off assets or negotiate a takeover (see Grant, 2008d, e; Shepherd, 2008). Critics accused the company of paying too much for Classic Media and its 'tired' brands and of marketing properties that were too parochially British (Grant, 2009a). One commented, 'Postman Pat is a British postman with a Royal Mail van. Rupert is a bear in tartan trousers. These are not global franchises' (ibid.). ER's presence in the US market was grounded neither on a current hit nor a first tier US channel presence on Nick Jr. or PBS, the real drivers of licensed merchandise. On 1 April 2009 it was de-listed, placed in administration, and its subsidiaries sold to Boomerang Media, an IP group backed by former Classic Media executives. The company had taken on too many risks, and combined with a worsening economic situation had demonstrated the fragility of a business model based on debt, stock market finance and licensing revenues.

Smaller companies have emulated aspects of the approach taken by the larger producer-distributors. The UK-based **Contender Entertainment Group** managed a small portfolio of preschool animated properties, in which it took either an investment stake (*Peppa Pig, Ben* and *Ben and Holly's Little Kingdom* from Astley Baker Davies), or complete ownership (*Tractor Tom*) or third-party representation (*It's a Big Big World*). However children's content constituted only a small part (six per cent) of a £25m business, focused mainly on home entertainment (Contender, 2007). The Canadian conglomerate, E1 Entertainment, acquired Contender in June 2007 for £49m (Reeve-Crook, 2007b). AIM-listed **Ludorum**, a small rights management entity, established in London by two former HIT executives in 2006, represents a further variation on the HIT model with a very strong emphasis on exploiting global licensing opportunities (Castleman, 2009a). *Chuggington* (52 × 10′), Ludorum's £4.4m CGI train-based series (Ludorum, 2007), made in China, launched on CBeebies in 2008, selling to 140 territories by 2009 including Disney in the United States. The funding model is also predicated on ancillary revenues. However rather than simply providing an advance, RC2, the master toy licensee contributed 50 per cent of the production budget for long-term rights in the property (Castleman, 2009a).

Canada represents a further significant base for larger consolidated producer-distributors and rights management entities, but with greater emphasis on production, because of the availability of substantial tax credits and production subsidies (Screen Digest, 2007) which make it an attractive co-production partner for American and European producers. **Decode Entertainment**, which became part of the publicly quoted DHX Media in 2006, is a prolific co-producer. Preschool productions in which it has participated include *Waybuloo* (2009 with UK-based RDF Media) and *Super Why!* (2007–08 with US-based Out of the Blue Enterprises). **Nelvana**, part of **Corus Entertainment**, which owns Canadian preschool channel Treehouse, has produced many preschool series including co-productions *The Backyardigans, Maggie and the Ferocious Beast* and *Max and Ruby* with Nick Jr. in the United States (Castleman,

2009b), as well as shows for older children. Through Corus, Nelvana is a one-third shareholder in the US multiplatform network, Qubo, as well as KidsCo, a global channel, launched in 2007 in partnership with NBC Universal and the Cookie Jar Group. The **Cookie Jar Group** (formerly Cinar) which includes licensing agency Copyright Promotions, is the producer behind preschool animation series *Arthur* and *Caillou* on PBS and live action show *The Doodlebops* on Disney (Kuzmyk, 2005, 2008) as well as animation shows for older children. In 2008 it merged with US producer DIC Entertainment, the programmer of CBS's Saturday morning block in the United States.

BBC Worldwide – a publicly owned alternative

While not a profit-making enterprise in the traditional sense, BBC Worldwide provides an interesting example of how commerce has been utilised to support the broader public service objectives of its publicly funded parent, the BBC. Established in 1994 BBC Worldwide is the BBC's commercial content arm whose profits are reinvested into the BBC's licence fee-funded content (Steemers, 2005).

BBC Worldwide is important for raising deficit funding on key CBeebies commissions, providing the BBC with a distinct advantage over commercial rivals for the most sought after independent programming. Worldwide is not obliged to invest in BBC properties, but will not invest in independent shows unless these have a CBeebies platform, a crucial adjunct for commercial exploitation. Its most successful properties have tended to be animation or costume character shows from independent producers rather than BBC in-house shows, because these tend to be 'presenter-led' which is 'always harder for licensing' (Banham, 2007). Worldwide's most recent success has been Ragdoll Production's £14m costumed character series *In the Night Garden* (2007–), in which Worldwide has a substantial investment. Other independently produced properties have included costume character show, *The Tweenies* (Tell-Tale Productions), which was financed with £4.6m from BBC Worldwide, and another costume character show *The Fimbles* (Novel Entertainment), funded with a £3.5m contribution (BBC Worldwide, 2002a: 6). *Teletubbies* (Ragdoll Productions), Worldwide's most successful children's property to date, had sold to 120 countries, including China by 2002 (BBC Worldwide, 2002b, 16), generating £116m in sales for Worldwide since launch and an estimated £1bn at retail (BBC Worldwide, 2003).

However, following the passage of the 2003 Communications Act and the implementation in 2004 of new terms of trade between terrestrial broadcasters and producers, independent producers are no longer obliged to use Worldwide as first choice distributor if they secure a BBC commission, forcing the company to work harder to secure the best independent properties. For example, in September 2006 it signed a joint venture with Ragdoll Productions to secure all UK and international broadcast sales and international licensing for Ragdoll properties. However, increasing reliance by the BBC on BBC Worldwide to fund budget shortfalls raises questions about future range and diversity on CBeebies as a balance is sought between creative and commercial priorities. The BBC Trust in its 2009 review of BBC children's services expressed concerns that the BBC's focus on 'fewer, bigger, better' children's commissions in order to compete on quality rather than quantity could have a negative impact on performance with more repeats and less diversity as main concerns (BBC Trust, 2009: 13). It also expressed reservations about the target of increasing commercial income 12-fold by 2010 (mainly from co-production) (BBC Trust, 2009: 13, 29). It concluded that this could be detrimental to the BBC's core purposes, by focusing attention on a more limited range of commercially and internationally attractive children's content from a small number of players (BBC Trust, 2009: 58–9), at the expense of programming that was relevant to British child audiences.

Children's content does constitute a key part of Worldwide's commercial activities generating £69.4m, about 8.5 per cent of BBC Worldwide's total sales (£810.4m) in 2006/07 (BBC Worldwide, 2007; Table 5.4). One indication of the importance of children's content was the fact that until 2006 it was the only area of content which was organised as a standalone business. This ceased in January 2007 following a period of unprofitability (BBC Worldwide, 2007: 26). In 2007/08 television sales were subsumed within Global TV Sales, while the rest (licensing, publishing and live events) came under Home Entertainment. Yet Worldwide's children's ancillary business based on DVDs and consumer products continued to generate losses in 2008 as some children's properties failed 'to break into the retail market' (BBC Worldwide, 2008: 31–2). In light of this, BBC Worldwide announced a 'radical' strategic review of its children's portfolio (BBC Worldwide, 2008: 32; Sweney, 2008). In 2008 the children's licensing business was renamed Children's and Licensing, and moved from Home Entertainment to BBC Magazines. This business (which includes some properties targeted at adults like *Dr Who*) generated £28m in sales and £1.7m in profits in 2008/09 (BBC Worldwide, 2009), an improvement on the previous years of losses.

Regardless of negative financial results in recent years, preschool content continues to be an important activity, underlined by Worldwide's investment in international channels under the CBeebies brand,

Table 5.4   BBC Worldwide – Children's sales (£m)

	2004	2005	2006	2007	2008*	2009*
Children's sales						
TV sales	15.0	11.5	12.9	15.8	n.a.	n.a.
DVD/publishing	10.7	9.5	14.3	15.7		
Merchandising and other	15.2	9.0	10.5	9.0	25.5	28.0
Magazines	27.4	27.7	25.2	28.9	32.2	32.7
Total sales (Children')	**68.3**	**57.7**	**62.9**	**69.4**	n.a.	n.a.
Total sales (BBC WW)	657.2	706.0	785.1	810.4	916.3	1003.6
Children's profits						
TV, DVD, merchandising (*)	−11.1	−6.6	−0.9	−1.6	−9.0	1.7
Magazines	−2.2	−2.9	1.6	3.4	3.4	2.0

Source: BBC Worldwide Annual Reviews.
*The 2007/08 and 2008/09 data combine DVD, publishing and merchandising revenues including some non-child properties (e.g. Doctor Who), but children's television programme sales are not now given separately, but subsumed within global TV sales.

rather than programming for older children. These counter declining sales of completed programmes elsewhere and provide a showcase for content and associated products (Steemers, 2004: 87). By 2009 BBC Worldwide was operating CBeebies channels in Australia, Hong Kong, India, Indonesia, Mexico, Poland, Singapore, South Africa and the United States (where CBeebies operates as a Hispanic service). According to David Weiland, Worldwide's Head of Programming, the channels represent a response to research that showed there was demand for softer educational programming that provided a balance between live action, puppets and animation, rather than simply animation (cited in Carugati, 2007). The marketing of these channels suggests ambitions, which place BBC Worldwide in a position to compete internationally with Playhouse Disney and Nick Jr.

Producers

Beyond consolidated rights-owning producer-distributors with a greater or lesser degree of vertical integration, there are numerous smaller specialist producers, driven by variable commercial, creative and educational motives. The vast majority are not global enterprises and do not operate their own distribution or licensing arms, relying instead on larger players to raise production finance, sometimes in return for an ownership stake. However, a growing number are keen to retain ownership in their creations, leading to different approaches to funding and exploitation.

Those preschool producers who concentrate on educational preschool programming are largely concentrated in the United States, serving the educational demands of the American marketplace. Foremost among these is **Sesame Workshop** (until 2000 CTW), which calls itself an educational media company. Although the Workshop produces content for older children, its most successful property has been *Sesame Street*, airing on PBS since 1969. In the fiercely profit-driven US market, Sesame Workshop is distinctive as a non-profit organisation, whose activities, as we established in Chapter 2, are informed by the conviction that the media are a powerful educational tool. Today the Workshop is engaged in the production of educational children's content across media platforms as well as international co-productions of *Sesame Street* with local partners, designed to address the specific educational and social needs of children in these countries.

While still pursuing an educational agenda, Sesame Workshop is by no means immune from commercial pressures, especially as a considerable proportion of the funding that sustains its activities derives from commercial ventures, associated with *Sesame Street* in particular. To diversify beyond *Sesame Street* and secure additional funding, it has sought to co-produce animation with commercial producers (*Dragon Tales* with Sony Pictures Television for PBS, 1999–2005; *Pinky Dinky Doo* with Cartoon Pizza for Noggin, 2006–) (Carugati, 2006; Dillon, 1999), as well as participating in alternative distribution outlets. In 1999 it teamed up with Nickelodeon to launch Noggin, but sold its half share in 2002 in order to expand internationally and pay off debt (Sesame Workshop, 2007: 63). In September 2004 it became a partner, alongside PBS, HIT Entertainment and Comcast in commercial joint venture, PBS Kids Sprout (ibid: 63). To sustain the *Sesame Street* brand, and maintain interest among an ever-younger audience, it has also launched *Sesame* spin-offs such as the claymation series, *The Adventures of Bert and Ernie* (52 × 5' with the Italian Misseri Studio in 2008).

Grants from government and other public agencies accounted for just 8 per cent of total revenues of $145m in 2008 (Sesame Workshop, 2008: 42). Combined with donations and corporate sponsorship (from

Table 5.5   Sesame Workshop – Revenues by source ($m)

	2005	%	2006	%	2007	%	2008	%
Program support (spon-sors/donors)	33.1	30.9	22.6	22.2	33.5	26.0	40.5	27.9
Distribution fees and royalties	25.7	24.0	32.5	31.8	43.3	33.5	52.7	36.3
Production licensing	48.3	45.1	46.9	46.0	52.3	40.5	52.0	35.8
Total revenues	107.1	100.0	101.9	100.0	129.2	100.0	145.2	100.0

Source: Sesame Workshop Annual Reports.

the likes of Kelloggs, Wal-Mart, McDonald's and Merrill Lynch) this accounted for 28 per cent of income (Table 5.5). Yet over 70 per cent of revenues came from straightforwardly commercial activities split between 'Product Licensing' (36 per cent) and 'Distribution Fees and Royalties' (36 per cent) attributable to television programme sales, home entertainment and publishing.

Clearly, the key challenge over the years has been in finding a balance between mission and money, between educational goals and commercial imperatives – and, of course, persuading the public (its ultimate source of legitimacy) and the government (an important financier) that it has succeeded in doing so. This involves 'walking a fine line', as outlined by Sesame Workshop chairman, Gary Knell:

> The Workshop has really tried to be consistent with its original mission – uphold the trust we've built with parents over the years, and not do things that would jeopardize that trust, or our brand equity. It's hard work. The more competition there is, the more pressure there is to sometimes dumb down or overcommercialize. We've walked a fine line – having product licensing support some of what we do – but that revenue gets plowed back into the educational research and production of the shows. That's been much of our economic base over the last few years. (Worldscreen, 2003)

The quote reveals the usual line of defence used by the Workshop to both justify its commercial activities as well as its continuing need for public funding – namely that all the money earned or received is ploughed back into educational research and content production – with 'Education, Research, Outreach' accounting for almost 8 per cent of expenditure in 2008.

The Workshop is still heavily reliant on the *Sesame Street* brand, but now faces more competition in educational preschool content both from Nickelodeon and Disney in-house productions as well as smaller preschool players such as **Little Airplane Productions** (*The Wonder Pets!* for Nick Jr.; *Oobi!* for Noggin), **Out of the Blue Enterprises** (*Super Why!* for PBS) and others who see commercial potential in preschool including **Wildbrain** (*Yo Gabba Gabba!* for Nick Jr.; *Higglytown Heroes* for Disney), **Scholastic Media** (*Clifford the Big Red Dog* and *The Magic School Bus* for PBS) and **Curious Pictures** (*Little Einsteins* for Disney Playhouse). The Workshop has also been squeezed by the economic downturn, cutting 20 per cent of its staff in 2009, following a decline in licensing income and 'volatility in the financial markets' (Grant, 2009b) which affected both its investments and donations from Wall Street firms (Runett, 2009).

By contrast Britain's **Chapman Entertainment**, established in 2001, represents a new generation of independent preschool production companies, who do not dispute their reliance on character licensing as a way of funding production (Chapman and Lynn, 2006; Midgley, 2006). However, they are also creatively led, in the sense that there is a strong desire to give the talent behind the intellectual properties greater creative and commercial control, rather than ceding ownership to a broadcaster or rights-owning producer-distributor in return for royalties (Carter, 2004, 2005).

Building on the company co-founder's track record (Keith Chapman is the original creator of *Bob the Builder*, whose rights he sold to HIT Entertainment in exchange for a royalty in the mid-1990s) Chapman Entertainment was established on the back of a 2-year development deal with Vision Video Limited (VVL), a division of Universal Pictures. The first project to be developed was *Fifi and the Flowertots*, a preschool stop-frame series about a half-flower, half-girl and her garden friends. Based on an idea from Chapman the series targeted girls as an underserved group. Chapman secured a broadcast commission from Five and Nick Jr. in Britain, but was forced to rethink funding in 2003 when VVL struck out of the deal following restructuring of its parent. Rather than approaching a producer-distributor and ceding a large ownership stake plus 30 per cent of sales revenues (Carter, 2004), Chapman turned to private equity investors to finance the show securing the backing of a small consortium of City investors who took a minority stake in the company, allowing Chapman to cover the production costs of *Fifi* (£3.5m for 52 ten-minute episodes) and develop other projects including *Roary the Racing Car* (Carter, 2004). The first series of *Fifi*, animated by Cosgrove Hall, debuted on Five's Milkshake! in 2005, quickly establishing itself as one of Britain's top preschool properties, and selling to over 160 territories. By 2007 *Fifi* had become a significant preschool brand generating £70m of sales at retail (Fry, 2007: 28). The boy-targeted stop-frame series *Roary the Racing Car*, launched on Milkshake! and Nick Jr. UK in 2007.

Chapman had typically relied on others to market and make its shows, appointing British distributor Target Entertainment to represent the distribution and licensing of *Fifi* in 2004. In 2007 Chapman appointed HIT as rights manager for Chapman shows in North America and Japan across broadcast, licensed merchandise and home entertainment (Hit, 2007a). Yet the company has indicated a keenness to control its own destiny. In June 2008 it announced the launch of its own animation studio for the production of the second series of *Roary* rather than relying on service studio, Cosgrove Hall (C21, 2008). In April 2009 it brought the licensing of *Fifi* in-house.

Chapman's emphasis on ownership and control contrasts starkly with another British animation producer, **Cosgrove Hall Films**. Established in 1976, and owned by UK commercial broadcaster, ITV PLC, Cosgrove was Britain's largest animation studio in 2006, producing 39 hours between 2003 and 2005 (Screen Digest, 2006). Although acclaimed for preschool stop-frame productions like *Engie Benjy*, the vast majority since the late 1990s have been service work, diminishing the company's ability to build its own assets and benefit from ancillary revenues (Grant, 2005; Pennington, 2006). Work for hire included *Andy Pandy* and *Bill and Ben* for BBC Worldwide, *Rupert Bear* and *Postman Pat* for Entertainment Rights, *Little Robots* for Create TV and *Fifi and the Flowertots* and *Roary the Racing Car* for Chapman Entertainment. However, a strategy of repositioning itself from a studio for hire to a developer and owner of properties (Pennington, 2006; Rosser, 2007) had not produced a tangible hit series by 2008, with job losses and a move from its studios to ITV premises in 2008 (Grant, 2008f, g). The situation was compounded by Chapman Entertainment's decision to move to in-house production in 2008 and ER's business failure in 2009. With turnover of £6m and pre-tax losses of £0.8m in 2007 (Cosgrove Hall, 2007), the company had not managed to profit from its own IP, a position not helped by the virtual withdrawal of ITV, its owner, from children's production.

British-based **RDF Media Group** by contrast provides a prime example of a large consolidated multi-genre producer and third-party distributor – a 'super indie' – that has recently moved into children's programming allured by the opportunity that *owning* children's content might offer in terms of exploiting intellectual property (IP) internationally. Founded in 1993 and launched on the AIM in 2005, RDF established a Family & Children's Television Department in 2006 under Nigel Pickard, former ITV director of television and ex-controller of BBC Children's. In 2006 it acquired children's producer The Foundation for £4m. The business rationale behind RDF's expansion into children's was explained by Pickard to trade magazine *Broadcast*, an explanation which reveals that companies are attracted to preschool because of the expectations of great rewards:

> There is lots of stuff that's there because it fulfils broadcasters' needs and obligations but there's some stuff that just breaks out and is fantastically successful [...] And if you're on the fantastically successful track it's not only great for audiences and broadcasters it's an extremely profitable business. The thing is, can you strike a path and hit those heartlands that get you everything? If you can, the rewards are fantastic. (Cited in Keighron, 2006)

Following commissions from CBeebies in 2007 for an arts and crafts show, *Mister Maker* (20 × 20′) and a live action animation hybrid *Big Barn Farm* (20 × 15′), RDF's largest CBeebies commission in 2008, *Waybuloo* (100 × 20′) represents the £10m 'cornerstone' of its bid to achieve 'franchise status' (Rushton, 2009a). Combining CGI characters (the Piplings) with 'real' children in stories that emphasise socio-emotional issues such as sharing, the series was co-produced with Canada's Decode Entertainment, underlining the importance of securing international partners with access to tax breaks and subsidies for the largest projects.

British veteran **Ragdoll Productions** presents an entirely different model again. Founded in 1984, by Anne Wood, a former schoolteacher and Head of Children's Programmes at TV-am (an ITV franchise), Ragdoll has earned a reputation as an innovator in preschool production, although its landmark show *Teletubbies* proved controversial in some circles for its targeting of children as young as two (Linn, 2004; Mitchison, 2004). Ragdoll does nevertheless demonstrate the importance of having both a strong track record and rights ownership. The global success of *Teletubbies* and the huge income generated by licensed merchandise allowed Ragdoll, who invested heavily in the production to keep US rights (the international rights and UK licensing rights were ceded to BBC Worldwide), to subsequently put in place a 'big brand' strategy (Oliver and Ohlbaum, 2007: 50) for new projects, without having to look for capital injections from private equity backers or the stock market. *Teletubbies* premiered in the United States on PBS in 1998, and became a hit in the world's largest market for consumer products, with the company generating £10.3m in profits from sales of £25.6m in 1999–2000 (Elliot, 2001). This provided the necessary funds to invest in research and develop new shows (Mitchison, 2004).

Since *Teletubbies* this 'big brand' strategy has involved the production of predominantly high-budget programmes, which do exhibit strong international and ancillary potential. However, pretty uniquely within a British context, but consistent with Ragdoll's emphasis on innovation, is the research-intensive approach to creative development and children's responses. *In the Night Garden*, Ragdoll's live action costumed character show for children aged two to three, also follows the 'big brand' strategy. The show was shot in High Definition using the latest technology in animatronics and CGI. Produced at an estimated cost of £14.5m for 100 episodes, it made its debut on the BBC and CBeebies in March 2007. Within a year of its UK launch it had been sold to over 20 countries (but significantly not this time to the United States), generating £11m from toy sales and £1m from publishing and DVD sales in Britain alone (Grimston, 2008). With backing from Hasbro, the master toy licensee, *In the Night Garden* exemplarily demonstrates the willingness of broadcasters and licensees to back companies with a track record in attracting audiences and generating licensed merchandise revenues.

However, unlike some producers, Ragdoll has eschewed building up a large licensing and sales arm. Since the production of *Teletubbies* it has developed a strong commercial relationship with BBC Worldwide. This relationship was consolidated in 2006 with the creation of a new joint venture, Ragdoll Worldwide. The deal gives BBC Worldwide responsibility for international broadcast sales as well as UK and international licensing of all Ragdoll properties on behalf of the new joint venture. Ragdoll retains all UK broadcast rights, and through Ragdoll USA (which opened in 2002 and is now part of the new joint venture), manages the Ragdoll portfolio in North America. In this way Ragdoll benefits from the marketing expertise and infrastructure of BBC Worldwide, which in turn secures programming for Worldwide's brand portfolio and international CBeebies channels (Waller, 2006).

Conclusion

The global market for preschool content is dominated by vertically integrated US transnationals, Nickelodeon and Disney, who are also significant broadcasters (see Chapters 3 and 4). To these can be added the publicly funded yet vertically integrated BBC, with a not insignificant commercial operation in BBC Worldwide. Another dozen or so smaller companies, in Britain and Canada, operate as significant rights-owning specialists in international brand management, but with varying levels of success, depending on the international attractiveness of their brands, their ability to secure broadcast distribution in the United States, and levels of indebtedness. Recognising their weakness in the value chain if they fail to secure a broadcast outlet, particularly in North America, some (e.g. HIT and BBC Worldwide) have invested in their own distribution outlets. Others, particularly Chorion and Canadian players, have developed co-production partnerships with major US broadcast outlets in order to stimulate ancillary revenues. A third much larger tier comprises many producers, of different size and scope, who are variously motivated by different combinations of commercial, creative and educational priorities. What is apparent is that there is no single business model. While some have covered their costs and even profited on the back of licensed merchandise revenues to fund further productions, other players experience a more precarious existence, focused on finding funding and distribution for each series on a project by project basis, while trying to maintain sufficient ownership in a property to safeguard future revenue streams where possible.

6
Production Preliminaries – Development and Research

As we have seen access to funding and broadcast transmission are key factors in determining whether a preschool production will actually get made. Looking beyond the institutional and economic facets of the production environment, this chapter considers those specific features of the development process that determine the nature of television for young children. According to Wartella (1994: 39), writing about US children's television generally, production is governed not only by the externalities of economics and industry frameworks, but also by 'internal constraints' which include producers' conceptions about their child audience ('what children are, what they like, how they watch, what they can and do learn') as well as the different practices they employ to make programmes. Focusing on this 'implicit model' (ibid.: 39) of children's television production, this chapter concentrates first on how ideas for preschool television are conceived and developed. Drawing on interviews and observations, primarily with British producers, it pinpoints how audience-centred, creative and commercial considerations take priority depending on different production circumstances. It then considers different attitudes to research in Britain and America, and how this impacts programme-making, before concluding with a case study of how curricular research is integrated in practice.

Coming up with a concept

All programmes start with an idea, preferably one that is sufficiently original to generate excited interest from broadcasters and funders, but not too different or risky to invite rejection. To avoid rejection producers need to be in tune with what broadcasters are looking for in terms of age, place in the schedule, programme form (animation, live action) or subject matter. For instance, in 2000 the development team at BBC Scotland successfully pitched *Balamory* as a long-running live action 'soap' (although it comprises self-contained episodes) in response to Nigel Pickard, the then BBC Children's Controller's wish for an 'aspirational' show with 'real people' (McLaughlin, 2007) rather than the costumed character shows that were prevalent at the time (*Tweenies*, *Teletubbies*). Sometimes an individual producer, writer, designer, performer or animator will come up with an idea (London, 2007: 78). For example *Bob the Builder* was based on an original concept by Keith Chapman. At other times a concept may be the outcome of collaborative endeavour.

Original ideas may stem from the perceived experiences of the preschool audience, 'moments of either what people's children are going through or what they went through as children' (Lloyd, 2007). This was the case with *Big and Small* (Kindle Entertainment and 3Js) a preschool live action show with puppets (52 × 11′) commissioned in 2007 by CBeebies and Treehouse in Canada. The idea emerged from the collective musings of the North American and British development team during a 'preschool day'. *Big and Small* centres on the friendship between Small who is 'fast, loud and exuberant' and Big who is 'slow, gentle and dreamy' (Brogan, 2008). According to Anne Brogan, Director of Kindle Entertainment,

> We talked for quite a long time about our experiences of being children, and what you remember and what matters to you, what hurts you, what makes you laugh. And out of that came the idea [...] of how important it is when you're little, the whole notion of size. All the adults around you are big. There are lots of things in your world that are big. There are some things that are small, and how compelling the notion of size is [...] So from that notion came the idea of having two characters, one called Big and one called Small, and immediately everyone could see that this could create a lot of physical comedy in their world. (Brogan, 2007)

In this instance the differences in size, personality and outlook provided the catalyst for stories centred on comedy conflict, which the characters then resolve 'with warmth and humour'.

A similar focus on small children's experiences inspired British live action series *In the Night Garden* (2007–) created and written by Ragdoll Productions' Creative Director, Andrew Davenport, for CBeebies. The

Illustration 6.1   Teletubbies Big Hug
Copyright Line: Teletubbies: © and TM 1996 Ragdoll Worldwide Limited.

idea stemmed from the anxiety often felt by parents and young children at bedtime. For Davenport (2008) this was an opportunity to reassure children 'that going to bed, or going to sleep – one of the few things that a child had to do alone – is a positive experience', that they did not have to go there alone. The 'calming' pace of the programme, which is designed to be enjoyed together with parents, gives children a metaphor to make sense of the experience of going to bed. In this case it is the blue character of Igglepiggle crossing the water in his boat to a magical land, populated by playful characters, 'that gives children and adults something to hold onto – to make sense of this difficult time of the day' (ibid.).

In other cases the driving force may be explicitly educational, focusing on literacy (*Word World*, PBS), mathematics (*Numberjacks*, CBeebies) or science (*Nina and the Neurons*, CBeebies; *Sid the Science Kid*, PBS). On other occasions the motivation may be more pointedly cultural. For instance programme-makers producing in Welsh for Welsh language channel, S4C, draw attention to language as a driving force. According to the producer of *Pentre Bach*, a live action series set in a Welsh village, 'I think it's more than making a kids' programme. It's making a kids' programme knowing that it will help my language, because if I can't implant that little tiny seed of Welsh-ness in a three-year-old I feel I haven't done my job' (Teifi, 2008).

Alternatively a series can be fashioned from pre-existing properties. In preschool television picture books, such as *Charlie and Lola* (written by Lauren Childs) and *Curious George* (Hans Augusto Rey and Margret Rey), are a rich source for animation series. Developing projects from publishing properties is a good way of reducing risk, because the audience and their parents may be familiar with the books. However, producers still need to negotiate creative input and ownership of the television series with authors, illustrators or other rights-owners. Also the existence of books does not necessarily mean a straightforward transfer to television. All book properties need to be adapted because television usually requires at least 26 episodes, and as 26 books are unlikely to exist, additional storylines have to be generated that work for television. This was the challenge facing British producers Tiger Aspect who adapted *Charlie and Lola* into a 2D animated series for CBeebies and Disney between 2004 and 2007. Focusing on the humorous relationship between Charlie and his little sister, Lola, they were attracted to the property because 'it contained those little everyday mundane issues that for a kid are full blown drama' (Lloyd, 2007). Yet according to series producer, Claudia Lloyd, the challenge of turning the childhood crises of falling out with a friend or losing your best friend's coat into a full-blown series proved considerable:

> I couldn't see how we would make the stories work, how we could turn sixteen pages of what's basically little moods really [...] that Lola confronts, into a story that could run and run and run because you really do need a minimum of 52 [episodes]. (Ibid.)

The solution in this particular instance was to work closely with the author Lauren Childs during the design and scriptwriting process 'to make that vision come alive' for television, while remaining true to the original concept, which was 'all about empowering children to sort out their own problems in their own way' (ibid.).

Another option is to create new series based on popular animated series from the past (TBI, 2003). With a raft of series dating back to the 1950s this has been a common strategy among British players including BBC Worldwide (*Andy Pandy*, *The Flowerpot Men*), Chorion (*The Mr Men Show, Noddy*) and Entertainment Rights, ER (*Rupert*). Just like series based on published properties, classic revivals offer a degree of certainty, because they might just resonate with parents who watched the originals, fuelling licensed merchandise in the process (Akbar and Carter, 2007: 11; Plummer-Andrews, 2006). However there is always a risk that the new version may not appeal, and concepts still need to be developed with stories and characters that attract contemporary children and international television buyers. For example, the revamping of *Postman Pat* (Entertainment Rights) in 2007 as the pacier stop-frame series *Postman Pat: Special Delivery Service* involved an expansion of the character base, a move to the urban environment of Pencaster, away from the original village setting of Greendale, and more vehicles, including a helicopter for Pat, to reinforce an expanded licensing strategy. The new *Mr Men Show* has been rejuvenated as a faster-paced sketch show for older children (4–6) rather than the single character shows of the 1970s and 1980s. Conversely Entertainment Right's 2008 reinvention of *Rupert Bear*, a combination of 3D CGI and stop-frame animation, is now targeted at a younger preschool audience. The characters are rounder and younger-looking than previous series, and the storylines are directed at 3- to 5-year olds, who constitute the main market now for toys.

Ideas are also generated with reference to what else is available. Chapman Entertainment's stop-frame series *Fifi and the Flowertots* was developed in 2001 to fill a perceived 'gap in the market' for preschool girls (Chapman, 2006). British animators, Astley Baker Davies, settled on the main character in their 2D series *Peppa Pig* (2004–) after a careful perusal of the retail shelves. Preschool is no stranger to anthropomorphic animals, but at this point there were no shows about a pig. From there they started thinking about what such a show might look like. According to producer, Phil Davies, they also pinpointed a gap for girls:

We started, I suppose, doodling [...] doing some drawings, because it's only when you start sitting down and drawing what the character might look like, that these sort of things all start to pop up. Then you think: 'Well, OK, is it going to be a boy or is it going be a girl?' We quite liked the idea of doing a girl because there was *Bob the Builder*, and Bob obviously is very much for boys. There wasn't anything targeted at girls. So, we chose the little girl pig. (Davies, 2007)

This need to be different extended to the main character, Peppa, who was a bit 'naughty' 'rather than the rather twee characters you get in a lot of preschool animations' (ibid.).

Development

There's a tendency in the business [...] to think there's a formula and those of us on the creative side are constantly going 'There's no formula. If we knew it we'd be in the Bahamas right now' [...] People like to think there are formulas, particularly people who have the money because they want it to be as risk-free as possible, *but this business is all about taking risks.* (UK Producer, 2007)

Once an idea has been generated, it has to be developed in to at least 26 episodes because broadcasters do not take short runs. Development is crucial as producers seek to satisfy the demands and expectations of broadcasters and other funders, amending their ideas accordingly (see Cantor, 1975: 116). During development target audiences are specified, and producers and writers will differentiate between younger (2–4 years) and older preschool (4–6 years) audiences in ways that seem largely determined by broadcasters' scheduling and commissioning requirements.

Development, this 'precious gestation time' (Wood, 2005: 16), is key for setting the creative and financial parameters of a show. As such it can be long, speculative and expensive with no guarantee of success if funding cannot be raised. During development show creators will think about concepts, characters, storylines and in the case of animation or puppetry, designs. They will consider how a production can be realised creatively, technically, cost-efficiently and on time, usually with far fewer resources than those available for adult television.

Development within smaller production companies is often, but not necessarily always 'creatively led'. As we saw in Chapter 5 within larger rights-owning entities like Entertainment Rights, Chorion, HIT Entertainment and BBC Worldwide development is defined by priorities associated with international sales and consumer products in order to generate profits, in much the same way as US media conglomerates. These considerations determine what gets developed. According to one British producer-distributor:

> Generally speaking, it has to be global, it has to be classic in feel. It has to be immersive and toyetic [...] And other than that gender doesn't matter. Classic means that it's got to have longevity. It's got to feel as though it's going to last more than a couple of years.

This focus on programming that works internationally and for consumer products requires projects to work as brands across different territories and product areas, not just television (see Chapter 9), narrowing choice against live action and presenter-led programming in favour of animation with licensing and global potential. Against this background a balance is often struck between the recognisable and the new with an eye to the commercial marketplace. Distinctive characters are important, because in the words of one producer 'if you just do another teddy bear show, there's no licensing and merchandising potential because it's just another generic character.' For animation, celebrity voices may be chosen to validate a show to broadcasters and parents, although these are unlikely to mean much to a preschool audience. For example Chapman Entertainment's stop-motion series *Roary the Racing Car* features the voice of veteran British racing driver, Stirling Moss. Joella Entertainment's *Underground Ernie* is voiced by former England soccer star, Gary Lineker. One noticeable trend has been the use of children's voices, prized for their natural performance and spontaneity. Examples include *Charlie and Lola* (Tiger Aspect) and *Peppa Pig* (Astley Baker Davies) in Britain and *The Wonder Pets!* (Little Airplane) and *Little Einsteins* (Disney) in the United States.

In this process of risk assessment producers with a track record have an advantage. According to one UK producer-distributor,

> We have more confidence in a property if people have done something before which has worked quite well. [...] because we know from dealing with broadcasters that they're more likely to get involved with something if it has a pedigree. That makes it easier for us to take a risk.

Beyond this, the process of developing and pitching a preschool show is not that dissimilar to pitching adult television (see Turow, 1984). The first stage normally involves writing a proposal or 'bible'. This will usually include a title and show description or synopsis, which succinctly captures what the show is about. There will be an indication of the target audience, a description of the world or setting with appropriate illustrations, the number and length of programmes, storylines, short character and story synopses, and often one or two sample scripts. For shows containing animation, puppets and costumed characters there will be character and background designs. On live action shows, there will be written detail on the look, tone and style of the show, where it will be shot (studio and/or location), and suggestions for casting. The aim is to provide backers with a clear idea of the rationale and look of a show. The pitch will also indicate costs. For example for live action, the use of studio settings combined with generic locations or montage sequences to link scenes would tend to suggest an economical approach that also meets the 'repetitive element' characteristic of many preschool productions.

A second stage of development for animation may involve producing a pilot to show prospective commissioners or at industry events like Cartoon Forum. This can be prohibitively expensive for smaller producers, which is why they may seek the support of larger players with deeper development budgets. A third stage, which overlaps with the first two, involves securing funding. Again this is a stage, which smaller producers may find difficult either to manage or fund, leading them to enlist the skills of a distributor, who may take an ownership stake in a property.

Once a series has been given the go-ahead, scripting can begin in earnest. With rare exceptions (e.g. Andrew Davenport at Ragdoll Productions), this is usually a collective, collaborative process involving several writers and note-giving from broadcasters and others. Individual writers or the head writer will come up with storylines, 'the initial spark', based on the original concept. If these pass muster they are expanded into a premise or brief, one or two pages which set out the story in three acts. If the show is destined for the North American market, educational consultants will be consulted on developmental and curricular issues early on because the United States demands a 'much more solidly overtly educational approach' (UK Writer, 2008). The next stage involves writing a treatment or outline of between five and 20 pages per episode, depending on the nature and duration of the show. A small amount of dialogue may be included to give it a 'bit of flavour' (ibid.), but there is a lot more detail about what is going to happen scene by scene. Only once the treatment and story structure have been approved by broadcasters and co-producers will the writer actually launch into a script with dialogue, because in the view of one writer,

> Dialogue is the least important thing about writing [...] The most important thing is the story. So it's getting the story to work and getting the story structure, which is really critical.

Scripts will involve a degree of visualisation with some stage directions and camera angles. Direction is particularly important for animators and storyboard artists, who need to be able to visualise what is happening. The script is also important for maintaining a project's overall vision, particularly in a situation where writers and animators may never meet. According to one writer:

> The rule of animation writing is three lines of dialogue and then an action line [...] If you just write the dialogue and then leave it and don't write the pictures in any sort of detail, two things can happen. One, a lazy animator can do nothing, so you just get talking. The other thing that will happen is that the animator can have lots of fabulous ideas which actually screw up your story [...] They'll have a character fall over when you haven't written it in because it's fun to have a character fall over [...] So they have someone falling over, and you see it, and you think why are they falling over. They fall over in Act Three. He's just pre-empted the big moment editorially, structurally and storywise.

Team writing under the supervision of a script editor or head writer tends to be the norm now simply because there are too many episodes 'to feed the series machine'. In Britain it is normal to have a script editor in charge of the writing, commenting on scripts and co-ordinating notes from broadcasters and other interested parties. In America, it is more usual to operate a head writing system. Unlike script editors, who do not write themselves, a head writer will write episodes as well as managing the work of others, tweaking premises and treatments to ensure unity of vision. At each stage notes are passed backwards and forwards between script editor or head writer, producer, broadcasters, co-producers and sometimes others including book authors, marketing and licensing representatives (see Chapter 9).

The use of research

Where British and American preschool programme-makers differ markedly is in their approach to research, particularly research that enhances the educational value of programming. In the United States, the integration of educational goals is more explicit with programmes such as *Sesame Street* and *Dora the Explorer* all based on a written formal curriculum, grounded in educational theory, applied by educational advisors (Kirkorian and Anderson, 2008). There is a recognised community of academic consultants, mainly drawn from psychology, who have developed strong relationships with preschool producers and broadcasters across many shows (see Hayes, 2008: 51). The expertise of this community is fore grounded on years of knowledge accumulated by academic experts, whose published research constitutes what Luke calls 'a founding tradition' and authority on the subject (Luke, 1990: 112).

This type of academic research, centred on developmental and cognitive psychology, and drawing heavily on the work of Piaget (1969), suggests that young children's ability to attend to and comprehend television is linked to their cognitive, emotional and social development, with the result that they understand television more as they acquire the skills that come with age and experience (see Anderson, 2004; Barr, 2008: 152; Bickham, Wright and Huston, 2001; Comstock and Scharrer, 2007; Lemish, 2008; Van Evra, 2004). Over time this includes the ability to understand simple stories, identify with characters and recognise some of the codes and conventions of audio-visual language (Lemish, 2007, 2008). Translated from the environment of academic research which focuses on children and their development, to the practicalities of formative programme research, designed to 'inform the creation or revision of a product' (Fisch and Bernstein, 2001: 41), this approach envisions children 'as active viewers', whose attention and ability to interpret and process what they encounter on screen is determined by the comprehensibility of what is on offer. Accordingly such research presupposes that appeal and comprehensibility can be enhanced by programme-makers' careful attention to programme structure, scripting, audio cues and editing, supported by rigorous testing with children to ensure educational effectiveness (see Anderson, 2004; Fisch and Bernstein, 2001).

The use of research to enhance the curricular value of programming stands in contrast to Britain where there is a much smaller body of academic work on the educational effectiveness of preschool television, and a smaller and less established community of educational consultants (see Messenger Davies, 2001a: 92; Oswell, 2002: 117–20). The incorporation of curricular goals is practically obligatory for US preschool programming – whether these are commissioned by PBS (Public Broadcasting Service), where educational rigour is usually linked to funding from federal agencies and philanthropic organisations (Ofcom,

2007a: 58; Palmer, 1988; Simensky, 2007), or commercial programmers like Nick Jr. or Playhouse Disney, where educational rigour is also associated with parental approval and ultimately commercial success as well (Beatty, 2002). Educational considerations do not usually extend to programming for older children on US commercial television, because it has always been assumed by the industry that children, particularly boys over six, will not watch 'educational' programmes (Lennard, 2004; London, 2007: 81; Stipp, 2007: 124).

However it is worth distinguishing between different types of research, because they are often conflated. First there is the curricular research undertaken collaboratively between educational and/or child-development specialists and programme-makers. This is the sort of research that had its origins with *Sesame Street*, and is quite explicit about promoting educational value, testing children's attention to and comprehension of educational content before or during production as formative research.

The spread of educational preschool programming in the United States beyond PBS since the early 1990s has, according to Fisch (2007), resulted in a number of different models for integrating curricular content. These range from the full-blown Sesame Workshop (formerly CTW) Model, where in-house content directors are integral members of the production team, working with a board of advisors, through to the use of out-of-house consultants with varying levels of involvement depending on internal production culture, available resources, perceptions of educational content and broadcaster expectations. Expansion has also brought a shift in emphasis away from the mainly cognitive skills (literacy, numeracy) associated with shows like *Sesame Street* to the softer pro-social goals of teamwork, sharing and perseverance evident in shows like *Barney and Friends* (Cohen, 2001: 573–4; Comstock and Scharrer, 2007: 138). This suits the commercial priorities of producers and cable networks because pro-social goals are more easily combined with entertainment, offering better chances of commercial success than more didactic material (Calvert, 2008: 470).

During the conceptual stage educational advisors will devise educational goals and in many cases review bibles and scripts for age-appropriateness (e.g. anti-social behaviour) and educational effectiveness. Sometimes their involvement will extend to formative research where storybooks or slide shows, and in some cases animatics (still images edited together and shown in sequence) are tested with groups of children to check their attention to and comprehension of educational content. Summative research to assess educational effectiveness and impact after transmission is rarer (Fisch, 2007: 100).

In the US formative research has helped to legitimise preschool programming on commercial outlets like Nick Jr., Noggin and Playhouse Disney, but the approach is also a hybrid one to the extent that it also allows for characters and stories to be tested for appeal and effectiveness in the wider marketplace as well as validating a programme's educational value in the face of regulatory and parental concerns (see Cohen, 2001: 578; Oswell, 2002: 160–1; Tracy, 2002). With research findings often used to underpin marketing campaigns, one commentator has likened the relationship between research and production to 'the clinical trials run by drug companies' (Hayes, 2008: 52). For the marketing aspects of research, as distinct from the educational aspects, are less about testing educational efficacy and more about whether a programme concept is hitting the spot with its target audience in terms of what children like, whether they will watch, who their favourite characters are and whether the show's popularity can be extended into other product areas (see Buckingham et al., 1999: 137–8; Wartella, 1994: 49–51). It serves to minimise risk.

Only a few British producers undertake research on this scale. First the formal integration and testing of educational goals has never been explicitly demanded by British broadcasters. UK preschool producers may integrate educational themes into projects in keeping with the broad learning values associated with outlets like CBeebies. They may also consult subject or educational specialists on the age-appropriateness and educational value of scripts, particularly if they want to unlock access to North America (Walker, 2002). For example when HIT Entertainment acquired Lyrick Studios, the US makers of *Barney and Friends* in 2001, it took on board Lyrick's approach to educational content, subjecting its own UK-originated properties, *Bob the Builder* and *Thomas and Friends*, to research with children to test appeal and understanding (Dudko, 2008a; Walker, 2002). However, in general formative educational testing on US lines is rare unless producers have deep pockets. UK broadcasters and larger companies like HIT Entertainment and BBC Worldwide do use focus groups, interviews, observations, viewing diaries and other forms of testing to inform a new or existing property's future content, development and branding beyond television. As a way of checking their own instincts smaller UK producers may test designs, colours, characters, storylines, music and completed episodes either informally with small groups of children themselves, or by using specialist research companies. Where research and curriculum are now central to American preschool production culture, their application and acceptance have been much more inconsistent in Britain for a variety of reasons.

UK producers' attitudes towards research

British producers express a wide range of opinions about the value of research, whether this is straightforwardly educational or simply product testing. First there are the 'recalcitrant deniers', those who are unreceptive and hostile towards any form of research, disputing the expertise of both researchers and their methods. These industry practitioners prefer to rely on their own personal experience of what works. According to one British programme-maker:

> I do think that research, particularly with very young children, is not much use at all because it's very hard to get them to tell you anything interesting. You either understand them as an audience or you don't. And our approach to programming is not governed by going out and finding twenty three-year olds and showing them something. It's governed by thinking this is a very good story and these are very strong characters and we'd like to develop it. (Interview, 2006)

Then there are others, the 'intuitive creatives', who prefer to trust their own experience, and are suspicious of the impact of research on creativity, creativity that is grounded on their 'gut instinct' of how to tell a story and entertain a young audience rather than what they perceive as the 'utilitarian outlook' of shows guided by developmental targets rather than story. They see research as a threat to their creative integrity, which in the case of educational research will simply lead to programmes that 'bore the pants off everybody' or in the case of market research turns programmes into 'vehicles for licensed product'.

However, in a more competitive marketplace, there are some, particularly on the marketing side who see benefits in learning more about the audience, what they like and don't like – in order to fine-tune a show for commercial exploitation. Yet research is rarely a significant item in production budgets, in sharp contrast to the United States, where Sesame Workshop, for example, devotes 8 per cent of its expenditure to research (Sesame Workshop, 2008). According to one British producer,

> I would like us to do more research, but research costs money and if there's any pressure on your budgets that's the first thing that goes.

For smaller producers this lack of funds translates into informal pre-production testing of storylines and characters in child care settings 'just to get a feel for the age', to see 'what kids of three can and can't do' and whether children 'get it'.

Ragdoll Productions is an exception as a company that has consistently used research or what the company prefers to call 'observations' to make programmes that 'understand, affirm, validate and appreciate the experiences of children' before 'reflect[ing] back to them something that they will intuitively know is meant for them' (Wood, 2005). This child-centred approach reflects the interests and experience of creative team, Anne Wood and Andrew Davenport, who have backgrounds in teaching and speech sciences respectively, and which according to Davenport makes 'it impossible for me to disentangle the creative work that I do from that background' (Davenport, 2008). Concern with the youngest preschoolers emerged from their realisation that 2-year olds and some 3-year olds found it difficult to follow one of Ragdoll's earlier series, *Tots TV*, because it was too complex. *Teletubbies*, its successor in 1997, constituted an attempt to appeal to children as young as two and was based on observations that suggested that younger children would benefit from and enjoy a different type of programme, one that saw them as 'natural makers of meaning' in their own right rather than individuals who needed to be taught top-down (Davenport, 2008; Wood, 2005, 2008). According to Davenport (2008), *Teletubbies*,

> [...] didn't conform to the prescribed view of what a preschool programme should look like. It didn't have a presenter telling us what we're going to learn today. It didn't have excitable puppets keen to sing songs about the red bus with the wheels going round. [...] It featured characters that from an adult point of view appeared to be arriving and going away again without anything significant happening. In fact, there was a rich and complex narrative there, but it was rendered indiscernible for some adults who naturally find it difficult to share the perspective that young children have of the world. They're literally not perceiving things in the same way.

What distinguishes Ragdoll from its US counterparts is that there is no separate checklist of educational goals or targets at the outset (Davenport, 2008; Wood, 2008). Instead, observations of children in a variety of settings are used to 'check our instincts', 'building up a picture' of the audience's reactions (Davenport, 2008), allowing adjustments to a show's content that take account of 'the child's own

Illustration 6.2   3rd & Bird! (From left to right, Mr Beakman, Rudy, Samuel and Muffin)
Copyright Line: Courtesy of Little Airplane Productions, Inc.

perception' and 'own way of learning' rather than adult expectations of what children should be achieving (Wood, 2008). Combined with dialogue with families over extended periods, and the occasional use of consultants, these observations inform a broader understanding of child development, which is educational 'in the more philosophical sense' (Wood, 2007). Interestingly, however, PBS' online video accompaniment to the series in the United States features Faith Rogow, an educational consultant, who was not involved in the show's development, explaining in retrospect and in great detail how a range of 'learning opportunities' are purposefully built into the programme's design (www.pbskids.org/teletubbies/parentsteachers/). Rogow's breakdown of the show's educational rationale furnishes far more detail than was ever provided in Britain. These explicit explanations serve to reinforce PBS' standing as a 'brand' that parents can trust, particularly in the light of the criticism that the show generated at the time (see Linn, 2004). Detailed references to what children are learning from the show are intended to reassure US parents, who are accustomed to educational preschool programming which addresses curricular concerns.

Case study: 3rd & Bird!

However, as British programme-makers and broadcasters work more with North American partners, US testing practices are finding their way into British productions. In this respect *3rd & Bird!* serves as a useful example of how a US research model was applied in a British setting – drawing on testing methods commonly employed for Nick Jr. shows in the United States (Brown, 2009; also Gladwell, 2000; Tracy, 2002). Launched on CBeebies in July 2008, *3rd & Bird!* (52 × 11') is an animated series produced by New York-based Little Airplane Productions in co-production with CBeebies and BBC Worldwide. Based on a group of anthropomorphic colourful birds who inhabit a treetop community, each episode features siblings, Samuel and Muffin Lovebird, and their friend Rudy. The series is animated in a distinctive photo-puppetry animation style where photographic images of animals and birds are digitally enhanced and 'cutified' to make them more appealing to young children. Colours are brightened, eyes are enlarged and legs and claws are made to look less sharp and pointed.

Each episode was tested simultaneously in 2008 with groups of American and British children to assess the appeal of the characters and scripts and the comprehensibility of the show's curricular goals. In stark contrast to some British producers, research is embraced as an integral and necessary part of the production process. According to Josh Selig, the company's founder and president:

> Ultimately if you're making a preschool show you can't do it without research anymore than you can do it without a writer or an animator. (2007)

Testing with children is used to fine-tune programming in an approach that prioritises children's comprehension over individual creative sensibilities. Referring to the testing of one particular episode, Selig explains,

> We re-wrote the script entirely based on the confusion that the original script was causing the children. That's a great example of a story that without the formative research would have gone right into production with the assumption on the part of the production company that 'Oh well the kids will get it'. But it seems pretty obvious to us that what we find time and time again is that however good we are at our jobs we can't get into their minds. We have to show them images. We have to tell them the story and hear directly from them, 'Are you

following this? Are you liking this? Is this too frightening for you? Is this fun for you?' And that very critical stage representing their culture clearly is what research does from my point of view. It makes sure that my team and I are creatively not missing the preschoolers' level and that is a critical intersection that determines the success or failure of a show. (Ibid.)

Director of Research and Curriculum and psychologist, Dr Laura Brown, undertakes in-house formative testing of every Little Airplane show, and together with the creators formulates what the learning goals of each show should be in a way that 'naturally fits with who the characters are and what the emotional tone of the story is' (Brown, 2008a). For instance, *The Wonder Pets!*, the predecessor of *3rd & Bird!* evolved as an idea about a team of animated superhero classroom pets without superpowers who rescue other young animals. This became an opportunity for children to learn about teamwork and problem solving, expressed in the plotlines and operatic songs sung by the three main characters – Linny the guinea pig, Ming-Ming the duckling and Turtle Tuck. However, a large part of the show's appeal also derived from the tension surrounding the predicaments that the young animals found themselves in (Selig, 2007). In this respect research was used to gauge how much tension could be inserted to make the show 'riveting' without being too frightening (Brown, 2007).

For *3rd & Bird!* the production team and broadcaster settled on understanding 'Community' as a curricular goal to reflect the neighbourhood where the friends live and 'Perseverance', a theme that recurs repeatedly as the characters encounter different challenges. These are both pro-social concepts, which children learn over time through regular viewing. Within 'Community' Brown defined a number of sub-goals. First children learn that the community and the individuals who inhabit it are 'a source of help'. Second the show depicts community events such as parades, picnics or scouting trips 'to familiarise young children with these things and show that the world beyond home is interesting and exciting'. Third the stories portray the social skills that are integral to the functioning of a healthy community 'like negotiating and sharing and understanding other people's feelings as separate from your own'. Finally the show 'models' awareness and acceptance of diversity and difference (Brown, 2008a, 2009).

Once the goals are set, the producers, director of research and broadcasters discuss the initial log lines and treatments exchanging notes and incorporating changes. According to Brown at this stage the main issues usually relate to *appeal* and *understanding* and how these fit with children's developmental capabilities:

> Is this going to be something that's going to appeal to children of this age? Is this something that children of this age are going to understand? If they're not going to understand it then what can we add to the story or alter in the story so that they will better understand it? And does this support one of the curricular sub-goals that we have set in every story? (2008a)

On completion of the second draft script, Brown produces a research protocol to test appeal and comprehension directly with children in a method described by Little Airplane as 'Show & Tell Research' (Selig and Brown, 2008). For this, each script is broken down into high quality 'fully-designed images' that 'more closely approximate the TV viewing experience' (Selig, 2008). As the screen images are shown a researcher reads the dialogue to the children, adopting different voices for each character, 'covering all the main story beats' (Selig and Brown, 2008). Animatics, where still images are edited together with dialogue, allow better reproduction of movement, but as a costlier and more time-consuming option, they are usually reserved for interactive series, allowing producers to test and time children's responses.

We observed the testing of two episodes ('Muffin's Plant' and 'Baby Jordan') at Little Airplane's London offices in May 2008. These were shown separately to three groups of British children in London and three groups of American children in New York on the same day, split according to age, with the 3-year olds separated from the 4- and 5-year olds. The 3-year olds only watched 'Baby Jordan'. Each group contained four to six children, mixed according to gender, ethnicity and social background. Not surprisingly the youngest children were more easily distracted, and more prone to responding in unanticipated ways, particularly when questioned after the story. Sometimes the youngest were not able to articulate verbally. These reactions reveal the challenges of appealing to a wide range of developmental abilities and personality. To address age differences the team work to 'layer' individual episodes, so that there is material that appeals to different developmental capabilities within the core three-to-five age range. To address diversity – between those children who are more gregarious and those who are quieter, for example – the team try to ensure that across a series there are different types of stories (Brown, 2008a, 2009).

'Muffin's Plant' is a story that focuses on Muffin creating a 'special' place in the community for her malodorous plant PU. The central themes are difference and acceptance of diversity. 'Baby Jordan' focuses on the feelings of jealousy encountered by Muffin, when a new young bird, Jordan, arrives in the community.

For each test a researcher read the illustrated story to the children, who were assembled on a carpet in a homely setting, with their carers seated close by. The Director of Research and core members of the creative staff observed the children via a live video feed from New York. An observer was allocated to each child, noting their facial, verbal and physical responses as every line was read out. During this observation phase, Brown is looking first and foremost at levels of engagement, interest and excitement and whether changes are necessary to improve appeal and reduce distraction, because put simply if a child is not watching, then they are perceived not to be understanding:

Behaviourally, are they engaged when the story is being read? Are they laughing? Are they smiling? Are they paying attention the majority of the time? If they're not paying attention, is there a pattern to where their attention is being lost, which will give me clues as to what's either not appealing or what's misunderstood? Often poor comprehension and low appeal go hand in hand. They don't like what they don't understand. Are there particular areas that are especially appealing that I can extrapolate from and use in the series going forward? (2008a)

The children were then asked a series of questions by the researcher, which allowed them to retell the story in their own words, itself an indicator of their enthusiasm and comprehension. In earlier sessions the children had been probed about character appeal (Who's your favourite character? Is there anybody you don't like?) allowing for modifications to personality or character design. In this session the questioning began with general probing trying to uncover flaws in the storytelling. The first set of approximately ten questions tested understanding of the story (What was the story about? How did Muffin feel about Baby Jordan?) and whether the children could identify the central issue from each episode. Some questions were reinforced with pictures that allowed children to point to characters in response to simple questions (Did Jordan the Bird or the worm come to visit?). The next set of questions tested the children's appreciation of the story (Did you like the story?

A lot or a little?) and their more detailed understanding of the issues and outcomes. At this stage according to Brown (2008a):

> I'm looking at general comprehension. Do they get the main story beats? And then within that, specific story beats, places that I'm concerned that they're not going to understand. [...] So I start on a global main idea level and then I get more specific.

The assumption being made is that if children like what they see and have good recall then the story has made sense, and they have in some way identified with the characters.

Brown's subsequent recommendations are then discussed with the production team and broadcaster before revisions. Recommendations are negotiated with the aim of achieving a balance between telling a story 'that the kids will want to hear' as well as integrating curricular goals (Brown, 2008a). This requires a researcher who according to Selig is 'sympathetic with the need to tell a great story', but there are clearly potential pitfalls in balancing the two, a fact acknowledged by Selig:

> There's constant negotiation, but it's a very amicable negotiation because we both have the same goals. If you have an adversarial relationship between creative and curriculum and research, then that can be a source of tremendous trouble. But your creatives should never be separated from curriculum [...] Your creatives should be trying to weave these themes in, and the artistry of a good writer is that they can do it in a way that doesn't feel shoe-horned in, that doesn't feel preachy, doesn't feel stiff, but is very organic to your story-telling process. (2007)

For the 'Baby Jordan' episode, the report recommended a change in dialogue so that Muffin could express her internal feelings about how she felt about Jordan, allowing the children to better understand her feelings of jealousy. The report also recommended changing the clothing of Baby Jordan to distinguish him from an adult bird, Mr Beakman. In the 'Muffin's Plant' episode the name of the plant was changed from 'Poo Poo' to 'PU' to avoid any possible unpleasantness surrounding the name. Brown felt that the British children were more 'conflicted' about whether the plant's name was something 'that they should really think is funny' (2008a). They laughed at the name 'Poo Poo' but spoke much more than the US children about how they disliked that the plant stank. The tests also appeared to show that the children did not understand that taking PU to a 'special' place would solve the problem of its pungent smell. This was made clearer through minor script adjustments and the introduction of a wide shot which established the distance between the plant's 'special place' in the community and the place where the characters lived.

The fact that the show was tested simultaneously with both American and British children raises some interesting questions about the cultural specificity of curricular goals and the context in which they are tested. According to Brown there were no huge differences between the two sets of children in terms of what they liked, but 'these two cultures are relatively similar' (2008a). The outcomes could of course be quite different in cultures, which are less proximate (see Hendershot, 1998). Brown also felt that the British children appeared to be more hesitant to call out than their American counterparts, possibly because US children are more used to shows, which invite them to respond (2008a).

As with any type of testing there are limitations (see Buckingham, 1993: 13ff; Hendershot, 1998: 168–70). As a method it is quite narrowly designed to produce findings that can be mapped onto specific learning objectives, which have been determined in advance. This can lead to an artificial situation, focused on establishing children's reactions to a text, which is seen to have a fixed meaning, and which subject to children's recall is then fine-tuned to maximise the desired levels of attention, comprehension and learning (see Buckingham, 1993: 13; Hendershot, 1999: 141). Within such testing it is not possible to take account of the broader 'social and interpersonal aspects' which inform children's individual 'viewing experience' and the diversity of their cultural understanding (Buckingham, 2005: 473). Also testing is never like viewing at home where children are subject to all kinds of other unpredictable distractions and social interactions with siblings, parents and so on – and at home there are, of course, no researchers, asking you questions.

As a method it is also understandably constrained by the production process. The research has to be focused on the practical purpose of providing timely and usable information, which will help programme-makers create a show that is both educative and entertaining within the required timescale (Fisch and Bernstein, 2001: 41). Unlike academic research which focuses on the impact of programming on children over a longer time-period, formative research is designed to inform and improve the appeal and comprehensibility of a *particular* television programme within a day or two (see Cohen, 2001), leaving little time to address the deeper qualitative aspects of community or diversity, for example. Nevertheless, it does constitute an approach to children's content that goes beyond 'gut' instinct or received wisdom. As such it could potentially reduce the risk of failing to connect with children, by trying to establish a degree of interaction and feedback, which allows programme-makers to build on their previous experience and acquire some informed insight into what might just enthuse, enlighten and entertain their young audiences – although this is always necessarily limited, and could, in some cases, work against innovation if interpreted too narrowly.

Conclusion

This chapter has provided an opportunity to map out the process of creative development in preschool television production and the extent to which it is shaped by a mixture of creative, commercial and curricular considerations. In terms of development there are clear divergences between British and US programme-makers, stemming from the more purposeful integrated US approach to educational goals and formative research, as opposed to the more intuitive informal approach adopted hitherto in Britain. However there are some indications of convergence between Britain and America, not least because of growing levels of co-operation between British and North American producers and attempts by British programme-makers to satisfy US channels' requirements for educational content. In one sense this may be a positive development because it compels producers to be more accountable to their young audiences, rather than simply relying on creative vision or untested assumptions about children's expectations and needs. As we have learnt, undertaking research and observations with very young children demands particular skills and is not unproblematic. However in the right situation there may be possibilities for 'dialogue' through observation, listening and letting children speak and act for themselves (see also Buckingham, 1995b: 38). The issue, however, is in disentangling what constitutes research and who does it ultimately serve, particularly if marketing objectives associated with product development become conflated with loftier ambitions associated with developmental and/or educational considerations.

7
Production Checklists, Rules and Assumptions

> When you work in children's you're working for an audience that you're not part of and you can't be part of. You might have been once upon a time, but you're not part of that anymore. (British Producer, 2008)

> We wanted to take this programme and focus it down into the child's world. That's why everything you see on the set is nearly twice life-size. [...] We're under the table. We're right down at their level. We're looking at what they're doing and it's all about that, their knowledge and their understanding of the world. (British Producer, 2008)

As the first producer above indicates, determining what will work in children's or preschool television is difficult because programme-makers are not part of that audience any more, but producers do need to get 'down into the child's world'. As we learnt in Chapter 6, in the United States this anomaly is tackled by marketing and developmental research. In Britain research has traditionally been less formal and more ad hoc, but the importance of the American market is focusing attention on incorporating educational goals into programme proposals, which presupposes more concern with the audience's needs, parental concerns and the concerns of society in general. For example *Waybuloo* (2009–), RDF's hybrid live action animation series for CBeebies, is promoted as a show that encourages 'emotional intelligence' and 'emotional literacy', showing children how to be happy and how to get in 'touch with their feelings' (BBC, 2009) – in much the same way as *Dora the Explorer* was promoted in the United States as a show that encouraged emotional and social development as well as visual, language and mathematical skills, in keeping with the latest psychological theories (see Beatty, 2002; Gardner 1993, 2006).

Yet alongside educational and marketing considerations, programme-makers also have strong beliefs about what works based on previous practice and assumptions about the audience. Wartella (1994: 51ff) writing about US children's television generally, rather than preschool television specifically, pinpoints the implicit assumptions or 'rules of thumb' that producers and broadcasters make about child audiences and how these impact what they make. In the United States these rules of thumb have included the notion that children love comedy, the importance of repetition, recognisable stories and characters, the idea that there are gender differences in what children like and that they prefer to watch programmes designed for older children. Looking back at her research on *Play School* (BBC, 1964–88) in the early 1980s Messenger Davies also concludes that producers and directors have 'a working hypothesis' about the impact of particular conventions and techniques on their young audiences (2006: 24), which suggests awareness of children's development and what children are capable of understanding.

None of the British programme-makers we interviewed in 2007 and 2008 had a background in child psychology, but a significant number had a teaching background, and many had started their careers at the BBC before moving to rival broadcasters or independent producers. Rather than explicit reference to theories of child psychology or development, most appeared to engage in what Caldwell has called '*industrial self-theorising*' (Caldwell, 2008: 18) or what Havens refers to as 'industry lore' (2007; also Gitlin, 2000). This is usually grounded in some basic knowledge of child development, combined with reference to their own or other people's children, and their own experience of what has worked before, so that they instinctively know 'what a two or a three or a four year old will understand' (UK Producer, 2007; also Buckingham et al., 1999: 117; Wartella, 1994). Each show will, of course, have its own rules which are not imposed arbitrarily, but arise out of the discussions and negotiations that take place during the development process (also Wells, 2007: 90–2).

A key concern for all programme-makers is to ensure that children can understand and follow content, an acknowledgement of the fact that 'children have to learn television conventions and that some of television's "grown-up" grammar may be confusing for the youngest' (Messenger Davies, 1989: 7, 2006: 25; also Huston and Wright, 1983; Singleton-Turner, 1994: 22). What this means in terms of developmentally appropriate television for preschoolers is usually very linear concrete programmes which tend to be more colourful, literal, visual, less verbal, slower, more repetitive and simpler in terms of story, language, camera moves and editing style so that young children have the time and opportunity to attend to and actively make sense of what they see and hear in line with their skills and experience (see Anderson, 2004; Götz, 2007a, b; Lemish, 2008; McCollum and Bryant, 2003; Singer and Singer, 1998; Wainright, 2006).

This is challenging both creatively and economically because children change so much before the age of six, requiring levels of differentiation, which may not be economically viable. However differences are evident. A programme like Ragdoll's *In the Night Garden* aimed at 2- and 3-year olds is quite different to a programme like Tiger Aspect's *Charlie and Lola* targeted at 4- to 6-year olds, in terms of the complexity of story, editing techniques, language, design, music and pace, reflecting the different abilities of their respective audiences.

As we learnt in Chapter 6, in the United States these developmental considerations are highlighted by educational advisors, well versed in research findings relating to how content and the formal features of television (pace, music, animation, sound effects, editing techniques, camera moves) can encourage children's attention and enhance comprehension (Huston and Wright, 1983; Kirkorian and Anderson, 2008), and it is these considerations that shape the educational curriculum and content of shows like *Blue's Clues* and *Dora the Explorer*.

Blue's Clues provides a good example of how knowledge about child development informs the conception and execution of a production. Launched on Nick Jr. in the United States in 1996 as a mixed live action–animation format, the *Blue's Clues* production team were advised by psychologist, Professor Daniel Anderson. At the time the show was seen as pioneering, because of its focus on active audience participation. In each episode children are encouraged to assist the presenter, Steve, and his animated pet puppy, Blue, to find clues and solve puzzles. Anderson concentrated his advice on five principles designed to enhance children's attention and their understanding of the series' educational goals (Anderson, 2004: 256ff), but the principles are also more broadly indicative of the sort of developmental checklists (see Fisch, 2004; Wainright, 2006: 8) which inform the production of educational preschool programming in America generally.

Anderson's first principle seems almost blindingly obvious as producers are advised to ensure that their content is sufficiently comprehensible to attract children's attention. To achieve this the different problem-solving activities in *Blue's Clues* are layered in complexity to appeal to different developmental capabilities, but also employ 'scaffolding' so that children are guided through a number of steps, starting with easier tasks before moving to more challenging problems, yet always revealing how these can be solved, so that children can master concepts with repeat viewing and practice. Second, Anderson emphasises the importance of incorporating auditory cues (lively voices, music, sound effects) to attract the attention of children at key moments for learning. Third, he advises that transitions (cuts, fades, dissolves, wipes) are kept to a minimum (e.g. when the host moves through the house) or clearly signposted in advance, so that children are not confused or distracted from learning by sudden scene changes, or by what may have been left out during editing. Fourth, he emphasises the importance of maintaining a child's attention (attentional inertia) over longer periods through an engaging narrative so that they spend more time attending to the task (p. 261). Anderson's final principle involves audience participation, where the presenter looks directly at the camera and invites children at home to participate, pausing sufficiently to allow children at home the time to listen, look, think and respond before an unseen studio audience calls out the answer.

According to Gladwell this approach was key to enhancing the 'stickiness' of *Blue's Clues* over and above a heavily segmented magazine show like *Sesame Street*, because it concentrated precisely on those aspects – an attractive linear story combined with direct address and audience participation – which engaged children's attention over time and therefore their possibility of learning (Gladwell, 2000: 110–18; also Linebarger and Walker, 2005; Tracy, 2002). These aspects were reinforced by episode repetition during the rest of the week, enabling children to learn how to solve the problems with practice, gaining confidence as they learnt to predict the solutions (Anderson, 2004: 263; also Crawley et al., 1999; Gladwell, 2000: 126).

US preschool programme-makers are then clearly guided by educational and developmental principles, which link attention and sustained interest to children's ability to learn – at least in respect of the US context. However, in the absence, in most cases, of a written curriculum, developmental checklist or widespread formative testing, as is the case in the United States, how do British programme-makers ensure that their programming is also age-appropriate and appealing? How do assumptions about the audience determine the nature of what is made?

Story structures should be concrete and straightforward

In interviews British producers and writers, often without a background in child development or access to a great deal of specialist advice, talk about keeping formats and story structures simple, not too fast, 'concrete' and linear without going 'back and forth in time' so that younger children can follow the logic of what is happening or predict it based on prior knowledge. Stories should be written 'from a child's point of view' and communicated in a 'concise and precise way' so that they hit 'certain beats' and retain a child's attention. Stories should be appropriately paced, relevant to children's experiences, unambiguous and with a clear outcome.

For narrative-based programming aimed at 3- to 5-year olds, most writers keep to a simple three-act structure revolving around simple events with few sub-plots. Stories are often focused on helping others and problem-solving from a child's view. There's an introduction to the situation and the main characters, followed by the posing of a problem or complication and a resolution. However, while 4-year olds are thought to be able to cope with more complex cause and effect stories and character relationships (also Lees, 2005b), 2- and 3-year olds are believed to require a simpler approach, where they are not 'befuddled with details', but offered 'really gentle, glorious storytelling' which is appropriate in both its pacing and content, with occasional silent pauses that catch children's attention, implicitly encouraging them to anticipate and react in their own time (also Lury, 2005: 93).

This recognition of the different developmental capabilities of the very youngest is evident in the approach of Ragdoll Productions, which has developed expertise in making programmes for 2- to 3-year olds when most of its competitors appear to be targeting 3- to 5-year olds. Ragdoll's *Teletubbies* represented a radical departure at the time, because it assumed that 2- and 3-year olds did not follow or interpret what was happening on screen in the same way as older preschoolers. Instead of concentrating on presenters telling children what was going to happen, Andrew Davenport, the show's co-creator, concentrated more on the idea that tiny children are 'very interested in spatial conceptual events', and would therefore be attracted to the Teletubbies' physical activities in a landscape of rolling green hills, 'designed to enhance the physical relationships between here and there, up and down', between 'coming and going and appearing or disappearing' (Davenport, 2008). This approach is reflected in the more limited use of words to tell the

Teletubbies' story and the greater emphasis placed on body language and movement. *Teletubbies* is still based on cause and effect, but its four characters often participate in almost identical narrative situations. According to Davenport, for example a puddle might appear, and then each Teletubby encounters the puddle in a slightly different way. Thus 'a set of rules' were built up, which reflect what 'a child is equipped to learn at that time' (ibid.). As each Teletubby steps into a puddle, anticipation is built up with the narrative development occurring when the fourth Teletubby jumps into the puddle and enjoys the experience by splashing about. This, in Davenport's view, represents a 'development on' and 'a sort of creative reversal' and 'an upending of a narrative routine', which is appropriate for a 2-year old who learns by repetition and rule-making.

In the Night Garden, Ragdoll's successor to *Teletubbies* is targeted at a slightly older child with more advanced language skills. The stories are more complex, because creator, Andrew Davenport, felt less of a need to repeat the narrative through a series of routines. According to Davenport (2008) *In the Night Garden* is aimed at a transition phase when children start 'to play with things which stand for other things', when toys start to stand for people and vehicles. Unlike *Teletubbies* where adults are an almost marginal presence, there is much more emphasis on the parent–child relationship in an introductory sequence which shows a real child and carer engaging in a bedtime story as 'a shared moment' of 'silliness' (ibid.). According to Davenport there is a clear progression from the simpler story structures of *Teletubbies* to more complex narratives, which reflect a child's growing fascination with language, stories and for 'rehearsing real life situations' in 'a playful safe situation':

> Physicality is still dominant, but that's not all there is to it. Increasingly narrative emerges as an important tool. Children's rehearsal progresses from the chucking of the toy out of the pushchair to see if it comes back, to rehearsing social and physical situations, often using toys [...] taking your toys for a ride in a shoebox or making them fly out of the window. Play becomes about rehearsing real life situations like making friends or fighting – and becomes overtly dramatic. Everything begins to revolve around narrative. (Ibid.)

The simplicity of the story is still present, but it has moved on to reflect children's ongoing development and their growing interest in the world around them.

Repetition is important for both learning and entertainment

British programme-makers, like their US counterparts, recognise the value of repetition and predictability, both pedagogically as well as a means of recycling content to reduce costs.

Repetition occurs in several ways. At the most basic level the same programme is simply repeated again on the same day or over a longer period of time, in much the same way as *Blue's Clues*. In the case of *Teletubbies* the live action segments of each episode are repeated within the same programme after the Teletubbies cry out 'Again, Again', allowing children further opportunities to understand. However, repetition can also involve the use of similar storylines, story structures, routines, music, sound effects and catchphrases across a series, allowing children to become familiar with and predict the format. For example in the stop-frame series *Bob the Builder* (HIT Entertainment),

> [Bob] will talk about what they're going to do. Then you will see what they're going to do. Then you will see them doing it. Then they will talk about what they've done. So it's sort of different ways, of showing a building job [...] and it's different ways of approaching the same thing. So it is repetition in a certain way [...] it's just a certain kind of storytelling that you do for really young kids. (UK Producer and Writer, 2007)

Similarly the live action series *Balamory* (BBC Scotland/CBeebies) follows a predictable narrative format that starts each time with preschool teacher Miss Hoolie singing about the weather before she opens the nursery. One of the series' ensemble of characters comes to the nursery and outlines a problem. On Miss Hoolie's advice, they go away and solve the problem with the help of the other characters. The character returns to the nursery to explain how the problem was solved. At the end of the show, the story is recapped by Miss Hoolie, accompanied by a series of still images, allowing children the time to reflect on what has happened. Repetition can also simply just involve verbally repeating information in the form of dialogue. For example a character might repeat what another character has just said to reinforce the story.

Frequently programmes will repeat generic material throughout a series, just like the animated sections or Muppet inserts in *Sesame Street*. For example *Balamory* drew on a bank of library material comprising a long opening sequence that sets the scene, location shots, characters singing and dancing in different clothes or settings, which are interwoven into new footage to connect different parts of the story, and serve as points of recognition or cues for attention, as well as helping to keep the show within budget.

Stories should create a world and characters which children can identify with

On the one hand identification with appealing characters and settings would appear to serve a clear commercial purpose. Kline, without, according to Buckingham (1995b: 31–2) much evidence or understanding of why young children might be drawn to ' "one-dimensional" characters and "predictable" narratives', argues that 'contrived' and highly formulaic US shows like the *Care Bears* in the 1980s created an imaginary universe populated by a community of characters which children could literally buy into; where the characters functioned as 'emotional symbols employed to further the child's identification with and bonding to a toy' rather than as allegories 'to help children make sense of their feelings' (Kline, 1993: 292–3). Where expectations for ancillary revenues are high (see Chapter 9), this is certainly a priority for a show's financial backers. However, content creators also want to create characters and situations with whom children can identify to enhance children's enjoyment and where necessary their learning (also Wainright, 2006: 14; Wells, 2007: 92–3). For example in animation vocational characters, who children can emulate, who mend things, 'put things right', and help others like *Bob the Builder, Fireman Sam* or *Postman Pat* are always perceived to be popular (also Wells, 2006: 116) – as are child or childlike anthropomorphic characters (animals, vehicles) with whom children can empathise in terms of the situations they find themselves in and their curiosity about life like *Dora the Explorer* in the US or Britain's *Peppa Pig* (also Wells, 2007: 16).

For example the facial expressions and reactions of Igglepiggle, the little blue costumed character in Ragdoll's *In the Night Garden*, are designed to encourage children's identification with him. This extends to his childlike gestures, including throwing himself onto his back when he encounters something new, because 'children meet things that are physically or conceptually too big for them all the time' (Davenport, 2008). For creator, Andrew Davenport, Igglepiggle is part of 'a diverse community of different characters resembling a 'nursery rhyme book', and it is Igglepiggle who represents the child's entry into this magical world:

In that sense it's a journey Igglepiggle makes at the beginning of the show and a journey that the child viewer also makes. Now that metaphorical journey can stand for going to sleep, or a journey through the day or a journey though life, but it's about what it is to be a child, to be that innocent, unprejudiced, supported creature going out to meet the world, blanket in hand, with no particular place to come from or return to. He arrives in that world and things happen around him or to him. He is our way in. The child goes with him into the programme. And he's that little child.

Like many other characters in preschool television, Igglepiggle is therefore designed to encourage empathy and understanding among the audience, but as we shall see, it is precisely this recognisability that generates economic value in licensed merchandise (Chapter 9), even if this is not a primary motivation for the creators.

Language should be age-appropriate

For some the apparently 'inane dialogue' of preschool television is almost impossible for most adults to endure (Kline, 1993: 289). Yet these programmes are not meant to enthral adults, with the exception of *Sesame Street* which developed a tradition of in-jokes for adults to encourage joint-viewing by parents and children, although possibly at the expense of children's understanding (Gladwell, 2000: 112). These misgivings and criticisms about language became very prominent in the apparent use of 'babyish' language like 'Eh-oh!' for 'Hello!' in *Teletubbies* – in spite of the presence of a very authoritative-sounding male narrator and children's voices in the show's live action inserts (also Bignell, 2005: 385). The creators defended the Teletubbies' use of language as part and parcel of the show's accessibility to very young children who 'love to play with language' including nursery rhymes and nonsense verse (Wood and Davenport, N.D). However, in other respects *Teletubbies* is also exceptional as a broadcast programme targeted at 2-year olds, who have only just started to combine words, compared to the more complex use of language by older preschoolers (see Messenger Davies, 1989: 17).

Looking beyond *Teletubbies*, writers of preschool television aimed at 3- to 5-year olds, talk about language being marked by short sentences, simple words, natural-sounding dialogue, frequent repetitions and questions that reinforce the message. With older children, aged four to six, you can, according to one writer-producer 'push it up in terms of vocabulary and pace' and this makes it easier to incorporate humour and 'be funny', a defining feature of content aimed at older children (also

Lees, 2005b; Wartella, 1994: 52). However, word play and puns (with the exception of *Sesame Street*) are usually avoided. Among scriptwriters it is assumed that young children will find it more difficult to comprehend storylines that are too 'talk heavy', so there is more emphasis on non-verbal communication, slogans (like Bob the Builder's 'Can we fix it? Yes we can!'), visual humour, sound effects, and character/facial expression. In some cases the absence of dialogue (*Pingu, Timmy Time*) can offer distinct cost advantages, particularly if a show is sold overseas and requires no dubbing (Calder, 2008c). The language level also needs to connect with the look and feel of the show. Several British writers pointed to frequent discrepancies between the 'young look' of a show and language, which was too sophisticated, both confusing the youngest or 'turning off' older children, with potentially serious economic consequences for shows designed to generate ancillary revenues. For example, it is interesting to note that the new CGI version of *Bob the Builder* (2009–) is designed to appeal to a slightly older audience than the original stop-frame version, through the use of 'more sophisticated' CG character expression that matches the story-telling (Hume, 2008).

Shot selection, editing and pace should reflect children's developmental capabilities

> I don't know if I would be able to say at two years old I would do this, but I wouldn't do that. I think you just have to feel that the story that you're telling has to be that much simpler if the children are that much younger. So does everything that goes with it. [...] Certainly you would make the camera move much more simply. You would make whatever is in the frame less cluttered, trying to have the characters at the centre of the frame, not depending too much on leading the viewer with the movement of the camera. Then as the children get older you can be slightly more complex. You could have slightly more complicated frames, or objects within the frame, things that are close to the camera or further from the camera [...] and certainly you do make the cutting faster. (British Preschool Director, 2008)

Much like their US counterparts (Anderson, 2004; Van Evra, 2004), British academic Maîre Messenger Davies (1989: 14) and BBC producer Roger Singleton-Turner (1994: 23–5) draw attention to how rapid editing and 'technical tricks' (panning and zooming) which leave out information can overstretch the 'intellectual abilities' of preschool children in terms of the time they need to process information and their ability to follow and understand what is happening on screen. Singleton-Turner goes on to recommend keeping shots uncluttered, avoiding fast cutting, not editing out too much 'real time' and letting characters 'move in relation to a relatively still camera' to avoid confusion, aspects acknowledged by the British director at the start of this section and common in US shows such as *Blues' Clues*.

In fact many British programme-makers argue that there is little that you cannot do in terms of shots and editing (also Lury, 2005: 29), pointing out that everything relates to age, context, type of programme and the experience of programme-makers who simply avoid 'confusing shots', 'bizarre angles', 'multi-cutting' and anything that 'messes with time'. Wide shots are used 'to establish where everybody is in relation to everyone else', with close-ups used to focus attention or provide clarity. Close-ups of costumed characters and puppets are sometimes avoided for practical reasons associated with their limited range of facial expressions and visible stitching. Events should happen on screen not off it, so that children can see the connection between cause and effect. When someone is speaking you should see them speaking. If a presenter or character is demonstrating something, programme-makers will cut to their hands so that children can see what is happening, because while 'you can imply action' for adult audiences 'with preschool you show action' (BBC Editor, 2008). There is also acknowledgement that in general programmes for 2- and 3-year olds need to be slower and 'more concrete' than programmes for 4- to 6-year olds. For older preschool children 'the camera can lead the story', with different shots and angles to add pace and even heighten the drama in a more theatrical, stylised way. Pace is also dictated by a programme's place in the schedule. For example *In the Night Garden* is deliberately slow as a programme that works at bedtime in contrast to more energetic programmes that reflect children's daytime activities.

However, according to one British writer-producer, drawing developmental distinctions between 2- and 3-year olds on the one hand and 4- and 5-year olds on the other is something which British programme-makers find difficult, because there is less developmental awareness, with the result that many programmes, particularly stop-frame shows, are shot, paced and scripted 'in a similar way' at the expense of younger children's understanding:

> The vast majority [of preschool] is pitched at a slightly generic age range between 4 and 5 like *Fifi [and the Flowertots]* or *Bob [the Builder]* [. . .] But you can't have something that's written for a two and a half

year old's developmental and cognitive stage and then shoot it like *Pingu* which is all wide and little [...] Actually when they're two. if you do a lovely little scene and you shoot it wide, and you've got little flowers here and characters running back and forth, you can't see it at two. So you put the camera there [gesticulates a close-up] and that in itself is a risk, because it breaks the rules. But everything else is shot like *Bob [the Builder]*. It's shot conventionally [...] for four to fives and the story lines are quite talk heavy and you're not going to understand that when you're three. You're going to watch it [...] but a three year old is only ever going to half understand most preschool stories. (British Writer, 2007)

This is not the case at Ragdoll where the show's creators have according to one director 'very specific rules that they think work for very young children, and if you don't adhere to those rules, then children won't be able to follow the story, won't be interested' (British Director, 2008). With such a strong vision about what they want to achieve based on their own expertise, Ragdoll's show creators, Andrew Davenport and Anne Wood, exercise much more control over direction and editing than is usual for live action shows, where directors usually determine the shots 'guided by visual language and what they know about how best visually to tell a story' (British Writer/Producer, 2008; Davenport, 2008). Within *In the Night Garden* and *Teletubbies* a static camera films the characters, usually in their entirety, moving in and out of the picture in long shot within a 'proscenium arch' with all the action happening within the frame, so that children see everything as it happens like a play. There are relatively few cuts. This style of filming is part of the creators' intention to raise young children's attention and therefore understanding (Wood, 2008) in much the same way as their US counterparts.

Received notions about editing may be challenged in other ways that reflect cultural differences in programme-making. For instance on Tiger Aspect's *Charlie and Lola* the British producers wanted to retain the graphic style, fantasy elements and black outlines of the original books by Lauren Childs, so that children could be transported from 'a bright red scene to an out of space scene' and then back to 'these lovely flat perspectives that just symbolise a school or symbolise a kitchen' (Lloyd, 2007). For US co-producers, Disney, who were more used to an editing style grounded in 'real worlds with corners and doors that they could walk through', these transitions from graphic scenes of domesticity to fantasy represented a challenge. Disney's argument was that 'young children don't like cuts, it's too hard on the eye' (ibid.). Yet the producers managed to convince Disney that hard cuts worked better with the more abstract and surreal fantasy scenes that children knew and loved from the books, although it should be noted that *Charlie and Lola* is targeted at older preschoolers and young school-age children (4–6 years).

Post-production also forms an important part of the narrative building process, particularly in live action where the story is reassembled from many different shots, in contrast to animation where this is predetermined during development and pre-production. As with any other programme, cuts are made to direct the attention of the viewer, to speed up or slow down action or reveal the location and relationships of characters. During this process transitions and sequences may be changed to improve the flow of the narrative. This knowledge appears to be based primarily on past experience of what is assumed to work. According to one BBC editor of live action programmes,

> Sometimes what happens is that something works on paper, but then actually when you film it and put it together with vision and sound – because the rhythm isn't right, because the pictures aren't right – you find that you actually have to start jigging it around a bit, because the story might be told better if that's stripped out, or that's put in there, or you put a piece of voiceover there. It's not always apparent on paper [...] So part of the job is saying: 'That's not quite working' [...] It is all about pace and rhythm. It's classic storytelling.

Alongside the visual elements, the addition of sound effects, voices and music are also crucial, functioning as cues to engage attention, allowing children to anticipate what will happen next. As Lury points out, in the case of *Teletubbies* the design and orchestration of different voices, music, sound effects as well as silences was central to the intentions of the show's producers, aimed at strengthening skills associated with anticipation, repetition and imitation (2005: 92–4) and giving force to the view of one BBC preschool editor, that 'You tell as much of the story through the sound as the verbal narrative' (BBC Editor, 2008).

Shows should encourage children's active participation

In keeping with recent US practice of addressing children directly and encouraging their participation in shows like *Blue's Clues* or *Dora the Explorer*, British programme-makers also consider interactive elements, especially where shows are specifically targeted at the US market and need an educational rationale or have broader multiplatform applications. A slower pace and direct address had always been a feature of more traditional presenter-led shows like *Play School* in Britain and *Mr Roger's Neighborhood* in the United States, and programmes like *Teletubbies* implicitly invite children to join in as well (Buckingham, 2002: 52).

However, before the demonstrable success of *Blue's Clues* this approach was, according to one British writer-producer, rather frowned upon on both sides of the Atlantic as 'patronising' because 'the child isn't really being spoken to, there isn't a real person there' (British writer, 2007). Among UK programme-makers there is still a certain reluctance to imitate US practice for the sake of emulation, particularly on narrative-based shows. According to one writer-producer, 'I think it's nonsense to argue that a show like *Bob the Builder* should have it [interactivity], because it's a story. That you would suddenly have Bob turn to you and say, "What do you think I should do?" That would be a different show' (2008). According to one British script editor,

> You don't want to ask children a question for the sake of it, because that's exploitative and empty. You don't want to ask them a question where there isn't a clear answer, because that's not fair. What if they don't get it right? It's not empowering for them. You don't want to ask them a question because then they feel patronised. That's a very important part of how you conceive a show. I respect that a child is able to respond, but I also respect that they may not have reached certain development points yet. So I need to get things to work within their parameters. (2007)

There is concern that interactivity may seem false or contrived if it does not serve a clear purpose, as is the case in *Blue's Clues* where it was always intended to reinforce curricular goals and esteem (Anderson, 2004).

Conclusion

The making of preschool television is shaped by a number of assumptions about the audience. In the United States, these assumptions are tested by academic consultants, with the goal of enhancing attention, understanding and learning. In Britain preschool television, as we have learnt, is not usually expressly educational. However, this does not mean that developmental considerations do not play a role in production choices. A lot of what takes place in Britain is inspired by programme-makers' practical consciousness and experience – it is often intuitive and infused with implicit public service priorities. Nevertheless, regardless of the lack of a written formal curriculum for many UK productions, along the lines of most American shows, there are still common assumptions about what works and is appropriate for the preschool audience in both countries. Where British producers usually differ is in the lack of any formative testing to check that the assumptions for individual shows are valid – a factor, which potentially limits access to the US market unless British shows can be retro-fitted to meet US requirements. With the rising importance of the US market to preschool producers (Chapters 3 and 5), a mounting requirement by public service operators like the BBC to demonstrate their distinctiveness in return for public funding, and public concerns about the impact of screen media, educational and developmental considerations are becoming more prominent. In the words of one BBC producer, 'you have to back up what you say with research from people who know enough to be able to say it' (Stewart, 2007).

8
In Production

> The challenge for production companies is to create high quality given the budget that you have and that might require innovation. It might mean you have to build around one character instead of five characters. It may mean you have sets that are made out of fabric, instead of sets that are made out of CG animation. There are a million choices that a production company makes and the idea that somehow you can only work with a big budget isn't true. (US preschool producer, 2007)

Chapters 6 and 7 covered the parameters and culture of preschool television development and production. They considered how programming is informed by programme-makers' conceptions of the audience, derived from a combination of professional experience, institutional practices and research which may focus variously on what children like and want or on what is believed to be developmentally or educationally appropriate. This chapter moves on from these production practices and beliefs to the specific and changing production circumstances underpinning television production for young children. First it provides insight into the broader context of production – how productions are managed both creatively and logistically in relation to different production structures (in-house and outsourced), forms (live action and animation) and contexts (domestic and overseas). The inclusion of a case study – *What's Your News?* – serves to open up important aspects of contemporary preschool production for further analysis. In particular it reveals how small producers make use of technology to innovate in cost-efficient and creative ways. Of course creative and technological innovation is not exclusive to preschool television, but in a production environment characterised frequently by low budgets and the need to be both developmentally appropriate and aesthetically distinctive, these choices are important in shaping what is produced.

Production structures

Alongside production practices and beliefs, organisational structures are also key in shaping the work of media producers, serving as a framework for the conventions and values which determine the collective endeavour of programme-making (Croteau and Hoynes, 2003: 156). Yet these organisational structures have changed markedly in response to the emergence of a multi-channel, more market-led environment and the segmentation of audiences and revenues across many media outlets since the 1980s.

In Britain a large share of preschool television production, like other forms of television production, has shifted from the vertically integrated in-house production units of the BBC and ITV to independent producers, as broadcasters have sought to reduce their cost base and risk (see Deakin and Pratten, 2000; Robins and Cornford, 1992; Starkey and Barnatt, 1997). However, it is also worth noting that since the 1950s, British preschool animation production had always been a predominantly independent enterprise, focused on small companies (Smallfilms, FilmFair), producing short series runs for BBC or ITV on shoestring budgets (Home, 1993: 65; Lury, 2005: 41–2). With the expansion of the international marketplace from the mid-1990s (Chapter 3), larger animation production houses emerged (such as Cosgrove Hall, HOT/HIT Entertainment) to cater for the higher volumes demanded by overseas markets. With the production of live action shows shifting from broadcasters' in-house units as well, independent producers are now responsible for producing a larger proportion of original preschool hours. However, the amount of preschool originations commissioned by public service broadcasters (BBC, ITV, Five) had sunk to 132 hours by 2006 from a high of 403 hours in 2002 (Ofcom, 2007a: 30). The BBC is virtually the only in-house producer-broadcaster since ITV announced the closure of its in-house production arm, ITV Kids, in 2006. Forty-five per cent of approximately 100 hours originated by CBeebies annually are made by independents and 5 per cent by international partners (Carrington, 2009), as the Corporation seeks to open up production to outside suppliers through the WoCC, which guarantees in-house producers a 50 per cent share of originations by volume, while opening up a further 25 per cent to competition with external suppliers, alongside a 25 per cent quota guaranteed to independents. As a consequence the expertise, professional culture and public service ethos traditionally inculcated with the training that took place within the BBC and ITV have become dispersed across a small number of larger companies (HIT Entertainment, Chorion, RDF) with preschool expertise. Additionally there are an estimated 300 animation companies (Optima, 2004: 6), not all of whom are focused on preschool production, and an indeterminate number of boutique operations who usually have neither the resources and/or inclination to provide formal training in children's television (Buckingham et al., 1999: 73; Oswell, 2002: 155; Saundry and Nolan, 1998: 421).

This shift in Britain from in-house to independent production is a feature of the trend towards the flexible firm (Atkinson, 1984) and 'flexible specialisation' (Piore and Sabel, 1984) that became evident in the 1980s following the establishment of Channel 4 in 1982 as a 'publisher-broadcaster' without any significant in-house production capability, and the requirement of the 1990 Broadcasting Act that the BBC and ITV source up to 25 per cent of their originations (excluding repeats, acquisitions and news) from independent producers. These structural changes had an impact on how production was organised with more of the management responsibility and financial risk of programme-making shouldered by independent producers, but with broadcasters retaining a large degree of creative control through their commissioning function (Barnatt and Starkey, 1994; Dex et al., 2000: 285–6; Tunstall, 1993). As elsewhere in television production, this shift towards 'flexible' production networks has been characterised in preschool television production by a shift towards more freelance employment on a project-by-project basis (Barnatt and Starkey, 1994: 254; Davis and Scase, 2000: 122; Saundry and Nolan, 1998: 418–22; Ursell, 1998). Focused on single projects, 'latent' (Starkey, Barnatt and Tempest, 2000: 299), informal networks of programme-makers, writers, performers and technicians with specialist expertise in preschool programming, children's animation and children's television reassemble periodically to work on projects, drawing on their combined expertise and trust in each other. For broadcasters these latent networks offer the security of manageable risk based on the innovation, reputation and track record of established producers who co-ordinate and manage the contributions of others (ibid: 300–1).

The disaggregation evident in British production stands in stark contrast to the United States, where preschool television production is largely consolidated within the diversified activities of vertically and horizontally integrated media giants Viacom (Nick Jr., Noggin) and Disney (Playhouse Disney) (Alexander and Owers, 2007: 62). With the exception of PBS (Public Broadcasting Service), which does not produce or own its programmes, production of preschool programming is dominated by the studios of the major media conglomerates, who produce for their own preschool outlets with series production serving as 'a focal point for brand extension and global expansion' (Sandler, 2004: 62). The studios do employ freelancers, independent production companies and service companies to execute production and frequently outsource animation overseas, but they remain in overall ownership and control, and barriers to other suppliers are high (Allen, 2001: 488). According to Cahn et al. it is impossible to create 'an economically viable' series without Disney or Nickelodeon (2008: 33) because they reach potential audiences of over 90m viewers in the United States alone.

As we saw in Chapter 5 there are a small number of US independents specialising in the production of high-quality educational preschool programming for PBS, Nick Jr. and Disney Playhouse. Yet there appear to be fewer openings for genuine independent production than in Britain. The revocation of the 'fin-syn' (financial syndication) rules in 1995, that restricted production and programme ownership by network broadcasters, resulted in consolidation as major studios with broadcast and cable interests acquired a number of independent studios, and started to programme their own outlets with their own content (Jeremy, 2002; London, 2007: 86; Westcott, 2002: 71). Disney acquired ABC in 1995 and Viacom acquired CBS in 1999. The US preschool market does provide a small number of openings for European and Canadian productions but these are limited – not least because the most important preschool outlets have been preschool blocks (Nick Jr., Playhouse Disney), rather than standalone channels (Noggin – rebranded in 2009 as Nick Jr.). Moreover smaller producers that successfully pitch to major US cable outlets often cede a large measure of ownership and control in exchange for funding and the considerable resources needed to market a property across markets (Alexander and Owers, 2007: 66; Steemers, 2004: 136). In contrast the stranglehold of UK terrestrial broadcasters over rights was broken with the 2003 Communications Act. In return for a licence fee, broadcasters acquire a limited UK broadcast licence, with all other rights retained by the producer. The downside of this approach is that British producers increasingly have to deficit finance gaps in funding as broadcasters reduce the amounts they are willing to commit to new productions (see Chapter 3).

Production forms and contexts

Preschool television, like children's television generally encompasses a range of forms (live action, animation) and genres. However, as we saw in Chapters 3 and 4, live action is often a more difficult proposition. Unless it comprises mainly costumed characters, it tends to be too culturally specific for overseas sales, with animation comprising up to 80 per cent of children's channels' schedules (TBI, 2006b).

Although it is less prevalent on commercial channels, live action is often cheaper to produce than animation, particularly if it is studio-based and predominantly focused on a limited number of 'real people' dancing, singing, talking and presenting (TBI, 2007a). However, once you start to add special effects, computer-generated animation, sophisticated costumed characters or puppets with animatronics, and detailed computer-generated backgrounds, costs inevitably escalate. For example Ragdoll's *In the Night Garden* is reputed to have cost £14m for 100 thirty-minute episodes (Lane, 2007), but is undoubtedly a complex production involving differently scaled costumed characters, shot separately, which are then brought together through compositing techniques. Similarly the £10m set aside for 100 episodes of *Waybuloo* (RDF) involves a complex combination of 3D CGI and live action (Rushton, 2009a). Moreover extra costs are incurred when children are used in live action shows, because they can only work for limited time periods, and they also require the support of tutors and chaperones (Hofmann and Schmid, 2002). To keep live action costs in check producers do employ a number of strategies – including voiceovers rather than actors to deliver dialogue, long introductions and the use of generic pre-recorded material that can be interwoven into different narratives, thereby generating savings as well as satisfying the notion that children enjoy repetition (see Chapter 7).

Animation by contrast is usually a more pre-planned industrialised process, where standardised tasks can be parcelled out between geographically distant and more cost-efficient locations (Winder and Dowlatabadi, 2001: 145ff), a process made considerably easier by advances in electronic communication (Tschang and Goldstein, 2004). Yet approaches to outsourcing vary markedly. The creative skills of British stop-frame animation specialists at HIT Entertainment (HOT studios), Cosgrove Hall, Aardman Animation and model builders like Mackinnon & Saunders ensured for many years that the production of stop-frame preschool series like *Bob the Builder* remained in Britain, because these skills could not be easily replicated overseas and this 3D look seemed to appeal particularly to preschoolers (Burns, 2005; Wood, 2004: 24). Conventional wisdom also suggested that specialised creative industries benefit creatively from clustering in close proximity to each other allowing frequent face-to-face interactions both within companies and between partners (see Cole, 2007: 893; Scott, 2004: 199). However, the balance appears to have shifted with technical advances and cost reductions in 3D CGI in particular, challenging stop-frame and allowing animation to take place at lower cost overseas (Hume, 2008). Poor exchange rates, rising labour costs, reduced levels of broadcaster funding and an emphasis on producing for global rather than national markets have all combined to focus the attention of British companies like HIT Entertainment, Chorion and Ludorum (see Chapter 5) on the cost benefits of 3D CG animation in the Far East, particularly as labour costs account for 60–80 per cent of production expenditure (Tschang and Goldstein, 2004: 3). This reflects US practice where outsourcing to Asia has occurred over many years (Lent, 1998, 2001) including for preschool productions such as Nick Jr.'s *Dora the Explorer* and *Ni Hao Kai-Lan*.

In this vein HIT Entertainment took the decision in 2007 and 2008 to cease stop-frame production of its *Fireman Sam* and *Bob the Builder* series respectively, and outsource these as 3D CGI productions – a momentous decision given Britain's reputation for stop-frame shows (HOT, HIT's Manchester-based studios continue to make *Bob the Builder: On Site*, a hybrid live action and stop-frame brand for the DVD market). The same decision was made for the 2D publishing-based property, *Angelina Ballerina*, and the live action train-based model series, *Thomas & Friends*. HIT's decision to produce its two most popular series *Bob the Builder* and *Thomas & Friends* in CGI was certainly influenced by a desire to 'refresh and update' the properties, a desire which had been reinforced by focus group research, which suggested that CGI techniques that allowed 'greater character expression' might improve the 'emotional connection between the characters and viewers' and improve appeal to the two-to-four target age group (Christopher Skala Senior VP Production, cit. in Buxton, 2008; Hume, 2008). Alongside aesthetic, audience and cost considerations, HIT would also have been aware of the international success of other CGI series such as Disney's reworking of Winnie the Pooh, *My Friends Tigger and Pooh* (2007–) and another builder-based property *Handy Manny* (2006–).

Yet there are risks if a rejuvenated property proves to be less well loved than its predecessor, notwithstanding the considerable investment required upfront in designing and building 3D characters, sets and locations (Wells, 2006: 125). For larger producers like the US studios and UK producer-distributors like HIT, Chorion and Ludorum, whose business is much more focused on ancillary and international rights exploitation, outsourcing represents one way of balancing the books and ensuring a return on investment. However, most companies are mindful to retain those activities, which constitute the creative core of a production in the originating country. These include development, scripting, voice recording, design, storyboarding, creative supervision and post-production, leaving more mechanistic humdrum processes to the outsourcing destination (Hume, 2008; Lent, 2001: 240; Tschang and Goldstein, 2004).

While some preschool animation specialists embrace the notion of outsourcing, others prefer to retain greater control. For many smaller creatively led producers or those involved in experimental forms of animation, there is a strong desire to remain close to the production process as a source of creative strength and innovation (Selig and Tilert, 2008), without seeing creative energies dissipated trying to administer production from afar (also Tschang and Goldstein, 2004: 11–12). Unable to compete with overseas studios on labour-intensive CGI projects or traditional 2D animation, smaller British companies like Tiger Aspect (*Charlie and Lola*), Astley Baker Davies (*Peppa Pig*), Illuminated Films (*Little Princess*) and King Rollo Films (*Mama Mirabelle's Home Movies*) have sought to innovate creatively with cost-efficient 2D computer animation, foremost CelAction2D from £300,000 an hour instead of £500,000 an hour (Burns, 2005; Wood, 2004). This has allowed most aspects of the production process to be retained in-house, reinforcing creative interplay and dialogue between members of the on-site team and 'the absolute singularity of vision' of any show. For one British animation producer outsourcing simply does not suit their internal creative processes:

> There is this idea that you can write down everything on the page and then it gets shipped off to Japan. It's just a job of work making series to the brief. We'd never make films like that, to be honest. It's too much of an organic thing. It develops while you're making it.

Some animators argue that it is harder to keep track of quality overseas, however much groundwork has been done beforehand in terms of story and design. Keeping production in one place allows small, but important changes to be made at any moment, rather than having to resort to electronic file transfers and notes, which are much more likely to be misinterpreted. This sense of a versatile creative process that allows for minor adjustments to characterisation or visual style is underlined by the producer of *Peppa Pig*:

> It's all to do with process [...] I remember a Canadian animator. He did the original skip cycle in Peppa. I can remember walking past his desk, and Peppa had just come out of the door. She was just skipping down the hill, going out to play in muddy puddles in Episode One. You look at it and think 'Wow that's great!' And the editor was saying to the animator 'Why don't you just tweak that?' [...] I saw it a couple of days later, and the character was completely different, purely because there's been a very small change in the way the animators animated a leg or an arm. (Davies, 2007)

The point being made is that it is small details and flexibility that often matter, making a show distinctive and possibly more successful as well. Some producers argue that this can only occur if an animation team work in close proximity and communicate in person so that they understand the philosophy behind a show. According to the producer of *Charlie and Lola* this distinctiveness risks being diluted if a production becomes too dispersed risking less personal investment in the show, less cultural affinity with the underlying philosophy and less personal interaction:

> How an animator would animate in Russia or Hungary or China would be different to how we would do it [...] If you contain the sense of humour or the tone of the show under the same roof, everybody just gets it by osmosis so it becomes a much purer product [...] with a true voice. That is what makes shows rise to the top because if too many people over too many countries have too much input it becomes diluted into yet another show that is probably selling a toy [...] It's just nuance and skill and experience. That doesn't mean that overseas animators don't have it. It just means that if you contain it in the same studio everyone is singing from the same hymn sheet. (Lloyd, 2007)

However, it is worth noting that some smaller creatively led British companies are not averse to outsourcing animation overseas if there are compelling cost reasons. Examples include Collingwood O'Hare Entertainment (*Harry and his Bucketful of Dinosaurs*/Taiwan, *Gordon the Gnome*/China) and The Canning Factory (*Ebb and Flo*/Vietnam). Some like British company Hibbert Ralph Animation (*Fireman Sam* for HIT in China; *Tractor Tom* for Contender in Romania) have even developed specialist expertise in managing outsourced productions for others. Co-productions provide another countervailing argument against the 100 per cent retention of a production in one location. Notwithstanding some organisational and creative disadvantages (see Chapter 3), co-productions also offer a more collaborative and negotiated creative solution to the top-down contractual relationships that determine outsourcing.

Case study: What's Your News?

As we have seen the shifting structures and global orientation of production combined with different production contexts have an impact on how, where and by whom shows are made. In such a rapidly changing and financially challenging market, producers will look to innovate, using technology to bring down production costs, but also to give their shows a distinctive look (Burns, 2008). This was certainly the case for Nick Jr.'s *Blue's Clues*, which used cost-efficient desktop computers to create flat 2D cut-out animation in a 'storybook animation' style which also featured a live action character, setting it apart from other preschool shows (see Tracy, 2002: 95ff).

Yet how can smaller producers utilise technology to compete? Some producers have looked to computer games techniques for creative inspiration and cost savings (see TBI, 2006c). *What's Your News?* (26 × 22 minutes), acquired and launched by Nick Jr. UK in 2009, provides one example of the changing context of preschool production, and the extent to which producers adapt and innovate in response to technological change, funding restrictions and a competitive marketplace. The case study also serves as a useful illustration of development and production practices addressed in Chapters 6 and 7.[1]

Produced by British production company TT Animation (a subsidiary of Traveller's Tales, acquired by Warner Brothers in 2007), *What's Your News?* is a news show for 4- to 6-year olds. According to the show's co-creator, producer and head writer, Jocelyn Stevenson:

> I always wanted to do a news show for kids that was about their news – news that they care about. Not *Newsround* [BBC] or *Nick News* [two news shows for older children] not things about obesity or green issues, but about falling down and skinning your knee, or learning how to ride a bike. You know, when you have kids, they're full of this news. And all the time the grownups don't pay much attention to what they're saying. But for them it's big news.

Illustration 8.1 What's Your News? Antony, Grant and the *What's Your News?* team
Copyright Line: Courtesy of TT Animation. WHAT'S YOUR NEWS? and all related characters, names and indicia are trademarks of and © Warner Bros. Entertainment Inc. 2008.

The show focuses on breaking news stories told from a child's perspective. Each episode is based on a real story, which a child told the writers. Structured like a news show, *What's Your News?* features two animated studio anchors – Grant, an ant, and Antony a much larger childlike anteater, who thinks he is an ant. Antony is the character with whom children are most likely to identify as he frequently addresses them directly. In each show a real child calls in with a news story, whereupon

Gi Ant the show's roving *correspond-ant* sets off in his vehicle to report back to the studio. As Gi reports back, we see his animated form inserted into a live action setting where he interviews real children about their news. Each show also features interviews by Grant and Antony of three real children and one baby, who appear on a screen in the animated studio, to give their 'expert' unscripted advice on some aspect of that episode's news story. The baby's comments are translated by another *correspond-ant*, Gooblee. There is breaking news, traffic news from Avi Ant in her helicopter, weather reports from Flickaboo, the weather bird, and updates as the drama unfolds.

The show employs a variety of news conventions, because assumptions were made that children of a certain age will be familiar with news formats – the musical stings, the layout of the studio, presentation techniques, the way the interviews are conducted. However, it is also noteworthy that Stevenson was advised early on by potential broadcasters to raise the target audience from 3–5 years to 4–7 years because of the show's themes. She believes this proved beneficial, because it allowed the writing team to inject more complex scripting and pace, which younger preschoolers would have found difficult to comprehend:

> That immediately made it easier to be funny [...] to just push it up in terms of vocabulary and pace. So just moving it up a year like that, really transformed the show for the better. (Stevenson, 2007)

In keeping with many other preschool shows there is a basic three-act structure and a considerable degree of verbal repetition. For example a child relates his or her story, and the reporter and news anchors reinforce the telling through questions and restating what the child has said or done throughout the episode. This kind of questioning and repetition is a feature of news formats, but also fits with the repetition inherent in preschool shows. In common with most British shows, there was no formative testing or checklist of curricular goals, but the series is broadly educational in its thematic concerns, focused on a child's achievements and growing confidence.

Where *What's Your News?* is designed to stand out is in the way it combines animation and live action to give the series a distinctive look, a crucial factor in a crowded marketplace. Of course the combination of live action and animation for preschool audiences is not uncommon (*Numberjacks*, *Blue's Clues*). Where *What's Your News?* differs is in the seemingly spontaneous interactions between the animated characters and the children, providing a sense of an animated show that in the words of its creators is actually 'performed'. A similar emphasis on the spontaneity of children's reactions to animated characters can be observed in RDF's *Waybuloo* (2009–, CBeebies), which is aimed at a younger audience.

Finding the technology to give the show this distinctive look was clearly a priority during development. As a former chief creative officer at HIT Entertainment, Stevenson had already encountered digital puppetry, where computer-generated characters are given movement and expression through animatronic controls linked to computers by puppeteers and performers rather than animators. A proprietary system had been developed by William Todd-Jones, Rob Tygner, and Matt Denton, who would later become chief performer, first-time director and technical advisor, respectively on *What's Your News?* However, like more sophisticated forms of 3D CGI, digital puppetry had proved hitherto prohibitively expensive for the limited budgets of British preschool television – one of the reasons being that each character has to be built in CGI in advance. Yet a show that mixed live action with more formatted animated characters, in this case ants, seemed a potentially more realistic prospect, particularly if computer-generated figures could be built quickly and cheaply. Motion capture, a procedure, that involves attaching sensors to human performers, who then act out the character sequences that make up the animation, also promised a cost-efficient and creative solution.

With a creative idea in place and the beginnings of a technological solution, Stevenson, and her co-creator, designer Chris Dicker, needed to secure financial backing. They were reluctant to approach traditional distributors, fearing that the core concept might be diluted in a quest for multiple sources of international funding. Instead they approached Jon Burton, Dicker's previous boss at Traveller's Tales, a British computer games developer based near Manchester. Burton was interested in digital puppetry and agreed to fund the production and undertake the render, using the TT games render machine, a procedure which gives 3D CGI animation texture and depth (through the addition of fur, skin, clothing etc). The rendering of 3D CGI has traditionally been prohibitively expensive, but the use of game engine technology offered a more cost-efficient solution. In this way a latent network of preschool television specialists was brought together with a different network of computer games specialists.

A subsidiary of Traveller's Tales, TT Animation, with Stevenson and Dicker as Creative Directors, was established in 2006. A 5-minute pilot, *News with Mee Mee* was produced in December 2007 to test the concept and the production pipeline. Underwritten by funding from a games company and subject only to the requirements of a broadcast acquisition by Nick Jr. UK, the producers found themselves at greater liberty to pursue their creative vision without interventions based on other considerations – such as pilot testing or licensed merchandise. With Toronto-based distributor Lenz Entertainment in place for international sales, filming of the live action elements began in August 2007.

Each show comprises 7 minutes of pre-edited scripted live action footage of children filmed prior to the production of the animated elements. Filming children aged between four and eight represented a challenge as they had to look as if they were talking to an animated character, which of course they could not see. To get the eye lines right the children were encouraged to talk to a small model or a strategically positioned member of the crew. Although the live shoots were scripted, the children were 'guided' about what to say to ensure a naturalistic performance, that inevitably diverged from the original scripts. As a consequence the animated characters' dialogue had to be re-worked by the producer so that it fitted in with the children's responses. The result is a complex multi-layered scenario, where animated 'ant' characters (Grant and Antony) in an animated television studio talk to a television screen in the studio, depicting live action footage of children being interviewed by an animated character, Gi Ant.

The effect is achieved through the combination of motion capture 3D animation techniques, which draw heavily on gaming industry expertise, and digital puppetry which draws on the traditional performance skills of puppeteers. This in itself was a creative and logistical challenge involving the coming together of two different production cultures – preschool programme-makers and computer games specialists who not only had to learn what they could and could not do creatively and technically, but also how to work together. Studio filming took place between October 2007 and March 2008. In the studio there were no sets, no cameras, no lighting set-ups, no camera operators and no lighting technicians. The team was divided between a small core of creative personnel (director, producer and performers) and a larger cohort of technical staff (first assistant director, production assistant, video assistant, sound technician, runner and three editors), a motion capture producer and two motion capture technicians. Most of the TV production team had a background in children's television, predominantly preschool, and many had worked together in the past (*The Hoobs, Mopatop's Shop; Construction Site; Bunnytown, Tikkabilla*) suggesting common beliefs about the purposes of children's television and how it should be produced. Interestingly the younger members of the team had no or limited experience of children's television and unlike the older crew members expressed no specific commitment to it, because they were uncertain where their next job might lead them.

Studio performances were guided by the script and the pre-edited live action footage. There were no storyboards. The movements of four human performers playing the roles of the *What's Your News?* 'news' team were 'captured' through sensors attached to their black suits as they acted out their roles. The captured data were fed via 36 fixed cameras to computers, where the performances were corrected and transformed by motion capture technicians into basic animated characters, pre-designed in 3D CGI. Studio performances were complicated by the fact that the animated characters differed in size. For example in the animated version Antony, the anteater, is more than twice the size of Grant, his co-anchor, necessitating complicated settings and awareness of how the performers' movements and positioning related to each other and the animated or live action setting into which their character was inserted. They did not perform to their actual positioning in the studio, but to the positioning of their characters in a motion capture grid, a basic unrendered version of the scene, which the actors viewed through headsets.

The complications arising from these settings led to frequent interventions from the performers who were all puppeteers and actors with past experience of preschool television. In rehearsals and repeated takes they made suggestions to the producer and director for minor script amendments (cuts or additions) born of their experience of performance and timing, which might make a scene work better. One remarked that their role is to 'imbue it [the technology] with performance'. This constant dialogue stems from the face-to-face nature of puppetry, unlike animation where workers are often physically separated from each other. Here there was a strong collaborative feel with the core creative team (performers, director, assistant director, producer, production assistant) sitting down to 'read' new scripts together prior to filming – in keeping with the experience of performers who are more used to teamwork and dialogue to find solutions to technical problems and script inconsistencies, particularly in a situation where the performers had to perform in new ways.

Capturing between 6 and 10 minutes of motion capture animated footage a day the process has obvious advantages over keyframe animation, where it can take a week to animate 1–2 minutes. The second advantage in terms of cost and authenticity is that unlike traditional animation, voices were not pre-recorded but occurred live with the actors' studio performances as they interacted with the pre-recorded and partially edited live action performances of the children.

The basic animated body footage with voices was then passed to three post-production performance animators who refined the animated images and studio performances through digital puppetry, operating the animated characters in a CG environment. They added facial expressions, hand, tail and antennae movements, and ear twitches with hand-operated animatronic controls connected to computers. Digital puppetry can also save time and money compared to CGI animation, allowing each post-production performer to animate 3–5 minutes of an individual character a day, compared to 9–12 seconds a day in traditional animation. For the performers the added advantage is that they can inject their experience and knowledge of live performance into CGI characters, bringing these to life. This is technological innovation, which puts puppeteers back into the picture (literally). Having been pushed out in recent years by the onward march of 3D CGI in overseas locations, digital puppetry blurs the boundaries between live action performance and animation. From here the post-produced footage was sent to computer games specialists Traveller's Tales where more detailed backgrounds and props were added, and the footage was rendered and lit in such a way that the animated characters were given a textured 3D look with the addition of skin, feathers, fur and clothing – more quickly and cost effectively than traditional animation.

What's Your News? provides an example of the importance of technological and creative innovation in flexible television production networks (see Barnatt and Starkey, 1994), where creativity is a combination of vision (from the top) and its interpretation (from the bottom) (see Tschang and Goldstein, 2004: 11). The innovative use of cheaper technological solutions combined with the traditional creative skills of performance, scripting and design allows smaller production enterprises like TT Animation to compete with better resourced and larger companies who are better placed to take advantage of more globally dispersed production solutions.

Conclusion

As previously discussed, production is shaped by both external and internal influences and constraints. It is also a collaborative process, where those involved have to agree on the creative, organisational and financial terms on which they will operate for each project. This is complicated by the changing organisational structures of production and different production contexts, which mean that no show is ever the same in respect of how, where and by whom it is produced or financed. The case study presented here provides insight into how technology is harnessed by small production companies in innovative ways allowing competition with better-resourced and larger rivals. In this sense it satisfies the features of organisational creativity outlined by Davis and Scase (2000: 19–21) in respect of structure (the division of labour), production culture and the work process. First, there is sufficient *autonomy* within individuals' work roles to allow for some experimentation, adaptation and adjustment within the creative process. The second organisational attribute involves acceptance of some degree of *nonconformity* in the way that individuals tackle tasks in contrast to the more mechanistic, routine nature of *some* animation productions, which are organised more as an industrialised, dispersed process. The creative process is also characterised by some measure of *indeterminacy* in operational practices, with creative work reliant 'upon the interactions of relatively autonomous employees' (p. 21) who negotiate and discuss their contributions, rather than a top-down approach to the management of creative work. These levels of creative autonomy, nonconformity and indeterminacy stand in contrast to those productions which are determined more centrally by commercial and corporate priorities.

Note

1. Evidence is based on interviews with the production team between 2007 and 2008 and a week long production observation in January 2008.

9
Spinning off Profits: Ancillary Exploitation and the Power of Retail

> Creative projects are the result of marketing strategies and children's imagination is tied into the market economy. Programming evolves not from the rituals of storytelling but rather the imperative of the marketplace. (Pecora, 1998: 59)

As Pecora indicates, at the heart of children's television including preschool television, there is often a very basic conflict of interest. However much broadcasters and producers emphasise the creative integrity, educational value and age-appropriateness of their preschool offerings, there are always suspicions among parents and cultural critics (see Engelhardt, 1986; Kline, 1993; Linn, 2004; Schor, 2004) that these shows are little more than 'giant toy ads' (cited in Hayes, 2008: 127) for a wide array of branded merchandise ranging from toys and DVDs to dubious fast-food promotions. These concerns are partly borne out by the wider context of production. Although many preschool programme-makers are strongly committed to and motivated by the needs of the audience, they have to operate within the economic constraints and market dynamics that define the sector as a whole. As the resources to produce television have diminished in a fragmenting market of multiple broadcast platforms, revenues from merchandise licensing have become a vital component of programme funding, paying for current productions and sustaining future output, reinforcing the 'commodity flow' of brand images both within and around programming (McAllister and Giglio, 2005).

For preschool content this association with commerce is possibly more difficult to reconcile than for children's entertainment generally, not least because young children, unlike older children, cannot be portrayed as 'savvy' sophisticated consumers (see Lindstrom and

Seybold, 2003), and programming and products have to appeal as much, if not more, to parents rather than their offspring. Difficulties also stem from the fact that many preschool projects are not only originated from within a public service (PBS, BBC) or non-profit framework (Sesame Workshop), but also because they are often promoted on the basis of their educational credentials, which might be considered cynical or ill-conceived if a property is perceived to be overly commercial (see Brown, 2002; Jarvik, 1998; Pecora, 1998: 103ff; Raugust, 1996: 8).

Bearing these tensions with commerce in mind this chapter examines the importance of merchandise licensing in the preschool television market and how programmes are shaped by consumer product considerations, drawing mainly on interviews with British players. It begins by focusing on the wider debate about children as consumers, before examining producers' perspectives on product licensing. Following a brief overview of how licensing works, it then considers what conditions a preschool property should meet for licensing success, and how different programme-makers reconcile the competing demands of creative and commercial interests.

Recognising reality – children as consumers

The relationship between merchandise licensing and children's television is one of many elements in the wider debate about consumer culture and 'the construction of children as a distinct audience for media products' (Buckingham, 1995b: 18). In the United States and Britain this targeting of children as a distinct and constructed audience can be traced back to the late nineteenth century with the evolution, promotion and exploitation of mass markets, including mass-produced media (Kline, 1993; Pecora, 1998). In the field of audio-visual media, Disney demonstrated its mastery of branding and the licensed spin-off as early as the 1930s (Gomery, 1994; Kline, 1993; Wasko, 2001: 48–9). Even *Muffin the Mule* broadcast from 1946, at the height of the BBC's public service monopoly, proved a commercial success with character merchandise, generating £0.75m in turnover in 1952 (Oswell, 2002: 59) for its creators.

The difference then was that merchandise licensing was usually considered as supplementary revenue after a programme had been made. It remained peripheral to the business of children's television as long as broadcast production budgets were deemed sufficient to fund output. This changed in the 1980s as a combination of shrinking advertising revenues, fragmenting audiences and deregulation put pressure on production funding. As recounted in Chapter 2, the FCC's removal of advertising restrictions around children's programming in 1984 opened up US broadcasting to product-based programmes (*Strawberry Shortcake, He-Man and the Masters of the Universe, My Little Pony*) funded by toy companies and licensing agents without fear of sanction (Engelhardt, 1986: 76; Hendershot, 1998: 128; Pecora, 1998: 73). By the mid-1990s the wider commercial potential of the preschool audience and their parents had also been recognised by media conglomerates Viacom (Nickelodeon) and Disney, stimulating production for this audience (Chapter 2). At the same time producers were identifying the possibilities of an expanding domestic and international market for preschool properties (Chapter 3 and 5).

This expansion of marketing to children through a variety of media platforms including television and more recently online media has increased anxieties about the impact of the commercial world on children's health and well-being (see Buckingham, 2007a), extending earlier critical evaluations of children's television (Postman, 1982; Winn, 1977) to marketing and the dangers of consumerism (Linn, 2004; Mayo and Nairn, 2009; Schor, 2004). On the one hand there are those who see the onward march of marketing and consumerism within children's culture, including television, as harmful and manipulative of children's desires. Kline, for example, has argued that the encroachment of electronic media and commerce into the child's world has 'undermined the traditional healthy preoccupations of street play, peer conversation and just wandering in the garden long associated with a happy childhood' (1993: 12), leaving children vulnerable to cultural products which will 'never inspire' 'high ideals or positive images' (ibid.: 350) because they 'are ultimately motivated not by an interest in the desire to enlighten, integrate, or even educate the child, but by economic considerations' (ibid.: 19–20). Without explaining why children might enjoy this type of content, Kline's argument is that the combination of programming and licensed product signals the further commoditisation of childhood. For Seiter, the targeting of children and their parents is more complex (Seiter, 1993: 224). She argues that attempts to shield children from consumption ignore the importance of consumption choices in defining children's identity, play and participation in a shared culture (1993: 7–8). This is also true of small children for whom 'Consumer culture provides a shared repository of images, characters, plots, and themes' as well as 'the basis for small talk and play' (Seiter, 1993: 7; also Buckingham, 2007a: 20). Rather than undermining creativity, she suggests that the formulaic nature of mass-market toys and television may actually enhance the ability of preschool children to engage in 'group, cooperative play, by encouraging children to make up stories with shared codes and narratives' (1993: 191).

Buckingham too argues that the divide between culture and creativity on the one hand (good) and commerce on the other (bad) is by no means clear-cut, not least because of the blurring of public service and commercial goals (Buckingham, 1995b, 2007b: 83). Programmes shown on public service channels are used in promotions for fast food outlets, and both PBS (PBS Sprout) and the BBC (overseas versions of CBeebies) are involved in commercial channel ventures. Commercial producers with an eye on broadcast exposure and profitability provide programming at low cost to non-profit broadcasters like the BBC and PBS. PBS benefits from corporate sponsorship and ancillary revenues on independently produced shows like *Barney and Friends*. Since 1999 it has earned between $7m and $10m annually as back-end revenues (predominantly from children's programming) although this represents only a small proportion of its total $624m income (PBS, 2008; USGAO, 2007: 50). The BBC benefits even more from the commercial success of preschool properties, through the revenue generating (publishing, DVD, international sales, consumer products) and fund-raising (co-production) activities of its commercial subsidiary, BBC Worldwide. Non-profit Sesame Workshop also relies on ancillary revenues to fund its production slate with product licensing accounting for 36 per cent of total revenues in 2008 (Sesame Workshop, 2008). Conversely it could be argued, that Nickelodeon has managed to 'combine the economies of commercial television with the components of a public service mandate' (Sandler, 2004: 53) through its educational preschool programming.

Mirroring these debates many preschool programme-makers feel uncomfortable about the sector's reliance on ancillary revenues, but argue that these are often the only way they can sustain production and economic survival. This represents a further shift from what Blumler calls 'principled diversity' based on assessments of children's needs to 'pragmatic diversity' which is better suited at satisfying regulatory demands (1992: 22–3) as well as managerial and commercial priorities. Rationalising reliance on commercial revenues, programme-makers argue that consumer products and consumerism are 'a way of life now really' where 'children almost expect the extras, cereal, and game' that accompany children's media, and where 'if kids like the show they want to have a plush toy'. Even those working within the seemingly protected public service confines of the BBC point out that they now 'have to be concerned about the marketing' of their projects as well as the creative aspects. During development many producers talk about the need to understand 'what the show is doing off air' and 'how to sell the concept'. For the producer of one 2D animation series, licensed merchandise 'was absolutely at the front of my mind' when they started to pitch the concept.

Yet many producers and broadcasters are also keen to emphasise that the creative concept has to 'drive' any licensing campaign. In the words of one marketing executive, 'if the programming doesn't work, the kids won't want to play with it.' Talking about *Charlie and Lola* (Tiger Aspect), a ratings success for CBeebies and a commercial success for BBC Worldwide, CBeebies Controller, Michael Carrington (2007a), underlines the primacy of ideas and characters, which connect with children and may just possibly contribute to some form of commercial success as well:

> These are well-crafted stories, they're well-crafted characters with true personality and integrity. That's what's shining through is that children are having an emotional connection with them, and therefore they want the pencil, they want the whatever. Whereas, you know, you could do something else that has a fire engine and all of the knobs on it, but without a story it's not going to have an emotional connection so it won't work.

What worries some is that whereas in the past producers were 'left alone to make the show for a bit' now the creative process is much more entwined with commercial exploitation from the start because the financial risks are much greater. The fact that licensing executives might be present at all suggests that creative personnel are very aware of the commercial imperatives behind their production efforts. According to one CBeebies producer:

> There is a really, really hard fight – and it was going on long before people were making a lot of money – surrounding what you allow in terms of the content of the programme when you know there's a sell-on capacity. Nowadays as a programme goes into production it's got all its franchising and things in place. And it was clearer in the old days that the television programme was first and foremost what you were doing. And if anything happened off the back of it, fair dos. Whereas now it's harder and harder to actually see where the content drives the merchandise or vice versa.

The concern is that growing reliance on revenues from licensed merchandise is affecting the content of preschool television in nefarious ways, as development becomes a struggle around the inclusion of characters and settings that serve commercial interests rather than what interests the audience.

However, it is also important to keep commercial exploitation in context. With the global success of *some* preschool properties such as *Sesame Street, Teletubbies, Barney and Friends, Dora the Explorer, Bob the Builder* and *Blue's Clues*, it is all too easy to assume that the link between preschool television and licensed consumer products is a foregone conclusion. Indeed British regulator Ofcom has suggested that preschool programmes have better potential for commercial return precisely because they are more likely to benefit from secondary revenues than other forms of children's programming (2007a: 198). This assertion is partially supported by the stock market launches of British companies involved in the rights management of preschool television properties from the mid-1990s onwards, led by HIT Entertainment, Entertainment Rights and Chorion. *Bob the Builder* is estimated to have generated over £1bn at retail since 1999 (Carter, 2005: 23), and Winnie the Pooh is estimated to generate a staggering $1bn a year for Disney (Milmo, 2005), but any perusal of the retail shelves reveals that the number of globally successful preschool brands is limited to a handful of properties.

Industry overview

Notwithstanding a brutally competitive retail market and a global recession from 2008, which suggests that a funding model based on product revenues and declining DVD sales is already being placed under considerable strain (Thompson, 2008), licensed characters are a very large business indeed. The preschool licensing market in Britain alone was estimated to account for £800m of the £2.5bn generated from licensing for children at retail in 2007 (NPD cited in Fry, 2007: 26). Where the preschool market comes into its own is its close affinity with toys, with two-thirds of the £31bn generated each year from global toy sales originating in the United States (Roberts, 2006). As older children graduate to computer and video gaming earlier, it is mainly children under-six who play with toys and have toys bought for them, giving manufacturers only a short window to market their products. According to Brown Johnson, President of Nickelodeon Preschool in the United States, it is this continued willingness of younger rather than older children to engage with toys, which sustains and drives the preschool television business (also Clark, 2007; Linn, 2004), because 'Kids over six don't buy toys: they're turning to technology' (cited in Hayes, 2008: 7).

However, royalty rates are low, with licensors receiving only 5–15 per cent of the wholesale (not retail) price of each item sold (Raugust, 1996; Tashjian and Naidoo, 2007). Disney and Viacom are major licensors generating $26bn and $5.5bn respectively of licensed product sales at retail in 2008, although preschool television only generates a proportion of these (License, 2008). Other players active in preschool licensing include HIT Entertainment (responsible for $2.4bn in retail sales), Sesame Workshop ($1.5bn), Chorion ($900m) and Entertainment Rights ($439m) (ibid.).

To launch a preschool property licensors need to secure licensees for the key categories of toys, publishing and DVD as part of a co-ordinated brand management strategy which treats brand components such as character poses, backgrounds, logos and so forth. as carefully controlled brand assets. One step on the road to commercial success is to secure a master toy licence early on, not only because toys have production lead times of up to 2 years, but also because toys can account for more than 50 per cent of licensed product sales (Raugust, 2004a: 109). Some licensees are preferable to others because they have a global presence, good retail contacts and can invest in product design, research, packaging, advertising and marketing (Clark, 2007; Raugust, 1996, 2004b). Key players in the highly consolidated global preschool toy market are Fisher-Price (owned by US giant Mattel), US-owned Hasbro and Denmark's Lego (Clark, 2007; Vogel, 2007) with smaller players (Character Options Tomy, Martin Yaffe, Vivid Imaginations) in national markets like the United Kingdom (Fry, 2007).

However, while relationships with licensees are vital, relationships with large retailers are arguably more important because of the 'power of the shelf'. According to one home entertainment executive, 'Without a doubt retail's king. They determine whether your product does well or not.' In a crowded retail environment, dominated by a small number of multiple (Tescos, Argos and until recently Woolworths in Britain; Wal-Mart and Target in the United States) and specialist retailers (Toys "R" Us), whose shelves are already dominated by a handful of preschool brands, there is little room for new brands to make a mark (Fry, 2007). To secure or simply maintain an in-store presence, licensors and licensees will invest in costly promotional space for toys or DVDs, often in conjunction with discounted offers. This type of co-marketing tends to favour larger players with deep pockets to fund the promotion and pay for additional advertising. Even in a small market like

Britain the co-funding of promotional space in store can cost anything in excess of £60,000 over 2 weeks. Even so licensors are under constant pressure by retailers 'to refresh the brand' to satisfy retailers' short-term sales targets and cyclical demand for novelty, which can conflict with the licensor's wish to nurture a longer-lasting 'classic' brand (also Tashjian and Naidoo, 2007: 168). If a major retail partner, particularly in the United States, decides to de-list a brand or reduce shelf-space dedicated to preschool products, rights-owners can find themselves facing considerable revenue downturns (see HIT, 2004: 4).

What works in licensing?

There is no sure-fire recipe for licensing success in preschool television, but most licensing executives will point to a core set of requirements (See Table 9.1).

One priority is broadcast exposure. Broadcast sales are no longer a key income generator for companies like HIT Entertainment that generate over 90 per cent of revenues from consumer products and home entertainment (see Chapter 5), but broadcast slots and frequent repeats are regarded as crucial for generating awareness. Without broadcast exposure there is no preschool licensing business, because retailers demand a mainstream broadcaster, which children watch in numbers before they will stock products. The 'power of the shop shelf', which can only accommodate a small number of proven preschool brands, dictates the small number of properties most likely to succeed. In the United States

Table 9.1   Licensing checklist

Frequent broadcast exposure on a mainstream outlet to attract retailers.

Enough episodes (minimum 26) to generate awareness and sustain longevity.

Online applications (games, downloads and 'immersive' interactive experiences) that extend the brand beyond television.

Costumed character and animation shows rather than studio-based or live action formats.

3D animation rather than less 'toyetic' 2D animation.

Teams of characters to generate collectability, including vocational, vehicular or animal characters.

Detailed backgrounds and worlds (for play sets).

Props (vehicles, pets and accessories) that can be marketed as toys.

Distinctive non-generic characters that stand out on shop shelves.

'Classic' properties that resonate with parents.

Properties with 'educational' value that appeal to parents.

Nick Jr., Playhouse Disney and PBS are the broadcast outlets of choice (Cahn et al., 2008: 33). In Britain there is a clear preference for CBeebies because of its reach both as a block on terrestrial service BBC2 (100 per cent availability) and as a digital channel available on cable, satellite and free-to-air to 87 per cent of homes (Ofcom, 2008a: 227). According to one UK producer-distributor, colleagues in licensing are loath to accept any other platform,

> The key thing for them is whether or not the broadcast platform [...] is going to be good enough for the retail guys that they deal with. If we say we have this project and we feel that it's something that would work very well for Nickelodeon, the first question that M. will probably ask me is 'But would it not work for the BBC?'. If I say 'I don't really think it is something that will work for the BBC', he would say 'Well, I don't really think that it's going to work for us because that's the best platform in the UK.' The BBC is still viewed as being the prime place to go with your preschool property. Nickelodeon is a very good platform and is getting better and better. But amongst the retail environment, that's still the number one choice.

Sufficient episodes (at least 26), repetition and an online presence that extends the brand beyond television, including direct links to e-commerce sites (not permitted on CBeebies) are also regarded as important for sustaining awareness.

Second licensing executives are seeking properties whose core characteristics will draw licensees and retailers in. They look for a strong cast of characters and recognisable locations that have what those in the business call 'toyetic' qualities, which go beyond the ability simply to sell train sets and cuddly toys, and extend into a concept or a 'world' where children can immerse themselves in play (see Calder, 2008d). In the words of one British licensing executive,

> I have my dull list of preschool conditions [...] I think if it's got vehicular content, if it's vocational, if it has a world and a universe around it, primarily stop-frame that would probably tick quite a few boxes for me. Because when you look at it you can go through them all, *Postman Pat, Fireman Sam, Bob the Builder, Noddy.* They've all got vehicles. They all live in a world. A defined universe is incredibly important [...] Vocational is fantastic, because kids love acting out a role [...] You have the thing that the child can be the director of

it all [...] I think that's incredibly important for a preschool child – that it's part of their play pattern.

Clearly animation properties with a number of distinctive characters, accessories, background environments, imaginary worlds, communities and storylines that lend themselves to imaginary friends, play sets (houses, garages, castles), collectability and line extensions in the form of new characters are popular with licensing executives (also Caves, 2000: 213; Hendershot, 1998: 99; Pecora, 1998, 53). In the case of established properties the incorporation of new vehicles, characters or environments is an integral part of ongoing development, designed to ensure longevity in the marketplace. According to one product development executive the format of these shows is designed to encourage collectability,

> That's the success of Thomas [the Tank Engine] that they're constantly bringing in new trains and new characters. That's how it works because it becomes collectable and the kids want the new train that's in Thomas. In Bob [the Builder], in the first ten series they only really had six core vehicles, and that's the biggest part of Bob in terms of continual products. That's most of what gets sold, the vehicles. So now they're bringing more vehicles into Bob and more characters.

In Britain 3D animated properties, based around farm (*Tractor Tom, The Little Red Tractor*) and building vehicles (*Bob the Builder, Construction Site*), racing cars (*Roary the Racing Car*), fire engines (*Fireman Sam, Finley the Fire Engine*) and trains (*Thomas the Tank Engine, Chuggington, Underground Ernie*) which are instantly recognisable, particularly to small boys, who can spot them on store shelves really matter – to the extent that 2D animation is considered 'a tougher sell'. Toys that look exactly like they do on television are important because they provide an instant point of recognition for children who cannot read or who may have limited exposure to advertising (also Seiter, 1993: 197). For example on *Postman Pat: Special Delivery*, product development executives at Entertainment Rights (ER) thought at length about how 3- and 4-year-old boys might 'want to interact' with the programme off screen. This led to a show that is not only 'vehicular' with 'lots of action', but also included 'a sorting office, that's going to have lots and lots of action holes, cycles, cogs, because that's what will work for boys.'

There are of course many other preschool properties that appeal to both genders (*In the Night Garden; Teletubbies; Blues Clues, Barney, Lazytown*) usually at the lower end of the preschool age range. Indeed an updated version of *Rupert the Bear*, 'a classic' publishing-based property, was re-launched in 2006 as a more 'gender neutral' younger skewing series which would appeal to girls through 'the use of colour and flowers and the frequency of certain female characters'. Similarly *Postman Pat: Special Delivery* was updated to include more female characters that appeal to girls. However as children get older (4–6), gender differences become more pronounced with boys' preschool animation shows concentrating more on heroes and action (*Bob the Builder, Roary the Racing Car*) and girls shows (*Fifi and the Flowertots, Angelina Ballerina*) marked more by pastel colours, 'cuteness', and emotional pro-social stories. These differences are also reflected in the shop aisles, as girls' and boys' toys become segregated onto different shelves (Tashjian and Naidoo, 2007: 169).

Certainly this preference for 'toyetic' animation or costumed character shows works against presenter-led live action or storytelling formats which are not 'toyetic' and are seen as being too British in their look to appeal to overseas markets (also Ofcom, 2007a: 198). In the case of the BBC this has worked against in-house productions, which tend to be 'lower budget' 'bread-and-butter stuff' with 'real' people, which do not fit the commercial priorities of the BBC's commercial subsidiary, BBC Worldwide. Of course, there are always exceptions to this rule – such as BBC preschool drama *Balamory* which proved a commercial success in Britain, or shows that mix humans with puppets, costumed and animated characters (*Blue's Clues, Sesame Street, Barney*) also succeeding internationally. Nevertheless according to one BBC Worldwide executive, in general:

> Using real people is always harder for licensing. They just have not had the right sort of fit and ticked the right sort of boxes for us to be able to be guaranteed of generating income out of them. More of the sort of scale of show has really come out of the independent sector. *Teletubbies* was probably one of the first big ones [...] There's the job shows – the Postman Pats and the Bob the Builders [...] So they all tick the enormous boxes for us from a commercial point of view. You can see very clearly how a range of toys could evolve from them.

Plainly therefore a series like Ragdoll's *In the Night Garden* ticks many of these commercial boxes. This is not to argue that Ragdoll have deliberately created the series simply to appeal to international buyers and toy manufacturers – and Ragdoll Productions expends a great deal of effort to ensure that its programmes are carefully researched and child-centred. Nevertheless there are clear possibilities here, and BBC Worldwide would not have raised a large proportion of the £14.5m needed to make the show it if did not expect a commercial return. In this sense creative and commercial priorities appear to co-exist rather well. First there are sufficient episodes (100) to generate awareness and longevity, reinforced by exposure on CBeebies, the UK preschool broadcast and online brand with the largest audience reach and highest parental approval (Ofcom, 2007a), immediately reassuring potential licensees and retailers.

There are no human presenters in the show, which is populated by a cast of distinctive costumed characters, which are not just collectable, but also stand out in a crowded retail environment, again reassuring licensees and retailers. In the words of one marketing executive,

> If you've created something that's going to be integral to the programming but it actually looks generic, then it's not going to work. If someone's going to have a pet rabbit, and it's just a grey rabbit, that's not going to be ideal because if you try and make a pet rabbit as a toy and it's just a plain grey rabbit, then why pay a royalty for it being Rupert Bear's rabbit, for instance? He'd need a discerning feature to make him unique, because if you're looking to do licensing off the back of it, consumers are going to be paying more for a licensed product because of the royalty structure involved. They've got to be able to understand why they're paying that.

For instance Igglepiggle, the blue character who starts each episode of *In the Night Garden* is teddy-like, but his colour and design mark him out as different from a generic teddy, as a character that a small child 'can hug, cuddle and take to bed'. The colourful world he visits with its props and vehicles also 'ticks' the right boxes in respect of perceived play patterns and how children might recreate that world. The Ninky Nonk train, the Pinky Ponk airship, Upsy Daisy's bed and Makka Pakka's trolley translate almost seamlessly to the toy shelves as pull or push-along toys. The property has a reassuringly 'educational' feel that resonates with parents, reinforced by exposure on CBeebies. Broadly educational or classic properties are particularly popular because they have 'trusted credentials', and according to one marketing executive, 'in preschool if you're trusted, you're 90 per cent of the way there'.

Of course not all properties 'tick' the right licensing boxes, and television demands more content than can ever be accommodated on the shop shelves. While a small number of animation and costumed character properties are hugely successful across many product categories, the exploitation of others is much more limited to DVD or publishing, if that. However, from what licensing executives reveal, the demands of licensing would seem to favour certain types of programming, which raises the question of the extent to which licensing considerations actually impact programme content.

Impact on programming

As Buckingham points out what licensing executives want may 'conveniently coincide with producers' creative instincts' (Buckingham, 2002: 42). What we found in discussions with British programme-makers was that the extent to which consumer product considerations influence content varies widely depending on the players involved and the nature of each production.

For some projects with strong licensing potential, and where this is really a priority for a show's financial backers, there may be clear efforts to influence the direction of a show in ways that are all about selling toys rather than producing an interesting show for children. In such instances a producer or writer may find themselves at odds with marketing colleagues. While the producer may be concerned with a character's role in a story, marketing executives may be much more concerned with how the character functions as part of a commercial strategy – and whether it can translate into a range of marketable products that children and parents will buy.

Such interventions occur early on during script development as broadcasters, executive producers, script editors and increasingly licensing executives give notes on premises and treatments. In some cases interventions or suggestions might be considered as seemingly benign, revolving perhaps around the design of a vehicle, logos, character names or the use of specific colours to enhance the appeal of products on shop shelves (also Castleman, 2009a; Raugust, 2004a: 111). In one instance animators were encouraged to introduce more music into the second series for use in other media (online, live appearances). On another series, it was suggested that the main character should dress up occasionally as a fairy princess, so that 'fairy princess' merchandise could be developed. Licensing executives will also bring their experience of the retail marketplace (knowledge of similar properties) and compliance issues (name registration and trademarks) into discussions. In other cases interventions are more substantial, involving the amendment of storylines to reinforce and promote particular characters and situations. According to one British writer such discussions might proceed as follows:

> "We believe this character needs a vehicle. It should be his story a bit more because we would like to show him more on screen. We would like to see this character in her bedroom, because we've got a really nice bedroom set and we'd really like to use it."

Which you can interpret as being,

> "We'd like to show a bit more of the interior of this house, because we've got a really good licence deal and we want to sell it in Toys R Us."

Yet we also found instances of non-intervention where development never touched on marketing aspects at all. It depends on the internal culture of the production company and the programme. For larger producer-distributors, consumer products and home entertainment are regarded as revenue generators, and those working in development and production are expected to co-operate with licensing. For other production entities consumer products and toys may be a more marginal concern, because these are comparatively low-cost productions. Funding may be in place and there is less licensing potential for shows that take place in a studio setting or mainly feature human beings as opposed to anthropomorphic trains, cars, animals and so forth. At CBeebies, which broadcasts many more programmes with human performers than its rivals (up to 76 per cent of transmissions), because of its service licence commitment to range (BBC Trust, 2008a), there are sustained efforts to garner the investment interest of the BBC's commercial arm, BBC Worldwide. Yet many CBeebies productions proceed without BBC Worldwide support and without paying particular attention to potential pyjama or toy sales, because they meet CBeebies' broader public service objectives. Whether this will always continue is subject to debate, with some indications that the BBC has been considering a more commercial approach to origination, and co-production finance in particular (BBC Trust, 2009: 58–9; Rushton, 2008b). Yet for many small privately owned British production companies simply making programmes is at the forefront of their minds with merchandise licensing comprising just one component in the funding mix. According to one creatively led animation producer:

> We didn't think about toys when it came to writing a story or the original design or anything [...] We never thought, 'We'll put a vehicle in there because we know that vehicles sell.'

Others are much more adamant about keeping commercial influences out of the development process:

> We would never create a show on the basis of a toy company saying, 'Make this product'. We sell our toy licenses and other things on the basis of there's a programme that's going to be made, it's going to entertain children, there's going to be an interest out there, and a toy or a book or clothing are going to play a part in their [a child's] life.

Levels of intervention in the creative process therefore depend on the interplay of a variety of factors at any one time. These include:

- The degree to which those managing a production are willing to protect the creative process from commercial pressures.
- The creative and/or financial standing of producers, and their ability to withstand commercial pressures.
- The degree to which marketing considerations constitute an integral part of an individual company's operations.
- The degree to which a project actually exhibits licensing potential.
- The money needed to fund a project.

Yet influence during development is only one part of the story. It does not tell us how many projects simply never get beyond the concept stage, because they fail to tick the right licensing boxes and are not sufficiently 'toyetic'. If a smaller producer is looking for substantial investment they have to convince larger players with an interest in ancillary rights that their project is worth backing, which may 'compromise what the programme itself is trying to do'. According to one producer this is difficult because those involved in licensing and international sales are often too narrowly focused on reducing risk and relying on what has worked before,

> That in itself becomes a filter against original programming because what you get is a company like a distributor who's got their own in-house licensing department. They will look at a programme. They will ask their international distribution what they think. They will ask their licensees what they think. If the licensing department can't

see immediately what the merchandising should be, they knock it back as being a bad project.

What we identified in our interviews and observations were four different responses to licensed merchandise. These responses depended on the different motivations and priorities of producers at any one time, and producers could find themselves in any one grouping depending on each project's circumstances. These different responses are entirely in keeping with the diversity of the British preschool production sector, which extends from the largest IP-owning producer-distributors with global ambitions to the smallest creatively led production teams.

First we identified those who pursue an *integrated approach*, ensuring that any television project is entirely in tune with a company's consumer product, branding and home entertainment strategy from the start. Rights-owning production companies will weigh up carefully whether a preschool property will have a life beyond television before they are prepared to invest in what Kinder has called 'a supersystem' or 'network of intertexuality' (1991: 122–3) – where co-ordinated promotions, events and licensed products all contribute to the awareness necessary to sustain a property's lifespan and maximise revenues (also Caldwell, 2004: 49).

What was noticeable was that this strategy was not necessarily confined to the largest producer-distributors such as HIT Entertainment or Chorion, who earn most of their revenues from consumer products and home entertainment. It was also a strategy pursued by smaller companies with one or two properties like Chapman Entertainment (*Roary the Racing Car*) or Joella Productions (*Underground Ernie*) who are very focused on commercially extending their projects beyond television (see Patrick, 2006). Those involved in the creative process in these circumstances are expected to work with licensing executives because according to one head of creative development 'what you do as producers, as animators, as directors, is fundamentally involved in revenue generation.' Licensing executives are therefore involved in development at every level:

> We're absolutely involved in it [development] because from my perspective if we are going to be investing […] the programme has to deliver a Return on Investment […] A vast chunk of that is going to come in globally from licensing so we need to make sure that I have a comfort level with how the series is developed whether it's going to be right in terms of driving revenue from consumer products. So I've

been sitting down with the brand manager and the production team looking at all of the opportunities that the new programme is going to deliver to us.

If a series has toy potential there will be discussions about character designs, how they might work as toys, how the colours of characters and backgrounds will translate to other products and media platforms, and how storylines might connect with particular products. A preschool television proposition has to work creatively. Yet it also has to show clear commercial potential – it has to be global, toyetic and long-lived. It has to work as a brand. As one British producer-distributor remarked,

> We don't make any secret of the fact that our series, as lovingly created as they are, as artistically beautiful as they are put together, it's very much to do with us being able to sell it as a brand. We launch the licensing and merchandising. We launch the DVD, in order to make sales, to make the money, to pull the money together, to actually make the show. Because unfortunately – that's the only way to do it. [...] It has to work at being more than just a television programme.

This approach favours internationally attractive animation over more culturally specific live action or studio-based formats.

Next we identified those producers who pursue a *balanced approach* between costly animation and costumed character shows with considerable international and merchandising potential on the one hand, and those programmes whose wider commercial outcomes are likely to be more modest, and which need to be funded in ways that take account of this more limited earning potential. Just as the integrated strategy is not dominated by the largest corporations, this more nuanced approach to preschool television is pursued by some of the very largest players in the industry, who are prepared to take risks on cheaper 2D animation, which is less 'toyetic' (notwithstanding the phenomenal success of *Dora the Explorer*) than 3D animation, but can be successful in other areas such as publishing or DVD.

So why would they take this risk? It's borne out of the realisation that global licensing hits are rare and that a company needs to have creative credibility to sustain its reputation and attract the best producers. No company can ever rely on achieving an international licensing hit like *Teletubbies* or *Dora the Explorer*. This means supporting shows that are popular on television but may not necessarily earn millions from toy sales. Producers will therefore sometimes take on more risky projects even if these do not have an obvious afterlife in licensed merchandise, if they can raise sufficient funding from co-producers and overseas sales to make the risk more palatable (Schreiber, 2006). In the words of one development executive at a producer-distributor:

> You've got to have a strategy that allows you to explore the creative landscape in a way that says 'I don't know what's going to work,' because that's the only thing we know about a creative business. It's that nobody knows what's going to happen. So we can look at XXX [a 2D animation series] and say 'The chances of that making any money in consumer products are just about one in a million.' But, if I can do it cheaply enough with enough co-production money and hedge the risk then we should do those properties.

A third *adaptive strategy* is visible among smaller specialised producers, particularly in animation, who have the creative credibility to play off funding partners, but who also engage with licensing and merchandising to get their shows funded. For example on a 2D animation series, they might mock up 3D versions of characters to show prospective investors how toys might look. As creative producers they want to push boundaries aesthetically, but they are also keenly aware of the need to secure funding beyond television and build on their intellectual property (IP) rights to ensure survival and seed funding for future projects. As one production company executive remarked: 'The reality is that if you don't create a business model from the IP that works, you don't reinvest, and you suddenly stop making programming. And there's an awful lot of people out there that that's happened to.' Ancillary exploitation is therefore a constant undercurrent during development,

> We're saying it internally all the time. We're saying, "That's a nice story but it's not going to sell. Can we make it so we can sell it, so that the kids can do it outside of the show?"

These producers take advantage of multiple sources of funding from broadcasters, co-producers, tax breaks, distributors, and protect their creative integrity, by ensuring that no one backer has too much of a financial stake to exercise too much control over their creative vision. Although some claim that 'when we're creating the show and the characters that consumer products don't play any role in why we're doing it or what they look like', they 'are aware of the demands that are put on *subsequently* to making a programme'. They become actively involved in

licensing decisions. There will be consultations and approvals on product lines, packaging and marketing as part of a collaborative effort. For
example the producers of the animation series *Peppa Pig* were consulted
at length about a camper van, on which they had final approval, and
which became a popular item at retail. Yet there is also in the words
of Buckingham et al. something of a 'Faustian pact' (1999: 162) going
on. Producers and writers are guided by their aesthetic and creative
ambitions and a child-centred approach to programming, but they also
recognise that consumer products and global sales are part of the deal if
they want to continue working. According to one writer:

> To be fair, we couldn't make the television without the toys. So I'm
> not anti toys at all and I'm not anti [the view] 'We need to skew
> this show, so that we see those locations often, because that will help
> when we want to sell the fire station or town hall toy.' Obviously
> part of the process is that the kids look at the fire station and say 'I
> want the fire station.' So you kind of need to write it in don't you? Or
> they can't see it. And if they don't get any branding or any licensing
> going, then we can't finance it. So to a degree one has to accept we
> make commercials.

Finally there are those who place *audience and creative concerns first*. In
the words of one US producer,

> There's a special talent in creating a children's television show which
> is different than a special talent in creating a toy. We strongly believe,
> and I think our partners do as well, that the show has to come first.
> If the show is a brilliant show, then those very expert toy people can
> come in and interpret your show and find interesting ways to market
> your show. But if those people come in too soon, your show is not
> going to be a hit anyway. It's going to be a commercial.

As we established in Chapter 5, a small number of producers put
research based on intensive audience observations and developmental
awareness at the heart of what they do, and do not tolerate commercial interventions in the creative process. In this vein one producer
remarked,

> You've got to really focus on who we're making it for. I want a level
> of feedback from the audience on what contemporary children, very
> very young children, are doing now [...] I suppose it's just reminding

ourselves that when we're working for children we're always trying to keep that relationship with them [...] Keeping that dialogue going just keeps us connected.

In some cases we found that suggestions from consumer products were overridden. For example *Pocoyo*, an animated series about a small boy and his friends co-produced by Granada Kids and Spanish animation studio, Zinkia, takes place against a white backdrop rather than a more detailed background environment. This went completely against the instincts of those involved in marketing who regard background environments and 'a defined world that you can exploit in terms of brand extensions' as really important for highlighting accessories, play and toy opportunities. Yet these were rejected by the programme-makers because they felt that backgrounds 'diluted' the 'clean look' envisaged for the show, making it less effective as an experience that children would enjoy (also Patrick, 2006). According to the show's script editor,

> We were told right at the start of developing the visuals that it was going to be a commercial problem because you need backgrounds to be able to make toys. You need a world to make children feel that they can be in that world and become those characters and play imaginatively and copy the play that they see. So in the first series, we did actually develop backgrounds and environments. So the first few episodes were put onto these background environments, and it was a huge amount of work. I think it was the first few stills that we saw. It had just lost its charm. And so a bold decision was made to go back to the white backgrounds because obviously it's all very well saying the toys will work if you've got backgrounds but if the show doesn't work then no-one's going to be interested in the toys.

Adding more detailed backgrounds was thought to have diminished the show's distinctiveness making it too similar to other properties. The decision to dispense with backgrounds might be interpreted as diminishing the commercial potential of the show, although this is also dictated by other factors, not least the consistent and widespread promotion of a show on broadcast television.

Among many producers there are then grave misgivings that some programmes have become too focused on commercial tie-ins at the expense of well-crafted stories and characters with 'true personality and integrity' with which children have 'an emotional connection'. According to one producer:

If you take your research not from your audience, but from marketing and sales and toys and licensees and what they want – if you start to build a programme around that then ultimately you're doomed to fail [...] It has to be about what the heart of your show is, what are you trying to achieve? There's no guarantee it's going to work, but you've got more of a guarantee by coming up with a really good idea that's strong on characters, good storytelling, and an overarching ethos that relates to your audience rather than worrying about whether a cat should be blue.

A clear distinction is made then between things that *might* emanate from a successful show *and* licensing and consumer products actually dictating the content or what type of characters might appear in it.

Conclusion

Among producers there is a clear spectrum of accommodation between those who prioritise what they do as a business, and those who are motivated much more by considerations of audience and creativity. It is important to recognise the variety of motivations, priorities and strategies behind different types of preschool programming and the different positions programme-makers take for different projects. This is not the same as claiming that 'Children's television shows are just giant toy ads' (Gary Pope, cited in Hayes, 2008: 127), not least because the retail market is too concentrated on a small number of proven sellers for this strategy to work for all shows. Moreover, there is a huge difference between the integrated strategies adopted by the largest multinational corporations (Disney, Nickelodeon) and larger IP-owning producer-distributors (HIT, ER, Chorion) with global ambitions and the more varied approaches of smaller producers, who may prioritise business or creative/educational concerns depending on their internal production culture and circumstances. What is clear is that dependence on tie-in merchandise can diminish the range of what preschoolers are offered, particularly for shows which are more culturally specific such as live action shows (Ofcom, 2007a: 198), shows that are more likely to be produced by public service broadcasters. The growing dominance of animation across many preschool channels and blocks and the difficulties of securing funding for preschool productions are evidence of this trend. It is important to recognise that some preschool shows will not sell many toys. For example CBeebies' *Nina and the Neurons*, a live action science show with a presenter and children in a studio setting, regularly rated as one of CBeebies' top shows in 2007 and 2008, but will never generate huge amounts from ancillary revenues. At the same time the industry is littered with children's shows that failed to ignite retail sales. To conclude it is important that small children, just like their older counterparts, have access to a range of voices, experiences and perspectives. Sometimes that will mean animation with characters that they can buy in the shops. Sometimes it will mean well-made programmes that will never sell a cuddly toy, but may still engage children's interest, imagination and curiosity. The concern is that growing reliance on ancillary revenues, particularly for narrative animation, will eventually reduce the diversity of what is offered to preschoolers, who have just as much right as older children to engage with content that reflects their lives and experiences.

10
Policy Interventions and the Crisis in Children's Television

Alessandro D'Arma and Jeanette Steemers

Children's television production does not exist in a vacuum. Like other areas of television it is promoted or constrained by policy and regulatory frameworks with profound and far-reaching effect. This is evident in the different historical development of children's television in the United States and Britain where commercial and public service priorities respectively have defined the different nature and scope of children's output. In this chapter, however, the case is made for a convergence in policy approaches with the United States, as British children's television comes to terms with a more deregulated media and communications environment. Reviewing recent regulatory and policy developments, we begin by highlighting those US policy features and interventions, which are likely to become more relevant for Britain, before embarking on an account of how the British children's television industry was plunged into a crisis precipitated by regulatory, technological and market change. In keeping with the thematic focus of this book, the chapter also draws out the specific implications of recent developments for preschool television in particular.

Children's television policy in the United States

In Britain children's television has always been viewed as a socially important area of programming, central to any conceivable notion of public service broadcasting (PSB). US children's television policy is, by contrast, embedded in a different broadcasting history with different legal and regulatory traditions – not least the lack of a strong tradition of PSB and the dominance of commercial broadcasting (see Chapter 2). While UK advocates of socially valuable programming for children have typically defended the 'great tradition' of PSB (Blumler, 1992), US citizen groups have campaigned more modestly for 'educational' children's programming as a compulsory staple of the schedules offered by commercial broadcasting, in addition to the educational children's television provided by PBS. However, such US policy initiatives aimed at limiting commercial broadcasters' editorial freedom, as well as initiatives aimed at curtailing advertising, have often been strongly opposed by both the industry as well as free-speech campaigners, on the grounds that they run contrary to the First Amendment of the US Constitution (Calvert, 2008: 456; Corn-Revere, 1997; Jordan, 2008: 237; Kunkel, 2007: 223–4; Lisosky, 2001: 830; Minow and Lamay, 1995). This conflict between regulating content on the one hand, and ensuring freedom of speech and the free market on the other, was exemplified in 1984 when the Federal Communications Commission (FCC), at that time dominated by appointees of Republican President Ronald Reagan, controversially removed all advertising policy guidelines adopted by the FCC in the previous decade (FCC, 1984a; Kunkel, 1999: 54–5; Kunkel and Watkins, 1987: 378–80). This allowed broadcasters to air advertising at their discretion, with the result that by the mid-1980s there was an explosion of toy-based animation shows, funded by toy manufacturers. In Britain the legal and philosophical principles underpinning broadcasting regulation are profoundly different and there has been, until recently, a wide societal consensus that the regulation of broadcasting content and advertising is a necessary tool to promote broadcasting's social goals as well as mitigate the potentially negative effects of children's exposure to certain types of content and commercial practices.

That said, it is still possible to identify two general features of children's television policy in the United States, which have some relevance for recent policy developments in Britain (for informative overviews of the historical development of children's television policy in the United States see Calvert, 2008; Kunkel, 2007 and Jordan, 2008).

First, there is the dual nature of US regulatory concerns, which have been dominated by two parallel yet different issues – regulating simultaneously for positive outcomes and against negative effects. On the one hand, there have been 'positive' content policies designed to ensure that educational and informational (E/I) children's content is a compulsory staple of the programming offered by commercial broadcasters. On the other hand, there have been 'negative' content policies designed to protect children from exposure to potentially harmful programmes (particularly violent content) and harmful advertising (Kunkel and Wilcox, 2001). The peak of both 'positive' and 'negative' regulation occurred with the passage of the 1990 Children's Television Act (CTA). This required broadcasters (but not cable channels, who do not use public airways and are therefore not subject to public interest obligations) to provide content that took account of children's E/I needs. It also re-established limits on advertising airtime during children's programming for both broadcast and cable channels (10.5 minutes an hour at weekends and 12 minutes during the week).

As in Britain these regulatory concerns are rooted in the belief that children are a vulnerable audience deserving special protection from the harsh realities of a commercial marketplace, whose objectives may run counter to the 'well-being, needs, wishes, rights and wants of children' (Messenger Davies, 2004: 10). Where the US differs from Britain, however, is in the application of these regulatory measures. The satisfaction of E/I requirements is only examined during licence renewal and only if a complaint has been filed (Jordan, 2008: 240; Kunkel, 2007: 210), as opposed to the institutional safeguards, which until quite recently, were enshrined across regulated British public service broadcasting including the BBC, ITV1 and Five.

A second important feature of US children's television policy is its political salience (Lisosky, 2001) in contrast to Britain where political debates about children's television are rarer. This political salience contributed to the passage of the 1990 CTA, which according to Kunkel stood as 'the sole anomaly involving any specific governmental requirements for delivering "public interest" programming' (1999: 60) at the time. It also contributed to the strengthening of the 1990 Act in 1996 after years of poor implementation and the classification of some rather dubious animation (*The Jetsons*, *The Flintstones*) as educational (Kunkel, 1998). According to children's advocacy campaigner Kathryn Montgomery (2007: 236–7) it was electoral considerations by the Democrat administration that persuaded the FCC to pursue a more active enforcement of the CTA's E/I requirements:

> Ultimately both the FCC and the White House realized that it was in the best political interests of the administration to take a leadership role in calling for quality children's media, particularly as the election year got closer, and political polls showed that these kinds of 'family value' issues were appealing to both liberals and conservatives, and thus could be valuable to Clinton's re-election campaign.

In 1996 the FCC adopted a rule requiring broadcasters to provide at least 3 hours of clearly identifiable children's educational programming a week, as well as defining what qualified as educational programming and specifying when such programmes were to be scheduled (FCC, 1996; Kunkel, 2007: 208). Yet there is still considerable legal dispute about what qualifies as educational broadcasting for children (Kunkel, 2007: 217) with up to a quarter of E/I programmes found to be only 'minimally educational' (Jordan, 2000, 2004).

However, the clearest indication of the political salience of children's television in the United States is the extent of public activism. While policy advocacy is a defining feature of US policy-making in general, in the area of children's television, public interest advocacy efforts have been strong since the 1970s. Founded in 1968 Action for Children's Television (ACT) forced the issue of children's television onto the policy agenda for the first time. By 1974 the FCC had issued a policy statement (lacking the force of rule) restricting the amount of advertising during children's programmes and articulating the principle that 'addressing children's programming needs was part of a television station's responsibility to serve the public interest' (Montgomery, 2007: 233; also FCC, 1974; Kunkel and Wilcox, 2001: 595). After the FCC removed most of its public service guidelines for broadcasters in 1984 (FCC, 1984b), ACT took the cause of children's television to the courts, and then to Congress. The resulting passage of the 1990 CTA and the reinforcing of the Act's E/I requirements in 1996 were historic successes for the advocacy movement. More recent policy battlegrounds to emerge in the 2000s under a broad coalition of public health and child advocacy groups have included online and interactive advertising and the extension of E/I requirements to digital multicasting alongside primary broadcast channels (Kunkel, 2007: 222–3).

The features of US children's television policy discussed here – the dual nature of the regulatory concerns that have dominated the policy agenda and the political salience of children's television policy issues (reflected in strong public activism) – have also begun to figure more in British children's television policy as regulation becomes less embedded within a public service framework and much more focused on co-regulation in line with US practice. So how did this convergence of regulatory concerns come to pass?

British children's television policy in the 1980s and 1990s

Until the 1980s British children's television was shaped and safeguarded by a public service ethos and a specific set of institutional and regulatory arrangements. It was the product of a pre-multi-channel broadcasting environment populated by a small number of channels, all of which, both publicly funded (BBC1 and BBC2) and commercially funded (ITV, and later Channel 4 and Five), operated within a public service regulatory framework.

With the arrival of multi-channel television in the late 1980s things started to change. Defenders of PSB feared that intensified competition for children's attention and advertising revenue would lead to a reduction in original programming, growing reliance on imported animation and a weakening of the public service ethos (Blumler, 1993: 417–20; Klein, 1988). These suspicions were reinforced by the Conservative government's radical proposals in 1988 for the deregulation of the commercial side of British PSB, ITV (Snoddy and Evans, 1988). However, in response to concerted lobbying by advocacy group, British Action for Children's Television (BACTV), the 1990 Broadcasting Act included children's programming in a list of 'protected' programming that ITV companies still had to offer as part of their PSB obligations, in return for access to the airways (Snoddy, 1990a, b). BACTV, which was only established in 1989, had argued that without such protection children's programming would not survive (Broadcast, 1989; Klein, 1988). The 'positive' programme requirements of the 1990 Broadcasting Act combined with lower-than-expected growth of multichannel television meant that throughout the 1990s the quantity, quality and range of children's programming was less affected than PSB's defenders had initially feared.

The 1990 Broadcasting Act required commercial PSBs – ITV and later Five – to devote specified amounts of time to children's television, including different programme types (ITC, 2003a). For example in the 2002 report of the pre-Ofcom regulator, the ITC (ITC, 2003b: 61), ITV complied with its annual broadcast quota of 520 hours of children's programmes, including 391 hours of in-house or commissioned children programming – of which not less than 70 hours were preschool programming. These arrangements guaranteed sustained provision of children's programming throughout the 1990s by both ITV and Five, in addition to the BBC's historic provision. However, with budget cuts at ITV's children's department, CiTV, in 2002, the Independent Television Commission (ITC) voiced growing concerns:

> There are signs that children's programming is the first genre to suffer from harder times. Repeats – traditionally high in children's programmes – rose on CiTV and Channel 4 (by two per cent in each

case). This state of affairs may well reflect the allotted budget: early in the year CiTV was cut from £42 m to £39 m, with reports of a further £6 m reduction later in the year (ITC, 2002: 37).

An independent study published that same year by the Institute for Public Policy Research (Cowling and Lee, 2002) also highlighted a number of worrying long-term trends among terrestrial broadcasters. The researchers found that imports, comprising mainly animation, had risen from 5.7 per cent in 1972 to 28.6 per cent by 2002 with repeats rising from one-third to two-thirds of total PSB provision. Of course, these concerns needed to be placed within the context of the overall massive expansion in provision, not least the launch of the BBC's own dedicated children's channels (CBeebies and CBBC) in 2002 (see Chapter 4).

After 2002 a combination of technological, regulatory and market developments would all contribute further to the gap between originations and provision of children's programming. The first (chronologically) and perhaps most important of such developments was the termination of the quota regime by the 2003 Communications Act.

The Communications Act 2003: From quotas to co-regulation

The Labour Government's 2003 Communications Act represented a major liberalising overhaul of British broadcasting involving the relaxation of media ownership rules and the establishment of single regulator, the Ofcom charged with the task of regulating all aspects of electronic communications. The Act's deregulatory thrust was particularly evident in the area of broadcasting content. Commercial PSBs were now relieved of the obligation to meet quantitative targets for children's programming. Instead the Communications Act stated that Ofcom must ensure that children's services provided by all PSBs (the BBC and commercial terrestrial broadcasters) 'include what appears to Ofcom to be a suitable quantity and range of high quality and original programmes for children and young people' (Communications Act, 2003, §264(6)(h)), but there were no measurable targets. Instead, commercial PSBs were simply required to publish an annual statement of programme policy and a review, based on self-evaluation, on how they had fulfilled public service commitments in areas where quotas no longer applied. As Ofcom pointed out (2007a: 12), 'it is ultimately for PSBs themselves to decide what to deliver'.

Ahead of the Act's passage, public attention was focused on media ownership rules with far less attention paid to the reform of content regulation. Unlike 1990, there was no sustained lobbying by children's advocacy groups. BACT had ceased operating in 1995. Its role had been picked up by the Voice of the Listener and Viewer (VLV), but only 'in a very part-time kind of way' (Home, 2007). Jocelyn Hay, founder of the VLV, admitted at the Westminster Media Forum on 6 December 2007, how at the time they were 'slightly naïve': 'We thought that we had secured something when children's programming was put in the Act [as one of the specified categories of PSB programming], where other genres were not, but then we realised it was the wrong Tier [Tier 3, where quotas no longer applied].' Similarly, Anna Home, Head of BBC Children's Programmes from 1984 to 1997, and chief executive of the advocacy group Save Kids' TV, commented how at the time 'nobody had really noticed that children's programmes had gone into Tier 3 rather than Tier 2' (Home, 2007). During the passage of the bill through Parliament, the issue of children's television barely came up at all. However, within 3 years it would take a prominent position on the broadcasting policy agenda. It was Ofcom's decision in 2006 to ban advertising of food high in fat, salt and sugar (HFSS) during children's programmes that would become one of the triggers of the campaign to 'save' British children's television.

The 'junk food' advertising ban

Debates about the negative effects of food advertising on children are by no means recent, with calls for advertising restrictions stretching back to the 1980s. During the 1990s the effects of TV advertising on children were regularly monitored by the ITC (1996, 2000, 2001). However, it was only in the first years of the new century that calls for restrictions on food advertising gained momentum because of mounting concerns about childhood obesity.

Before and during the passage of the 2003 Communications Act, the government was heavily pressured by medical and health bodies including the British Medical Association and the British Heart Foundation, and consumer groups including the Children's Food Bill Coalition (Sustain) and *Which?* to tackle childhood obesity (for information on the policy background see Ofcom, 2006b: 13–16). Research commissioned by the Food Standards Agency (FSA) published in September 2003, suggested that children's food preferences, behaviour and consumption were influenced by their exposure to food promotion (Hastings et al.,

2003), concluding that children's food promotion was dominated by television advertising. From that moment on the debate about food advertising became focused on *television* rather than advertising in other media. In December 2003 the Secretary of State for Culture, Media and Sport, Tessa Jowell, charged the not-yet officially established Ofcom with the task of considering proposals for strengthening rules on the television advertising of food and drink products targeted at children (DCMS, 2003). Although Ofcom had limited powers over broadcasting content, it did have considerable powers over advertising.

The first action undertaken by the new regulator in early 2004 was to commission research on the link between television advertising of food products and obesity in order to build a case for intervention (Ofcom, 2004a). It concluded that 'TV advertising has a modest, direct effect on children's food choices' and 'larger' but unquantifiable indirect effects (Ofcom, 2004a: 23). On this basis, Ofcom maintained that there was indeed a case for strengthening the rules on television food advertising to children, but it ruled out a draconian pre-9 p.m. ban as advocated by the pro-ban camp as this 'would be both ineffective and disproportionate in its wider impact' (Ofcom, 2004b). In March 2006 Ofcom published its proposals for new restrictions on television advertising to children (Ofcom, 2006b).

Overall, as recounted by Ofcom's Director of Research, James Thickett (2007b), both before the publication of Ofcom's regulatory options in March 2006 and during the formal round of consultations, the debate was dominated by those who supported an advertising ban. The government itself had made it clear that it was in favour of restrictions (Department of Health, 2004). According to Thickett's insider account (2007b), the anti-ban camp, comprising the food, retailer, advertising and television industries, did not really seriously engage with Ofcom during these consultations:

> ... the broadcasting industry and the food industry itself were very quiet. [...] [W]hat we found, as we developed our response, was that the debate was all very one-sided by the press, by politicians, by the government and there wasn't really an effective counter-argument.

One important reason that can be adduced in order to explain why broadcasters failed to really engage with Ofcom is that the stakes were not as high as they might have appeared. Thickett hints that by the time of the consultation ITV had probably already decided to pull out of children's television (see next section). Giving weight to Thickett's suggestion is the fact that in its written response to the Ofcom consultation, ITV's chief concern appeared to be that restrictions should not extend to adult airtime (ITV, 2006: 4). As for other commercial broadcasters involved in children's television, namely Five and the American channels, the most likely reason for their disengagement was again pointed out by Thickett (2007b):

> Five responded – it was probably a pre-emptive response – by moving from mainstream children's to preschool, where obviously that sort of advertising doesn't really matter so much. And then the American channels [...] well the likes of Disney, Cartoon Network, and Nickelodeon have been facing these issues in other markets for ten years, and they are much more reliant on subscription revenues [...] So in reality, the impact [of the ban on food advertising] was always going to be more muted. We calculated it between 3 and 5 percent of their ad revenues. But their ad revenues on average account for between a third and two thirds of total revenues.

Ofcom published its decision on 22 February 2007 (Ofcom, 2007d). Advertisements for HFSS food and drink products would be banned in or around programmes specifically targeted at children under 16 or of particular appeal to them. The new rules came into force in January 2008 except for dedicated children's channels who were given more time to adjust (until January 2009).

The future of public service children's television

The junk-food advertising ban dominated the children's television debate in the years following the passage of the 2003 Communications Act, but it was almost as if the production community had barely noticed it. It was not until 2006 that concerns emerged about its potential impact on plurality and range in the provision of public service children's programming – namely concerns associated with 'positive' as opposed to 'negative regulation' – surfacing forcefully at the Showcomotion Children's Media Conference in July 2006.

Ofcom's first PSB review: The breakdown of the 'PSB compact'

Ofcom set out the terms of the debate in its first statutory review of the whole of PSB between 2004 and 2005 (Ofcom, 2004c, d). The rapid take up of digital multi-channel television in Britain to over 80 per cent by the start of 2007 (Ofcom, 2007e: 101) combined with access to more channels reduced the audience share of the five terrestrial public service channels (particularly ITV1 whose audience share dropped from 24 per cent in 2002 to 19.7 per cent in 2006), intensifying competition for advertising revenues (Ofcom, 2007e: 166). Ofcom argued that the historical 'compact' in which PSB was provided by commercial terrestrial broadcasters (ITV 1, Five, Channel 4) in return for discounted access to analogue spectrum was eroding because of the diminishing value of this form of implicit subsidy. It called instead for explicit funding in order to maintain PSB plurality in the digital age (that is the funding of public service programming, including children's programming outside of the BBC) (Ofcom, 2004d: 5).

In its review, Ofcom also noted some worrying trends in children's television. Programming expenditure by the five terrestrial channels had dropped by 8 per cent between 1998 and 2002; and fewer first-run original programmes were broadcast (10 per cent less than in 1998), particularly factual programmes and those targeted at the over-12s (Ofcom, 2004c: 37). While children's television was singled out in a few passages of Ofcom's review as one of the PSB genres most likely to be negatively impacted by ongoing market and technological change, it had not yet become the focus of specific regulatory attention. A number of intervening circumstances contributed to move children's television to the centre of the broadcasting policy stage in 2006.

ITV's ongoing withdrawal from children's television

The 2003 Communications Act had already replaced quotas for children's programming with a new co-regulatory regime, leaving commercial PSBs free to decide how much and what to provide. While they are now required to consult Ofcom and take account of its opinion in preparing their Statements of Programme Policy whenever they plan to make a *significant* change to their schedules, they are under no obligation to follow Ofcom's guidance (Ofcom, 2007a: 12). Exploiting the leeway offered by the new regime, in 2005 ITV started implementing its withdrawal from children's television. In the eyes of ITV executives, children's programmes were no longer sustainable in a competitive market, because of the small amount of advertising revenue they generate compared to other types of programmes (ITV, 2007: 7).

A first move in 2004 by ITV to reduce children's programming on its main channel, ITV1 from 11.5 hours a week to 8 hours was agreed by Ofcom on the grounds that it would 'afford ITV a greater degree of flexibility in the delivery of its public service obligations' (Ofcom, 2005).

Then in the summer of 2006, having announced its decision to close its in-house production centre, ITV Kids, ITV approached Ofcom to further reduce children's output on ITV1 to 2 hours a week. This time Ofcom was of the opinion that ITV's proposed changes were not appropriate (Deans, 2006). Obliged to take Ofcom's comments into account, ITV subsequently stated that it would commit itself to broadcast around 5 hours of children's programming per week on ITV1 in 2007 (reported in Sweney, 2007). This was as far as the broadcaster was ready to compromise. In its annual statement of programme policy for 2007, ITV was vague and wary of committing to any quantitative target. It promised to 'broadcast a significantly higher volume of children's programmes than originally proposed to Ofcom, albeit a lower volume than in 2006' (ITV, 2007: 23–4). At the beginning of 2008, ITV consulted Ofcom again about reducing provision on ITV1 from around 4 hours on average per week (as aired in 2007) to 2 hours (Ofcom, 2008b). Ofcom again deemed the change inappropriate, but reiterated that it has no powers to compel ITV to maintain current levels of provision, as its responsibilities rest on ensuring overall provision not provision by one supplier. Ofcom was also aware that theoretically ITV could hand in its terrestrial licence and simply walk away from its PSB commitments, which would affect other public service content including news (Thickett, 2007b).

The industry wakes up

ITV's efforts to reduce its ITV1 children's schedule from 8 hours to just two amounted to an almost complete withdrawal from children's terrestrial television. ITV had launched a dedicated digital children's service, CiTV, in March 2006, but the programme budget was considerably less than the £25m it had spent in 2005 on ITV1, and this channel was largely reliant on repeats and acquisitions. One argument in favour of ITV's position, however, was that children's viewing has migrated to dedicated cable and satellite channels anyway. Whereas 55 per cent of children's viewing of children's television in 2002 had been taken by terrestrial television (ITV 1, BBC 1, 2, Channel 4, Five), by 2006 this had fallen to 18 per cent with 82 per cent of children's viewing of children's programming attributed to dedicated children's channels (Ofcom, 2007a: 97; Thickett, 2007c).

By the time Ofcom turned down ITV's proposed changes, the production sector, under the aegis of trade association PACT, and lobby group, Save Kids TV, had finally mobilised to lobby government and Ofcom. The series of 'threats' to children's television, which manifested themselves within a very short space of time in the first half of 2006, were a wake-up call for the industry. The closure of ITV's in-house production centre, ITV's plan to cut down its commitment to children's television on ITV1 and, finally, Ofcom's decision to introduce restrictions on junk food advertising galvanised the industry.

In 2005 Pact changed the name of its Animation Council to 'Children's and Animation Council', a clear indication of the new direction that Pact's lobbying efforts would take. In its response to Ofcom's discussion paper on the food advertising ban of March 2006, Pact had called for the creation of a Government-backed fund for children's programming, designed to encourage the production of original children's programming and offset the withdrawal of ITV and decline in advertising income (Pact, 2006). Pact had also urged the Government to consider production tax breaks as an interim solution.

Advocacy group Save Kids' TV also came to play an important role in raising awareness about the crisis and propelling the issue onto the political agenda. Established at the annual Showcomotion Children's Media Conference in Sheffield in July 2006 the group initially concentrated its efforts on campaigning against the 'junk' food advertising ban, but soon realised that it needed to shift its profile, strategy and objectives to achieve 'the best TV for British kids' without being seen as a self-interested industry group (Childs, 2007). According to Greg Childs (2007), SKTV's Secretary:

> The initial feeling was that we should fight the ad ban, but it became apparent to us very quickly that this was heading nowhere. The ad ban was going to go through one way or another. Tony Blair said so [...] We began to realise that we appeared to be yet another self-interest group like PACT. PACT were doing quite good work, but they were up against the fact that it was self-interest and they were about saving an industry. I think that it was at that time that we looked at two steps. One was to stop worrying about the ad ban, and actually stop responding if anyone asked us about it [...] And we also realised that we had to try to stop being an industry group and broaden it. We characterised ourselves, and always have done ever since, as an alliance of the industry, the audience, and concerned cultural campaigners and academics.

In December 2006, Ofcom (2006c: 32) announced that it would bring forward its review of PSB provision in the specific area of children's programming ahead of its second PSB Review (scheduled to take place in 2009). Ofcom's move appeared to constitute implicit recognition of the serious threat to children's television. In terms of reference published on 13 February 2007, it stated that the aims of the review were 'to explore prospects for future delivery of a wide range of high quality and original content for children' and, ultimately, 'to assess the desirability and scope of any public service interventions in this market' (Ofcom, 2007f).

Ofcom's report on 'The Future of Children's Television Programming'

Published in October 2007, *The Future of Children's Television Programming* was broadly supportive of some form of public intervention in children's television on market failure grounds.

The key finding of Ofcom's report was that despite the dramatic increase in the number of dedicated children's channels (from 6 to 25 between 1998 and 2007) and in the volume of children's airtime (from around 20,000 hours a year in 1998 to over 112,000 hours in 2006), expenditure by *all* broadcasters on first-run *original* children's programming (new UK-originated programming) had declined from £127m in 1998 to £109m in 2006 (Ofcom, 2007a: 60). Commercial PSBs – ITV1, Channel 4 and Five – were accountable for this decline (and certainly the bulk originated with ITV, although Ofcom provided only cumulative figures on expenditure). Commercial PSBs' aggregated expenditure more than halved in real terms between 1998 and 2006 – from £60m in 1998 to £27m in 2006. According to Ofcom, the scale of the reduction was the result of 'the increasingly unattractive economics of some types of children's programming for the commercial public service broadcasters, relative to other output' (Ofcom, 2007a: 1). Ofcom estimated that the opportunity cost borne by ITV1 of showing children's programmes in its traditional late afternoon slot up to 2007 (that is foregone advertising revenue from more popular programmes) was approximately £18m–£28m annually.

The decline in expenditure on original children's programming by commercial PSBs was not compensated by increases in programming investment elsewhere. The aggregated expenditure on first-run original programming by American children's channels remained fairly stable in the period under consideration, despite the launch of new dedicated services: it represented only 10 per cent of total investment in new programmes reflecting the fact that these channels rely heavily on imports from their US parent companies. The BBC's expenditure on first-run original programming between 1998 and 2006 did increase (from £51m to £62m), with a peak in 2004 (£85m) following the launch of CBBC and CBeebies in 2002. However, the BBC increase was not enough to offset the decline in spend by commercial PSBs. The result was that by 2006 the BBC had become by far the main broadcast financier of original children's programming, raising serious concerns about plurality of provision. In 1998 the BBC contributed 40 per cent of overall expenditure on first-run original programming, but by 2006 this had risen to 57 per cent with commercial PSBs down from 52 per cent to 33 per cent. Ofcom's assessment was gloomy: 'the future provision of new UK-originated content for children, particularly drama and factual programming, looks uncertain other than from the BBC' (Ofcom, 2007a: 1).

Preschool television – a safe harbour?

However, Ofcom's analysis suggested that market failure did not apply to all sub-genres and for all age groups. The report claimed that the real problem was with drama and factual programming for older children (9–12) and young teenagers (13–15). Ofcom argued that preschool children were well served: provision of programming had grown since 1998 following the launch of dedicated preschool channels including Nick Jr. and Playhouse Disney. Preschool children also continued to be well served by PSB – on BBC1, BBC2, CBeebies and Five's Milkshake! Qualitative research with parents of preschoolers appeared to show that they were more satisfied than parents of older children:

> Programming for pre-school children is seen to be good quality; there is a good range of genres available, a good mix of programmes made in the UK and from overseas and a good supply of new programming. Parents feel that their children are well served by PSB programming from CBeebies and Milkshake! on Five. Many of the preschool channels, across different platforms, air programmes which are perceived to possess PSB purposes and characteristics which parents see to be essential for preschool children. (Ofcom, 2007a: 136)

According to Ofcom, a partial explanation for this lay in the economics of preschool programming, which made it more attractive to both broadcasters and producers:

> For broadcasters, pre-school programming is appealing to commission because they are able to contribute less of the budget (typically 25%) to producers compared with other sub-genres of programming.

Pre-school programming is more resilient in terms of advertising revenues, as parents are target viewers. [...] For producers, pre-school programmes taken as a whole also have more potential [to] make a better commercial return than other children's sub-genres. Producers are able to secure initial funding and broadcast of pre-school programmes are more likely to benefit from secondary revenues than with other sub-genres. (Ofcom, 2007a: 198)

Following publication of the report stakeholders were invited by Ofcom to state whether policy interventions should be tailored to different age groups or types of programming. With the exception of Hit Entertainment (2007b) and Ragdoll (2007) (preschool specialists with a vested interest) and VLV (2007) and S4C (2007), the majority of stakeholders appeared to be in favour of tailored intervention. The BBC, for instance, stated that it agreed with Ofcom's segmentation of the children's audience by age group and that 'in order to secure greatest effectiveness and best value for money from any intervention policy interventions would need to be targeted accordingly' (BBC, 2007: 14).

Yet Ofcom's positive assessment of preschool television was based on some questionable methodological choices. Its analysis of broadcasters' output used BARB's classification of children's programming, which divides programming into five categories: cartoons, drama, factual, preschool and light entertainment/quizzes. As noted by other commentators (Buckingham et al., 1999: 80–1), this classification lacks consistency as it is based on overlapping criteria, namely the *form* or *genre* of a particular programme and, in the case of preschool, its *target audience*. It is therefore dependent on highly subjective judgments – on which basis, for instance, is a decision made about whether a cartoon should fall into the 'animation' or the 'preschool' category? The regulator appears to have been aware of these limitations and their implications:

> In the future, range within pre-school programming (which itself is difficult to measure but includes sub-genres like drama, factual, animation and entertainment programming) may become a concern if more funding is required from outside the broadcaster and may lead to reliance on sub-genres with greater potential for commercial exploitation or global sales such as animation. There may be less live action, presenter-led programming commissioned as a result (Ofcom, 2007a: 198).

The implications of the research design for preschool programming were also recognised by James Thickett (2007b) from Ofcom:

> I think there are a number of areas in preschool which appear to be under threat, although it didn't come out directly in the research. And I think that that really relates to presenter-led factual types of programming. So, you know, the classic studio-based presenter programme like *Play School* for instance, where it's basically the same problem as mainstream factual programming, in that it doesn't really have an international market. Most preschool programming is gravitating towards programming that sells on the international stage. There is a risk that you end up having a very redundant type of preschool proposition, or a sort of international proposition.

Ofcom also appeared careful to qualify its statement about the economic attractiveness of preschool television. It reported that some stakeholders had suggested that 'ancillary revenues from worldwide sales and merchandising (for preschool) tended to be a myth, with big hits like *Bob the Builder* or *Teletubbies* happening only once in a generation' (Ofcom, 2007a: 150). It also noted that while animation and preschool programming is less dependent on broadcaster support, nonetheless 'it is widely believed in the industry that commission funding and first showing by a domestic free-to-air broadcaster remain crucial to precipitating secondary revenue' (Ofcom, 2007a: 50).

In terms of number of hours of first-run original programming aired by PSBs between 1998 and 2006 preschool programming also appeared to be the 'sub-genre' where originations had declined the most: from 220 hours in 1998 to 132 hours in 2006, with a peak of 403 hours in 2002 following the introduction of CBeebies. In contrast the decline across other sub-genres was more moderate – in fact, provision of factual programming increased over the same period from 313 to 511 hours (Ofcom, 2007a: 30). The decline in hours was matched by the very small amounts spent by all broadcasters on first-run original preschool programming – £11m in 2006 with the BBC accounting for over 50 per cent of overall expenditure (£5.9m), commercial PSBs for approximately £1.8m (ITV, C4, S4C, Five) with possible expenditure of £3m by commercial channels such as Nick Jr. and Playhouse Disney (Ofcom, 2007a: 61; Oliver and Ohlbaum, 2007: 26).

All this passed uncommented and did not seem to have any bearing on Ofcom's overall positive assessment of preschool provision. What also passed unnoticed was the fact that concerns about the lack plurality in the provision of public service children's programming (with the BBC becoming more dominant as a commissioner) are as justified in preschool provision as they are in other sub-genres.

Throwing a lifeline to children's television

Ofcom's summary (2007a) of possible policy approaches proposed by stakeholders revealed no consensus, although the majority did advocate some form of public intervention, including a dedicated fund for children's commissions, tax breaks for producers (advocated by PACT) and the creation of a new online destination, advocated by SKTV (SKTV, 2007). Yet Ofcom was careful to stress that most of these would require government intervention and new legislation.

In April 2008 Ofcom published the first phase of its second PSB review (The Digital Opportunity) (Ofcom, 2008c). Earlier work on children's programming was incorporated into this wider analysis. Ofcom restated the case for targeted public intervention on market failure grounds, especially for original drama and factual programming for older children and teens. Policy interventions across the board, including interventions targeting preschool children were not contemplated. New figures released by Ofcom showed that expenditure on first-run original children's programming by commercial PSBs had declined further in 2007 – from £27m to £12m (Ofcom, 2008d: 15). Ofcom estimated that public intervention to pay for home-grown PSB children's programmes and maintain plurality of provision would cost £30m a year (Ofcom, 2008c: 129). A number of short-term corrective measures, that would not require legislation, were contemplated (2008d: 3) including developing the BBC's role for older children and extending Channel 4's remit to include older children and teenagers. Tax breaks, the most debated policy intervention, received a mixed assessment by Ofcom and some stakeholders as a short-term measure that did not necessarily solve the problem of securing distribution from broadcasters who had no wish to take on children's programming at all, however cheaply it is made (2008c: 132–3; Thickett, 2007b).

In the months following the publication of Ofcom's report on children's TV, ITV announced new funds for commissioning children's programmes (Rogers, 2007), albeit at £4m (Five, 2008b) far less than the £25m it had spent previously. The BBC Trust carried out a review of BBC children's provision in 2008, concluding that the BBC's children's services are generally performing well, particularly CBeebies (BBC

Trust, 2009). Yet the BBC was clearly not the problem. It had raised investment in original programming from £63m in 2006 to £70m in 2007 (Ofcom,2008c: 134), as well as tripling the guaranteed minimum volume of children's output on generalist channels BBC1 and BBC2 to 1,500 hours per year (BBC, 2008a) in response to Ofcom's earlier concerns that it could potentially reduce provision on these services (Ofcom, 2007a: 176). Five volunteered to reinforce its commitment to younger children (Five, 2008a: 7), but stated that it could only make a minor contribution to programming for older children, an area from which it had withdrawn in 2007 for commercial reasons. Finally, in March 2008, in a clear attempt to provide a tangible sign of its public service credentials and secure public funding, Channel 4 announced that it would establish a new £10m pilot fund over 2 years dedicated to programming for older children (10- to 16-year olds) (Channel 4, 2008a). However, with the worsening economic situation by the end of 2008, Channel 4 announced that the project had been frozen (Channel 4, 2008b). While each of these developments were welcome, it was clear that they did not represent a long-term solution to the structural and economic problems facing children's television in a post-digital switchover world.

In January 2009, Ofcom concluded its second review of PSB (Ofcom, 2009). Its key recommendation was that Channel 4 should become part of a new larger organisation with a strong public service broadcasting remit, but no extra direct public funding, possibly in partnership with BBC Worldwide or Five. Children's television campaigners expressed their disappointment at what they saw as the marginalisation of the children's issue (Brown, 2009). Ofcom did suggest that a new enlarged Channel 4 'could play an important role in delivering content to older children' (ibid.: 109), and that consideration should be given to providing additional funding on a competitive basis 'if resources permitted' (ibid.: 10). However, the issue occupied by now a rather marginal position in the general debate. Certainly there appeared to be no appetite for extra public money to be injected into PSB generally, and children's television in particular (see House of Commons, 2007).

This marginalisation was confirmed by the release in June 2009 of *Digital Britain*, the government's blueprint for future legislation and policy in the communications sector (BIS/DCMS, 2009). The government ruled out any injections of public money. Instead it endorsed the idea of 'top-slicing' the BBC licence fee and distributing a small portion of it to other content providers for 'competitive provision of essential public content' (ibid.: 141). Where children's provision was concerned *Digital*

Britain envisaged a continuing role for Channel 4 as a smaller public service provider alongside the BBC, with a new remit including, in line with Ofcom's recommendations, 'a solid commitment to children's content, with priority given to older children' (ibid.: 147), although the age of the children was not specified. The issue of how to guarantee Channel 4's long-term financial viability was not really addressed either. The government ruled out direct state funding, 'given other public spending priorities' (ibid.: 19), argued against Channel 4's merger with Five, and expressed reservations about a joint-venture between Channel 4 and BBC Worldwide, favouring instead, the pursuit of 'purely commercial ventures' (ibid.) between the two players as a short-term initiative.

Conclusion

Recent policy developments have demonstrated that British children's television is now less embedded within a public service framework and arguably more closely aligned to the US approach – both in terms of the growing salience of the debate, yet ultimate weakening of public service broadcasting in the face of moves towards co-regulation and the acceptance of commercial over societal priorities.

Recent developments in Britain can be seen as a textbook case about the limits of self- or co-regulation, which have been apparent in the United States for many years. The removal of scheduling quotas, ITV's reduced commitment to children's broadcasting, advertising restrictions, budgetary pressures and the competitive environment at home and abroad have all combined to reinforce the trend towards a contraction of broadcast funding and commissioning of domestic children's productions. What ITV's decision to drastically reduce its commitment to the commissioning and scheduling of children's television programming demonstrated is that in the absence of 'positive' programming requirements, which drive investment decisions in quality programming, profit-driven broadcasters may lack much incentive to provide socially valuable programming (also Messenger Davies, 2007) – unless they can discern real profit-making opportunities (from product licensing for example).

The BBC's dominance as a broadcast commissioner following ITV's disengagement has also raised questions about choice, creative competition and plurality in the marketplace (Ofcom, 2008d: 6–7). For British production interests, arguments have revolved around the idea that the production of British programmes is essential for 'children's cultural sense of themselves, of their identities and for the cultural life of the nation as a whole' (Brogan, 2007; also House of Commons, 2007; Messenger Davies, 2007). These arguments might, of course, betray a measure of self-interest (see Buckingham et al., 1999: 12), and in the case of preschool are irrelevant for that programming which is too internationally orientated to ascertain cultural origins. However, there is also an argument for recognising the wider benefits of a thriving domestic children's media production industry, which is not only capable of supplying quality programmes that have some affinity with children's home-grown culture, but also rests on specialist skills, that might be lost if the sector goes into decline.

However, these arguments are not accepted by all, and for some the current problems in the British industry are simply a sign of market contraction after phenomenal growth in recent years, contraction which may not necessarily harm the industry if production becomes focused on a 'few well-funded independents'. The BBC Trust's view (2008b: 80) has been that Ofcom has overstated concerns about the amount, quality and range of existing children's provision failing to account sufficiently for PSB investment in other platforms, (particularly online) and the contributions of other providers, such as Five, to preschool programming (ibid.: 88).

Of course television constitutes only one aspect of media provision, and increasingly policy has to take account of multiple delivery systems including on-demand, online and interactive media – raising important questions about advertising, harmful content, the plurality and quality of content and even the sustainability of regulation on a national basis, given that distribution is no longer confined to national borders. The scope and effectiveness of regulation is contracting ever more with rules in the United States and Britain confined largely to publicly funded PSB and diminishing provision by commercially funded free-to-air broadcasters, leaving other platforms such as the internet or television distributed via cable or satellite largely untouched by any rules relating to the range, origins or funding of children's content (Jordan, 2008). Based on political unwillingness to combine 'positive' regulation with workable funding models these circumstances are unlikely to change for the foreseeable future.

11
The Bigger Picture: Preschool Television in its Critical and Aesthetic contexts

James Walters and Jeanette Steemers

So far this book has concentrated on the production circumstances behind preschool television and the assumptions that those who produce, broadcast and market preschool content make about young audiences and the broader marketplace. However, beyond the focus on production practices and changes in institutional and economic circumstances, there are particular qualities and motivations underpinning preschool production, which allow an appreciation of the aesthetic achievements of those who inhabit the preschool production community. This aspect was highlighted at a symposium attended by members of the academic, regulatory and television production communities in January 2007,[1] when speaker Nick Wilson (Director of Children's Programming, Five) voiced surprise and concern that, at an event focussing on children's television, there had not been a single example of content shown or discussed. In an effort to correct this perceived omission, Wilson proceeded to screen an assortment of preschool programming from the past 30 years, prompting favourable nods and sighs of recognition. This would turn out to be the only showing of television content that day. It may well be the case that Wilson improvised his words to fit with the already-prepared footage, but had he anticipated in advance that no other speaker would deem it necessary to talk about the programmes, his suspicions would perhaps represent a shrewd appreciation of a general attitude towards preschool television. Even at public events such as these, there is often an assumption that focussing on the programmes is not an essential requirement; that as adult viewers (or critics, or producers) we understand what preschool television is well enough to avoid having to reacquaint ourselves with the content in order to appreciate its qualities and distinctions. This may derive partially from an understanding that preschool television diverges fundamentally from programming designed for adults and even older children in terms of audience taste and capacity for understanding, resulting in storylines that can seem obvious, thin or repetitive.

This chapter moves beyond surface definitions of this kind to concentrate more on the styles and formats of preschool television as a profitable, if infrequently performed, critical enterprise. Whilst not suggesting in any strong sense that the close study of preschool television has been unacceptably neglected thus far (there are many genres, styles, forms and formats of television which we could claim as being critically underdeveloped), this chapter explores some of the challenges and obstacles facing its interpretation and evaluation, as well as surveying those accounts that are exemplary in their careful description and considered analysis. Finally, the chapter returns to the programmes themselves, presenting a short consideration of British examples in order to establish a series of defining qualities and achievements. However, it is not the aim here to provide a comprehensive picture of the breadth and range of preschool television content. Rather, an emphasis is placed upon programmes that make strong interventions in debates surrounding aesthetic composition and creative merit. In this sense, such programmes might be seen to constitute exemplary cases, but scope remains for the critical practices outlined in this chapter to be extended across further examples of preschool television, which encompasses a wide variety of programmes with different motivations, styles, forms and tones. In many respects, the programmes covered here are implicitly regarded as extraordinary cases of achievement and quality in preschool television, a feature underlined by their widespread international circulation. Nevertheless it follows that further work might also incorporate a focus on the 'ordinary' or even the 'bad' to better understand what such terms might mean in relation to preschool and what we mean if and when we use them.

The speciality of preschool aesthetics

Interpreting any children's programme – and perhaps particularly one aimed at a very young audience – is fraught with difficulties. As adults, we are not the intended audience; and, as such, there is a significant risk of 'misreading', taking things too literally, or simply lapsing into pretentiousness. It is all too easy to dismiss such programmes as boring or simplistic, or alternatively to find them cute or anarchic or surrealistic – responses that could be seen as characteristic of how adults relate to children generally. (Buckingham, 2002: 58)

Buckingham's assertion outlines a series of issues and challenges facing anyone seeking to formulate interpretative and critical responses to preschool television. Furthermore, his position highlights some of the ways in which preschool programming can be seen to correspond unsatisfactorily with broad notions of quality and achievement in television, so that we might risk failing to understand properly its nature and tone ('dismiss[ing] such programmes as boring or simplistic') or instead impose a set of evaluative criteria that corresponds unsatisfactorily with the artistic aims and viewing context of the programmes ('alternatively... find[ing] them cute or anarchic or surrealistic'). Indeed, whilst there has recently been something of a resurgence in television scholars attending to questions of aesthetics in relation to quality and achievement (Corner, 2007), it is notable that the critical judgements contained within such readings are based largely upon the extent to which narrative themes are handled and shaped with subtlety and complexity within the programmes. Scholarship of this kind searches for the symbolic and the metaphoric in texts, a concern that perhaps emphasises its close relationship to analytical trends existent within the field of film studies, and literary criticism. So, for example, when writing about the work of Stephen Poliakoff, Sarah Cardwell sets out her critical concerns thus:

> At a stylistic level, Poliakoff's work increasingly employs a complex level of patterning – and this is particularly true of his television programmes. Whilst all television programmes employ repetition, rhyming and discernible narrative shapes or structures, Poliakoff uses these more repeatedly and with greater sense of awareness. He attains a complex coherence across all elements of his work, including images, sounds, music and dialogue, so that the patterning discernible in each element echoes, emphasises, highlights or counterpoints that found in its neighbouring elements. (Cardwell, 2006: 135)

Here, Cardwell establishes an analytical framework built around questions of depth, coherence and resonance in order to emphasise Poliakoff's artistic merit over, or at least in relation to, other television content. Cardwell proposes that in Poliakoff's hands potentially mundane or redundant features like repetition and rhyming take on a shape and significance which elevates them above other – by implication less accomplished – forms of television. It seems unlikely, for example, that Cardwell would choose to make the same claims for 'artistic originality' (ibid.: 140) about a game show such as *Deal Or No Deal* or a motoring magazine programme such as *Top Gear*, which might equally be seen to offer 'repetition, rhyming, and discernible narrative shapes or structures', but perhaps fall some way short of inventively shaping these features beyond the structural confines of quiz show or magazine programme formats.

The focus upon notions of richness, intricacy and complexity in television programming, inherent in Cardwell's work, derives perhaps from the very nature of 'textual analysis', a term often used to describe and encapsulate this type of interpretative criticism concentrated closely on the object of study. In many of these critical accounts of television, acknowledging programmes as texts implicitly involves an appreciation of their *texture*: the extent to which they are composed of different aesthetic layers requiring time and consideration in order to appreciate accurately how they are made meaningful *in combination* with each other. Such arguments derive from a sense that there is more to say than can be satisfactorily elucidated on first viewing: that crucial issues exist which require further deliberation and explanation in order to be fully appreciated. Examples of preschool children's television, however, do not match these criteria precisely because they are required to communicate their salient points directly and straightforwardly in order to be understood and enjoyed by the majority of the audience: preschool children. The themes of 'repetition, rhyming and discernible narrative shapes or structures', which Cardwell claims Poliakoff employs with a refined sense of artistic self-awareness, are evident in preschool children's television as fundamental storytelling tropes, unselfconsciously designed to help guide the target audience uncomplicatedly through dramatic scenarios. As Máire Messenger Davies explains:

> Dramatised stories, like *Postman Pat* and *Bertha, the Big Machine*, take simple events, like the rescue of a kitten, or a breakdown in Bertha's machinery, and turn them into mini-dramas. To understand even simple stories like these, children must have an ability to understand the underlying logic of events: that when Pat abandons his van, it is because a tree has fallen across the road earlier [...] Even in a very simple pre-school programme, like *Postman Pat*, there may be an intervening scene, featuring other characters, between the tree

falling down and the van being abandoned. If the sequence of events is interrupted, young children may have difficulty in maintaining earlier events in memory, in order to understand later ones. Thus they may be completely baffled by what is going on in the later part of the story. (Messenger Davies, 1989: 22–3)

In Messenger Davies' terms, the special demands of a preschool audience dictate that a story should be understood as a linear pattern of progression. Where the work of Poliakoff, for example, might encourage us to think retrospectively about the symbolic meaning of repetitions and structures, the repetitions and structures in preschool television facilitate the comprehension of storylines, allowing the primary audience to follow a narrative straightforwardly and thereby readily understand the events taking place.

Unlike drama, a category which has received perhaps the greatest critical attention in recent accounts of television, preschool television does not engage the adult viewer in an aesthetic debate over its construction as a means of understanding its artistic ambitions (in the way that Cardwell ascribes to Poliakoff's work). As Buckingham maintains, we patently are not the primary audience for this programming and, since it is only adults that are likely to write critically about television, careful consideration is required in order to avoid dismissing or over-elaborating certain themes and features (Buckingham, 2002: 58). For example, precaution is certainly required when assessing the behaviour and attitudes of characters in preschool television, given that for very good reasons they are not imbued with the same degrees of motivation and levels of complexity more usually associated with characters in adult drama, or even drama aimed at older children. Indeed, it would be a distinct problem if a character in a preschool programme were to behave in a psychologically opaque or inscrutable manner, as it would potentially hinder the target audience's ability to comprehend what is taking place at all. Whereas in adult-centred drama we might understand characters to have dual motivations, or a series of conflicting motivations or even motivations that are mysterious to them (Walters, 2006: 97), in preschool television we would perhaps be misinterpreting or at least imposing disingenuous interpretations upon the text if we were to talk about the complex motivational strategies at work in the characters of *Dora the Explorer* or Tinky-Winky, Dipsy, Laa-Laa and Po.

Contentions of this kind require careful handling as they risk making the inherent assumption that, because preschool programming strives for narrative linearity in ways that are quite distinct from other forms of television, its aesthetic construction is necessarily simplistic or lacking in artistic merit. However, understanding a programme's aims and objectives is never the same as understanding the means of achieving those goals. As a consequence, dismissing preschool television because it is easy to comprehend on a linear 'storytelling' level represents an inadequate critical strategy. There have been a number of contributions to scholarly debate around children's television which seek to move beyond surface understandings of content (see Bazalgette and Buckingham, 1995; Buckingham, 2002). In this sense, the case for attending more carefully to the features of children's television has been and continues to be made within the academic community. It is also true, however, that much of this debate has centred upon questions of television's educative potential and value, often contributed by scholars possessing a specialist grounding in issues pertaining to the viewing experiences and learning patterns of children. This emphasis upon education and development is due, in part, to a reaction against a generalised view – still held in some quarters – of television being inherently harmful to children and therefore lacking in cultural value (Davies et al., 2004). Whilst these education-centred debates are undoubtedly pertinent, closer consideration of preschool programmes in an *aesthetic* context offers an opportunity to reflect on the professional investment and creative aspirations of the preschool television production community itself. It is notable that during the course of our interviews, many different professionals including producers, writers, animators and directors – even licensing managers and heads of marketing – would consistently vocalise a critical engagement with the style and form of preschool television across categories and formats (observations that clearly inform, and are informed by, some of those individuals' pedagogical or commercial ambitions). Moreover, members of the production community frequently acknowledge the difficulties surrounding the public perception and critical appraisal of preschool programming, a notion illustrated by Melanie Stokes, company director of Kindle Entertainment, when commenting on the work of another company, Ragdoll Productions:

> You look at something like *Teletubbies* and it's hard to appreciate the craft and the skill and the imagination that's gone into that show, compared to if you watch a very modern version of telly like *Macbeth*. Everyone goes 'it was so amazing because they put it into a Scottish restaurant and the lighting was incredible blah blah blah.' It's much easier to appreciate the value of that than the value of *Teletubbies*.

But *Teletubbies* is every bit as hard, if not harder, because you've got to get under the skin of a child that can barely talk – and make them laugh! That's an amazing thing: to communicate with that little three-year-old and make them feel really excited and engaged and valued. But we don't appreciate it. There's a sense that television is bad for you still. (Stokes, 2007)

This assertion references the potential disparity between public critical reaction to a new televised adaptation of Shakespeare and a new programme aimed at preschool children. To echo a point made earlier in relation to the work of Poliakoff, this disparity may be in part related to differing modes of address in each programme, with the hypothetical Shakespearian adaptation perhaps *inviting* a critical response through its self-conscious use of conventions and aesthetic strategies ('they put it into a Scottish restaurant and the lighting was incredible'), whereas these features go almost unnoticed within *Teletubbies'* somewhat direct style of delivery ('to communicate with that little three-year-old and make them feel really excited and engaged and valued'). In this sense, the implication seems to be that programmes such as *Teletubbies* perform their function almost *too* well to attract critics and viewers to retrospectively debate their quality and value.

Teletubbies in a critical landscape

Stokes' remarks do, however, bring into focus one particular way in which preschool television might be critically discussed, namely as part of the 'television is bad for you' debate, which is periodically rehearsed by commentators such as Aric Sigman in public addresses and published work (Sigman, 2007). Such debates can be understood within their historical context as having consistently recurring themes and foci (Wells, 2001b: 98), but it is also true that at the end of the 1990s Stokes' choice of programme example, *Teletubbies*, notoriously brought about a renewed furore concerning the pedagogic and cultural value of preschool television. As Jason Jacobs points out, the anxieties surrounding *Teletubbies* ranged from its perceived infantilising of language, to the commercial exploitation of its viewers through merchandising, to the general role and responsibilities of the BBC as a public broadcaster (Jacobs, 2004: 205–6). Furthermore, while these kinds of public debates might at least merit consideration and hold value for programme-makers as well as social commentators, it is also true that

The criticisms of [*Teletubbies*] reached epidemic proportions with fears about children getting addicted to the show or pulling the television sets on their heads in order to give the Teletubbies a hug. Such criticism rapidly took on a predictable form of a war between self-appointed traditionalists and self-appointed progressives, so that US Reverend Jerry Falwell warned parents that Tinky-Winky (who is purple and likes his handbag) was homosexual, while media studies scholar Andy Medhurst claimed that the same character was the world's first pre-school gay icon. That the chosen terrain for battle was a show aimed at two to three year olds – at a time when news and current-affairs programmes were simplifying their formats and mode of address to be 'accessible' and focusing more on emotional human interest stories, and when documentaries chose increasingly sensationalist topics to the extent that some were faked – is indicative of the intellectual poverty of the debate. (Ibid.: 206)

As Jacobs makes clear, the moral debates regarding *Teletubbies*, fuelled by a general sense that television was in some ways 'dumbing down', grew to an extent that those outlining the issues began to lose any sense of perspective regarding the show's artistic ambitions and also its potential benefits to the youngest children. What becomes clear, then, is an inclination by critics, scholars and commentators to impose evaluative criteria on a show that do not befit its structure, tone, achievements or aims. As Jacobs concludes, 'such crude comparisons...miss the charm of *Teletubbies* and its important innovations' (ibid.). This is certainly the case, but it also true that such eccentric responses highlight the potential critical hazard awaiting anyone writing about preschool television or children's television generally: of assuming without question that the programme has been conceived for and is addressed to *them*. When those sorts of assumptions are held, aesthetic elements such as Tinky-Winky's bag hold interest not because it is a feature that is used creatively in the show (e.g., in episode 16 of series one when he collects items from Tellytubbyland and deposits them magically within the bag), but because it might indicate an effeminacy that could be read – unequivocally by some – as a coded sign of homosexuality. These kinds of responses are now taken somewhat philosophically by the creative team at Ragdoll (who conceived *Teletubbies*), but they can still recall the experience of receiving such astounding criticism. As Chris Wood, Director of Children's Responses at Ragdoll, explains in relation to perceived gay characters in their programmes:

I don't have a problem with any of that. What I have a problem with is them then trying to use their particular views and campaigns on a programme which is designed for two year olds who aren't interested in that. They project all that kind of angst – or whatever – because they feel they want to get at it. A lot of the time they'll put a headline on it, and I think what amazed me about Tubbies is how people got so wound up, and how it got caught up in so many different ways. It's always surprised me. It really starts to open your eyes up to the world that we live in now, and what people are about. [...] One of the things I'm really interested in is how we have difficulty as a culture in dealing with innocence. It's an area I'm really fascinated about. (Wood, 2007)

Wood's comments make reference to a certain propensity for sensationalism and scepticism on the part of the popular media, but they also reinforce the crucial need for critics and commentators to base judgements and evaluations of preschool television on the tone, nature and ambitions of the programmes themselves.

This is a need taken up and carefully handled in a selection of recent writings on preschool television, and in fact on *Teletubbies* specifically. The article by Jacobs already mentioned makes a case for quality and accomplishment in the show, in part as a rejection of the hysteria that had previously been directed at it, both from the popular media and the academy. In her book *Interpreting Television*, Karen Lury assesses in detail the ways in which sound design in the programme facilitates the pedagogical and entertainment ambitions of its creators, Andrew Davenport and Anne Wood (Lury, 2005: 88–94). Through careful analysis, Lury counters claims that *Teletubbies* is inherently nonsensical (an assumption deriving from notions that the Teletubbies themselves babble unintelligible nonsense or that their world is filled with surreal noise) by demonstrating the ways in which its soundscape, particularly, is governed by clear vocal logic and coherent spatial relationships. On these two points she asserts, for example, that:

Knowledge is achieved through close attention, through listening, questioning and then being rewarded with a visual response. This kind of audibly directed narrative is repeated endlessly throughout the programme in various different contexts. The voices and the sound effects in the programme, therefore, are organized carefully to meet with the pedagogical ambitions of the programmes' producers. (Ibid.: 92)

And

> [I]f and when the Tubbies enter the Tubbytronic superdrome and the camera remains on the outside, their voices can often be heard, but are relayed with both a slight muffle and echo effect. This is clearly designed to illustrate the fact that the Teletubbies have gone indoors (hence muffled), but also to remind the viewer of the spacious dimensions of the drome itself (hence the echo). (Ibid.: 93)

Lury's analytical response to this programme performs a key function of critical writing, whereby her own attention to detail helps to tease out and thus disclose the programme-makers' attention to detail (evident here in the audio layering and sound design within the programme). What is also striking in Lury's account of *Teletubbies* is her ability to formulate sophisticated readings of the programme's complex aesthetic structure whilst keeping in focus the preschool audience for which it was intended. In this way, she successfully relates her critical observations to the aims and ambitions of the programme itself, rather than imposing a set of criteria that it would fail to meet. It is this strategy that best serves her contention regarding *Teletubbies* that 'the design and orchestration of the sound effects, silence and music is fundamental to its integrity and success' (ibid.: 94). Integrity and success, for Lury, are themes related inextricably to the child audience that the programme is intended for, rather than abstract notions removed from the viewing experience.

Jonathan Bignell's article 'Familiar aliens: *Teletubbies* and postmodern childhood' charts a perhaps more theoretically biased course as he sets out to argue that '*Teletubbies* casts childhood as both familiar and alien – just as the Teletubbies themselves are – and poses television as a mediator of the uncertain boundaries between adulthood and childhood, familiar and alien, human and inhuman' (Bignell, 2005: 374). Although focussed less upon the actual viewing practices of children, and more upon conceptions of childhood – specifically its analogous relationship to postmodernism and technoculture – many of the article's key assertions are grounded within an appreciation of the programme's aesthetic forms and strategies. So, for example, when discussing the television screens embedded within the Teletubbies' tummies that show 'documentary' footage of real children, Bignell contends that:

> The television screen becomes part of the Teletubbies' skin, so it exists at the border between self and other, inside and out, body and environment. The fabric skin of the Teletubbies becomes a boundary that

both encloses their bodies and opens them into another world, mediating notions of subjectivity, identity and perception by confusing the distinctions between inner and outer, and between the 'this-here' of Teletubbyland and the 'there-then' of a 'real world' of children. Their bellies are windows and screens, bodily and material, but also spaces of virtual projection, 'in' Teletubbyland but linking it with the 'real world,' and thus they pose the viewer's television screen as a boundary surface that is both 'here' for its viewer and opens onto a multiple 'there' of possibility. (Ibid.: 377–8)

Although complex in its formulation of *Teletubbies*' postmodernist traits as exhibited in this collapsing of spatial distinctions, Bignell's assertions derive from an understanding of the programme's inherent structural complexity, as well as its imaginative approach to storytelling for young children. Indeed, he makes a point later in the article of drawing attention to programme co-creator Anne Wood's determination to move away from traditional models of 'instruction as learning' in television and develop a fictional environment, where children are encouraged to find their own logical meanings through imagination (ibid.: 385). In the course of the article, Bignell places his reading of the Teletubbies' tummy screens within a wider understanding of the careful rules and modes of logic that are established in *Teletubbies*, concluding that 'the programme makes rules in order to break them' (384). It becomes clear, therefore, that the more sophisticated claims he makes regarding the programme and conceptions of childhood rely upon a measured understanding and appreciation of its broader themes and structures. In this sense, he presents conclusions based upon a methodological understanding of information offered by the programme itself, thus returning to the site of the text consistently in his arguments, rather than imposing an analytical structure that fits uneasily with the style, form and – perhaps most significantly – the ambitions of the programme.

Each of these accounts of *Teletubbies* performs a crucial role in strengthening the case for a closer consideration of aesthetics in preschool television. In the work of Jacobs, Lury and Bignell, such an enterprise can be seen to reveal a depth, subtlety and complexity in programme-making that belies notions of simplicity, linearity or even banality. Furthermore, such critical interventions inherently possess a greater appreciation of the artistic *work* that goes into the creation of preschool television, presenting an attempt to understand the creative methods and practices at work in the formulation of the television programme. Related to this, at a fundamental level each of the writers pays attention at different stages and with varying emphasis to co-creators Anne Wood and Andrew Davenport, referencing the fact that *Teletubbies* is an authored work, replete with a series of creative intentions and pedagogical ambitions. Although reiterating an apparently straightforward fact, the acknowledgement of this authorship across critical readings contributes to and helps to construct notions of artistic integrity in relation to this particular preschool programme: somebody made it, and made it well. Thus, the style and structure of the show are seen not to simply conform to a set of formats and conventions associated with, and inherently expected from, preschool television, but instead marks a creative intervention from Wood and Davenport. The acknowledgement of authors working within preschool television proposes its relationship to other, more culturally revered, forms of television such as drama, comedy or documentary, where notions of authorship are already well-established and readily made use of by critics. In this way, Ragdoll becomes very much a special case in preschool television, given that reference is very rarely made to the creators of children's television at all. The emphasis on Wood and Davenport in these accounts (and elsewhere in media coverage and interviews) marks them out as authors working within the parameters of preschool television and, as a consequence, elevates Ragdoll's programmes beyond the confines of the ordinary or run-of-the-mill. This reputation was founded to a large extent on the success of *Teletubbies* and, as it has grown and endured, has meant that Ragdoll can take a series of creative and financial decisions not ordinarily available to the creators of preschool content.

Preschool title sequences and storytelling tones

A major challenge facing the critical study of preschool television, then, lies in handling the genre's apparent simplicity of form and perceived directness of narrative delivery. The accounts of *Teletubbies* discussed go some way to challenging this perception, highlighting the complex composition of this particular preschool programme. It is also the case, however, that preschool television can be as richly constructed and carefully planned precisely at the moments when it apparently addresses most directly and its attractions are seemingly most obvious. Title sequences, for example, have traditionally been taken to function as a means of relaying information to a distracted television audience, specifically by announcing the beginning of a programme through image and, crucially, sound. This might be seen as especially true in the case of preschool television, where audio-visual recognition can be seen to function as a direct trigger for audience awareness. In this sense, the evident 'functionality' of these title sequences may lead us to neglect their expressiveness and aesthetic ambitions. However, in a further article including a short study of title sequences from contrasting medical dramas, Jason Jacobs provides grounds for looking beyond their role as straightforward announcements:

> Title sequences have communicative and expressive functions; our judgement of them will not need to spend much time on the former since a basic competent rendering of the show's title and the repetition of its music is likely to be successful in that respect. But in terms of expressive content, judgement is likely to go beyond the acknowledgement of mere functionality. (Jacobs, 2001: 438)

Following such an approach, we may become sensitive to the ways in which title sequences in preschool television can establish a programme's aims and ambitions, as well as defining a set of dramatic and aesthetic boundaries that are continued and expanded upon within the show's main narrative.

Ragdoll's *In The Night Garden*, for example, features a title sequence, created by Andrew Davenport, that expresses a number of the show's narrative themes and stylistic concerns, thus meriting extended description and critical evaluation. We begin with a static shot of a black night sky specked with pinprick dots of effervescent starlight. A glockenspiel note is played on the soundtrack, which coincides with a star shining more brightly than the others for a brief moment. The suggestion is that the star itself produces the musical note, and this effect becomes a pattern as five more notes are played one by one, with five more stars flashing in turn. This six-note stanza becomes an underscore for a gently paced vocal melody, sung by a female voice: 'The night is black and the stars are bright, and the sea is dark and deep...' In combination with these words, the image cross-fades from the starry sky to a young child in bed, watching as an adult traces circles on the palm of their hand with a finger. The soundtrack then evolves again as the female voice hums the melody of the glockenspiel underscore, whilst a male voice is incorporated, speaking evenly and softly: '...But someone I know is safe and snug, and they're drifting off to sleep.' The humming ceases as the male narrator continues: 'Round and round, a little boat no bigger than your hand, out on the ocean far away from land...' The scene dissolves again to be replaced by a little blue character sitting in a small boat with a red sail, surrounded by the dark, deep sea and black night described in the narration. The voice continues 'Take the little sail down. Light the little light. This is the way to the garden in the night', and the audio track incorporates new elements again: the sound of water lapping against the boat and a richer, more complex rendition of the simple glocken-spiel tune played earlier by the stars, with the female voice humming the melody once again.

On screen, the little blue character takes down his red sail and hoists up a light on the boat's mast, which he then switches on, replicating the actions described in the narration directly before. These movements are captured in a style of stop-motion photography that renders the character's gestures into a series of still images, captured and shown in sequence. The move from one still image to the next occurs in time with the downbeat of the musical accompaniment (which now includes an acoustic guitar), synchronising audio and visual elements. The blue character's last action is to lie down and pull the sail over their body, so that it becomes a blanket, and drift in the vessel over the waves into the background. As this movement is completed, the underscore builds both

Illustration 11.1   In the Night Garden (From left to right Upsy Daisy, Makka Pakka, Igglepiggle and the Tombliboos)
Copyright Line: In the Night Garden: In the Night Garden™ and © Ragdoll Worldwide Limited 2007).

in volume and range of instrumentation, incorporating new orchestral elements such as wind instruments, strings and keyboards. In the sky above the boat, stars light up and remain glowing in time with the music. One star, located centrally within the frame, shines brighter than the others with a blue light, pulsating and eventually rising up into the sky, passing on through new stars that light up and open out to become blooming flowers with white petals and stamen of pink, yellow and blue. These flowers fill the screen and, when they dissipate, we find that they have become the blossom of tall trees, and the scene has shifted to a garden in daylight where the little blue character, red blanket in hand, makes his way towards a group of friends gathered in a gazebo (at the top of which sits a blue glowing light, matching the appearance of the star earlier). The camera cranes down to capture this scene, allowing us to glimpse the strange shapes and colours of the assorted characters that await their blue visitor. On the soundtrack we hear their vocal greetings, a collection of words and squeaks mingled with the musical score which has now reduced to an acoustic guitar and glockenspiel. The camera continues its descent, and the view becomes obstructed by a leafy hedge in the foreground of the shot which walls the scene that we have just been watching. The camera's downward motion concludes as it reaches ground level and then, distinct against the green of the hedge, the words 'In the Night Garden' fade up one by one in large white lettering, accompanied by a narrating voice reading them out. Finally, a blue star dots the 'i' of 'Night' and a single glockenspiel note is sounded in conclusion.

Even at the level of description, it becomes clear that a dense range of audio-visual layers and transitions are at work in this 'authored' title sequence, indicating an accomplished degree of technical endeavour and creative ambition on the part of the show's creator, Andrew Davenport. Moreover, the sequence provides an introduction to the programme's themes and concerns that advances it beyond a rudimentary signposting function. The musical stars at the beginning of the sequence introduce an idiosyncratic tone to the fictional world whereby events take place without clear cause and effect or, indeed, motivation. There are no rules of logic that can be applied to certain stars making noises like a glockenspiel and sounding out a tune, but that is not the framework of reason that the moment relies upon. Rather, it seems to draw upon the familiarity of 'Twinkle, Twinkle Little Star', a nursery rhyme itself hinging upon a speculation about stars in the sky, and use that point of reference to develop a notion of what stars could be: musical notes in the sky. The audio-visual pleasure of seeing the stars light up and hearing them chime in sequence is complemented by the satisfying pace of the action, which gently leads the viewer into a fictional world. It is an aesthetically reduced scene, especially in relation to the bright vibrancy of the world of the night garden itself, but it achieves a captivating effect in this simplicity, precisely by reducing down the spectrum of information available. For a programme designed to be watched just before children's bedtimes (Lane, 2007), this opening successfully introduces a mood of settling down, rather than waking up.

The nursery rhyme aspect of the imagery is furthered in the vocal quality of the singing female voice, which joins in with glockenspiel chimes and compliments their rhythmic balance and metre. The introduction of the voice more clearly replicates the practice of adults telling nursery rhymes to children, and this relationship of adult to child is made explicit as we cross-fade to the scene of the finger tracing circles on the child's open palm. Again, familiarity is in play as this scene references the central action of the 'Round and Round the Garden' nursery rhyme, providing a point of potential familiarity for both adult and child viewers, as well as offering a ritual that can be replicated in the home. Crucially, the pace of the circling finger is much slower than would be the case for the nursery rhyme, and the activity does not conclude with the tickling that is a routine final feature of 'Round and Round the Garden'. The tense anticipation of the tickling inherent in the nursery rhyme is thus negated and instead the camera steadily zooms in on the gentle action as it is slowly performed; soothing rather than stimulating. Again, as with the musical stars, there is no clear causal motivation for moving from the night sky to this scene, but neither are the two moments framed in isolation to one another, due in part to the female voice that carries over them both and binds them together. Indeed, the sequence appears to claim an association between the imaginary and the everyday in this transition, linking together a magical night sky with the routine of a parent putting their child to bed. Whilst perhaps not as pronounced as Bignell's claim for *Teletubbies* combining the familiar and the alien, we are reminded here of Ragdoll's particular skill as a production company in negotiating the relationship between the tangible and the illusory. Strikingly, these opening moments seek to blur the lines between real and invented experiences, opening out a halfway world of make-believe where some recognisable features apply – trees, grass and hedges – and some are particular to this world entirely – blue characters that sail to secret gardens and stars that turn into flowers.

A further recognisable bedtime ritual is evoked as the male narrating voice is introduced, (a feature that also pre-echoes a major element in the programme as Sir Derek Jacobi narrates events). In this opening, the male narrator performs the role of the bedtime storyteller, replicating the pace and tone that adults adopt when trying to introduce intrigue without perhaps over-stimulating the recipient. As the words carry over the image of the child's hand, their content does not quite make sense, containing none of the framing logic inherent in familiar opening clauses like 'once upon a time there was...' or 'there once lived...' and so on. To this degree, the convention of standard audio storytelling is withheld as the viewer is encouraged to associate the abstract words 'Round and round, a little boat no bigger than your hand' with the image of the circling motion of the adult's finger on the child's palm. In this sense, then, an acknowledgement is perhaps made to the need for personal invention to drive storytelling in the absence of a framing logic, encouraging the viewer to imaginatively relate voice and image. This process is rewarded emphatically as the scene slowly cross-fades to the little blue character in the boat, taking down the sail and putting up the light.

As described earlier, the stop-motion filming of the blue character reduces its movements to a series of static images. This distinctive style of animation also succeeds in lending the scene a picture-book quality, reminiscent of the books read to small children at bedtime. This feature complements the creative aims and intentions of the programme (relating directly to domestic bedtime rituals) and is furthered in the narrator's style of vocal delivery: slow, soft and tinged with familiarity as the words are spoken (particularly on 'this is the way to the garden in the night') as though this story has been told before and its outcome is reassuringly inevitable, very much like a well-known bedtime tale. Again, we might be aware of the extent to which the sequence draws upon familiar conventions of bedtime routine, but avoids making these connections straightforwardly – by having an onscreen narrator reading a story to a child, for example. Instead, it evokes the everyday procedures of bedtime inventively, blending real world with imagination to create a distinctive and at times abstract fictional space. In all of this, linear cause and effect logic is effectively suspended, so no explanation is offered as to why the blue character should need to take down his sail and use it as a blanket, or put on his little light. Instead, these actions become representative of an idiosyncratic character that in turn is representative of a highly particularised fictional storyworld, replete with its own sets of rules and orders.

This sense of the fictional world's distinctive internal logic is continued as the blue star rises up through the sky, its movement coinciding with the music building to a crescendo. There is no reasonable way to account for the movement of the star, much less the appearance of flower heads bursting open in the sky seconds later. Yet, the title sequence has thus far introduced a narrative pattern whereby events take place without clear motivation or logic, and so these occurrences take their place as part of a fictional world that continuously invents and reinvents itself. Whilst this strategy can be seen as particularly adventurous, given that it risks confusing or disorientating the viewer, it is crucial that the inventive transitions and transformations which take place are handled at a steady and evolving pace, guiding the viewer through a strange world rather than assaulting them with images they can barely comprehend. Further risk is exhibited when, having moved over into the realm of the night garden through the blossoming flowers, the camera offers only a brief glimpse of the blue character making their way towards a group of friends before continuing its descent behind a hedge, masking the scene from view. The decision to show the programme's main characters for only the briefest of moments in the title sequence not only represents a significant degree of confidence on the part of the programme's creator, but also reveals a strong understanding of, and inventive elaboration upon, storytelling conventions. The glimpse into the night garden becomes a tantalising hint of the story that is about to follow, allowing and encouraging viewers to recognise the main players for themselves at a distance rather than directly introducing the characters up close and in full, either by sight or by name. Later we find out that the blue character is Igglepiggle, and that Upsy Daisy and Makka Pakka are part of the waiting group, glimpsed fleetingly. This is certainly a departure from the conventional approach taken by most preschool title sequences whereby characters are explicitly shown and named, a technique employed to various degrees in programmes ranging from *Bob the Builder* to *Balamory*.

In the Night Garden perhaps constitutes an especially inventive use of a title sequence in preschool television, unquestionably displaying high production values (Lane, 2007), and therefore it is reasonable to define it as exceptional. Yet, although it is certainly distinctive in terms of creative ambition, the show's title sequence is representative of the potential depth, range and inventive drive inherent in the production of preschool television, observable even within its most direct and apparently straightforward elements. The case that has been made for artistic quality and achievement in *In the Night Garden* could be applied in vary-ing terms to further examples of title sequences. The animated series *Charlie and Lola* (Tiger Aspect) for example, successfully conveys a sense of its narrative tone and structure within a short opening sequence, embedding the programme's emphasis upon playful imagination and complicity between siblings and friends in each episode. The scope of childhood imagination is conveyed strongly in instances such as Lola's ribbon transforming into a butterfly, Charlie and Lola leaping from planet to planet through a galaxy, or the pair traversing a staircase made of crayon lines and then sliding down the loops and curves of a drinking straw. Through all of this, Charlie and Lola's affectionate alliance is rein-forced as they share these fantasies together: Lola calling Charlie's name excitedly when the ribbon becomes a butterfly, Charlie sketching the stairs that Lola magically runs up, and each hesitating at different points for the other one to match their progress. The pair call each other's name throughout the sequence, an act that perhaps performs a direct function of reinforcing character identity, but also expresses the bond between the characters, and the extent to which these fantasies only matter if they can be shared. These themes are taken up and expanded upon in the episodes themselves as Charlie and Lola negotiate the obstacles of childhood.

The pace and tone of the title sequence for *Charlie and Lola* is far more frenetic, immediate and vibrant than *In the Night Garden* (complemented by an upbeat, lively theme tune), effectively positioning the show's appeal to older preschool viewers as they are perhaps better equipped to comprehend the interchangeable duality of a real world and the characters' imagined world that exists within and forms the dramatic centre of the programme. The gentle establishing tone of *In the Night Garden* is eschewed as *Charlie and Lola* asserts its narrative complexities in energetic fashion. It is also the case, however, that simplicity, restraint and brevity can be employed in preschool title sequences to success-fully express a programme's thematic concerns. *Peppa Pig*'s (Astley Baker Davies) title sequence, for example, consists of nothing more than the central character walking onscreen and announcing 'I'm Peppa Pig' before introducing each of her family: 'This is my little brother George. This is Mummy Pig and this is Daddy Pig.' Each introduction is accom-panied by the character snorting, and underscoring the whole sequence is a fast-paced and uncomplicatedly repetitive musical arrangement. At the end of the introductions, the family laugh together, and their laugh-ter carries over to a title card stating 'Peppa Pig' and featuring Peppa announcing her name once again. Lasting no more than 15 seconds, the ease and simplicity of this sequence matches the tone and structure of the programme itself, which involves straightforward lines of causality focussed around a single narrative theme and locale (a feature complemented aesthetically in its even, 2D style of animation). Peppa's family are most regularly complicit in the progression of the story, although other characters such as various friends are introduced, and a key feature is their ability to resolve situations good-naturedly, often through humour. The short title sequence therefore encapsulates the tonal structure of the programme, emphasising its narrative simplicity and also introducing a strong focus upon family alliances and shared humour. Although certainly not as intricately constructed as *In the Night Garden* or even *Charlie and Lola*'s title sequences, this opening nevertheless represents a series of careful artistic judgements and creative choices that successfully convey *Peppa Pig*'s narrative tone, as well as its horizons of dramatic possibility.

Conclusion

By focusing on the aesthetics of preschool television, this chapter constitutes an attempt to appreciate the depth, subtlety and complexity that underpin the creative practices behind particular preschool productions that are defined by authorship and intense attention to detail. In this respect even a focus on title sequences can open up an aesthetic debate around preschool television that can be profitably expanded upon. The analytical focus here has been intentionally restricted, and in this sense considerable scope still exists for these critical evaluations to be developed and tested in relation to a programme's content in full, tracing some of the creative strategies as they manifest in the work as a whole. Even if the study were to remain concentrated on preschool title sequences alone, however, there are numerous variations available for consideration, taking into account national as well as historical specificity. The potential for these kinds of expansions cannot be explored here, but this chapter has sought to emphasise the level of creative ambition and intellectual achievement inherent in even a small sample of preschool television, highlighting the extent to which a sustained focus upon aesthetic composition can enhance our critical appreciation, thus helping to avoid unfounded assumptions or broad-brush definitions. Although distinct in many ways from other forms of television in terms of aesthetic style and narrative structure, preschool television has the capacity for diverse and richly textured content that results from the pedagogic and artistic dedication of its creators. As an area of critical study, therefore, it provides potent grounds for sustained analysis and evaluation.

Note

1. 'The Production Ecology of Preschool Television', an AHRC-sponsored event hosted by the University of Westminster, 19 January 2007.

12
Conclusions and Future Outlook

This book has attempted to map the historical, institutional and economic contexts that impact the creation of preschool television as well as the interlocking creative, business and regulatory interests which inform its development. This has been achieved through a 'middle ground' (Cottle, 2003a: 4–5) analysis, focused on organisational structures and professional practices, allowing an exploration of the relationships and dynamics that exist within the broader field or ecology of preschool television. This constitutes the environment where those involved in the creation of preschool television content co-operate, compete and interact to determine what is produced, negotiating their competing creative, curricular, institutional and commercial objectives in the process. The complexity of these relationships has involved examining not only how television content for young children is made, but also how it is funded and distributed across different platforms, territories and product categories. It is these complex relationships between broadcasters, producers, distributors, rights-owners, financiers, regulators, advocacy groups and licensed merchandise interests that make up the production ecology of preschool television.

Analysis of the origins of preschool television in Britain and America in Chapter 2 revealed how much has changed from the earliest days as well as the continuities, and those differences which distinguish British and American preschool television today. In both countries there was a strong public service rationale behind early preschool television initiatives in the 1950s and the 1960s. Yet there were clearly different understandings about what television should be achieving for this age group. The BBC concentrated on educating its young audience in the broadest sense in keeping with its public service ethos, an approach which continued even after it lost its monopoly status in 1955, influencing the practices of its regulated commercially funded rivals, ITV and later Five. The crucial difference was that the key 'moment' for American preschool television occurred only after commercial television had become firmly established. From 1969, PBS's, and more especially CTW's, approach with *Sesame Street* was narrower. Unlike British preschool programmes, *Sesame Street* was specifically designed as a tool for raising educational standards and school-readiness by integrating curricular goals, educational advisors and testing into the production process, embedding developmental and educational insight into the production culture of American preschool programming from that point on. *Sesame Street* is also significant as an early indicator of the funding arrangements that would later prevail in preschool television. From the very start CTW could never rely on full funding by PBS, relying instead on an ad-hoc mixture of sponsorship and federal funding, combined with growing proportions of income from international sales (including co-productions) and licensed product revenues.

For many years preschool television provision remained a worthy, but ultimately unrewarding economic activity for commercial interests in both countries, centred on a small number of iconic programmes (*Play School, Sesame Street, Mr Rogers' Neighborhood*) on a small number of broadcasting outlets – the BBC and ITV in Britain and PBS in the US. However, commercial success in the early 1990s of preschool brands like *Barney* on PBS attracted commercial players Nickelodeon and Disney. To enhance the legitimacy of their own preschool undertakings, they adopted and adapted to the educational testing regimes utilised for PBS shows, but also deployed preschool content as the basis for brands to be exploited across different platforms, territories and products. As detailed in Chapter 3, the emergence of preschool children's channels and blocks in the 1990s fragmented audiences and revenues, altering the funding base of preschool television and animation in particular, as producers sought to supplement declining broadcaster license fees with revenues from international pre-sales, co-production, licensed merchandise and on occasion stock market launches. This approach proved ideal for some preschool properties including animation (*Bob the Builder, Dora the Explorer*) and costumed character shows (*Teletubbies*), which could be easily adapted for international audiences, because they were not too culturally specific.

What had begun in the 1950s and 1960s as a public service endeavour, guided by concerns about children's development and well-being, but with little emphasis on commercial value, has now become more of a global enterprise at many different levels, from development and funding through to ancillary exploitation and production, with a growing number of British and American animation productions outsourced to cheaper overseas locations. Television, for the most commercially oriented shows, has become less of a revenue-generator than a promotional vehicle for consumer products, in a business dominated by US transnational corporations, Nickelodeon and Disney, and a second tier of rights-owning producer-distributors (HIT Entertainment, Chorion, Entertainment Rights, DHX Media, Nelvana), with a business strategy focused on the ownership and exploitation of all rights in character-based preschool properties with global potential. It has been this ability of *some* preschool shows to exist beyond broadcast transmission in international sales and licensed merchandise that has sustained the industry in America and Britain, allowing it to expand beyond domestic markets. However, America, which accounts for two-thirds of the global business in licensed goods remains the 'Holy Grail' for most preschool content producers, as reflected in the concerted efforts by some non-US players to satisfy the curricular demands of US channels.

Broadcast distribution on a major outlet remains key, particularly in the US, even if broadcasters invest only small amounts in originations. In the British market, for example, access to a broadcast platform like CBeebies or Five's Milkshake! block is the starting point for raising funding in other markets and generating ancillary revenues (see Chapter 4). However, the number of new broadcast commissions is small, and the global dimension of funding favours narrative animation over more culturally specific presenter-led shows, which tend to be confined to public service outlets like CBeebies or PBS, who are obliged to satisfy a broader range of programming than their commercial rivals.

The shift from local endeavour to global enterprise represents one dimension of preschool television production. Yet, as we saw in Chapters 6, 7, 8 and 11, productions are also an outcome of programme-makers' conceptions of their audience, their own creative ambitions, aesthetic judgements and ability to innovate utilising new techniques and technology. In spite of industry consolidation and the market power of the US corporations and larger rights-owning producers, the industry is still reliant on the creative input of individuals with specialist expertise in writing, animation, directing, performing, production management and marketing. These individuals have their own theories about what works, based variously on their own beliefs, their experience of what has worked before and their knowledge of child development, pedagogical goals and recourse to different types of research, which might inform them about what children actually enjoy as well as what is developmentally appropriate. Depending on the production culture of each production entity, concepts will also be adapted to meet the demands and constraints related to funding, resources and corporate objectives in other areas – such as international markets or ancillary products.

Where British and American preschool programme-makers have differed markedly is in their approach to research, with the US placing much more emphasis on the formal integration and testing of educational goals and the use of educational advisors. The commercial importance of the US combined with concerns about the impact of programming on children suggests that some British programme-makers are moving closer to the US testing model as much for marketing as for curricular purposes. This convergence between America and Britain is also evident in the realm of regulation and policy (Chapter 10) as the British children's television community comes to terms with a more deregulated environment that has more in common with the US experience of limited regulatory intervention rather than the all-encompassing public service framework, which had, until, 2003, also applied to commercially funded terrestrial broadcasting (ITV1, Five) as well as the BBC.

Alongside deregulatory pressures, there are also commercial pressures. Although many preschool television programme-makers are strongly committed to their young audiences, they also have to operate within the economic constraints and market dynamics that define the sector as a whole. As we learnt in Chapter 9, preschool television is no longer just television, but a platform for other products, attracting players who regard it as a potentially extremely profitable business for investors and shareholders. Even if the number of globally successful preschool shows is limited to a handful of properties jostling for shelf space in a crowded retail market, licensing considerations *do* influence programme content, favouring character-based animation. Among producers, however, there are a variety of responses to these pressures, ranging from the integrated strategies pursued by global corporations and IP-owning producer-distributors to the more varied responses of producers who prioritise commercial, creative or educational concerns depending on their internal production culture and the specific demands of each individual production.

Future outlook

Of course the preschool television market constitutes only one part of the children's media market, and an even smaller part of the wider television marketplace. Nevertheless the sector's evolving creative and business responses to channel proliferation, audience fragmentation, declining budgets and digital developments reveal how production cultures change over time in order to accommodate the demands of a more competitive and globalised production environment. In this sense the preschool television sector can be viewed as a microcosm for the production and funding issues facing television production generally.

By 2009, the preschool children's television market in Britain and America was saturated with content, and children's television production as a whole was dealing with the funding crisis afflicting television in general. This has forced producers of all types of children's programmes to think about new funding models and new approaches to content.

One response is focused on multiplatform content, where even the very youngest children, according to CBeebies Controller, Michael Carrington, are 'proactively recording, downloading and sampling content' requiring broadcasters to reach out to them in different ways 'through online, mobile and TV experiences' (cited in CBeebies, 2006). Larger producer-distributors who need to generate revenues from a number of sources 'are certainly looking at download, Web content, what can be downloaded to a PSP or a handheld' during development and are investing heavily in their own brand-based Web sites to drive sales in other areas. According to one Head of International Sales at a leading British children's television distributor, 'There is not a single production that we do that doesn't absolutely look at a 360 degree environment [...] The 2.0 Web experience is exactly where we're going.' Even smaller producers are thinking about programming as 'a concept, an idea that kids can follow wherever they're going' rather than simply as a television project.

For broadcasters, producers and rights-owners alike digital media signal both opportunities and challenges as they look to exploit digital media platforms (the Internet, gaming, mobile applications, video-on-demand) to bridge funding shortfalls and appeal to the 'digital natives' of the future. Among some producers there are hopes of reducing the dominance of broadcasters, because as one remarked 'it makes much more sense to go straight to the consumer'. Some, particularly in the US, are adopting a multiplatform approach making their programming available online as streamed content (KOL Jr) as well as on digital cable where programming is accessible in traditional linear form as well as on demand and online within a suite of content (Grant, 2007a, b; Waller, 2007, 2008). However, US multiplatform destinations like Qubo, PBS Kids Sprout and Kabillion Junior do not yet match the broadcast audience levels achieved by Nick Jr., PBS and Playhouse Disney, who operate their own Web sites, and are the bedrock of the licensing business.

It is true that younger children are now drawn to a wider range of media activities than just television (Marsh et al., 2005; Rideout and Hamel, 2006; Rideout et al., 2003). However, while older children are proving skilful users of online, mobile and interactive services (BBC Trust, 2009; Livingstone and Bober, 2005; Ofcom, 2007a), the industry's approach to preschool children is more concentrated on parents/carers, because younger children are less adept at using new technologies. Clearly children under six are less likely to be expressing their personality through social networking (Facebook, MySpace), file sharing (YouTube) or mobile applications. Also, most children's sites, including virtual worlds such as Disney's *Club Penguin*, the BBC's *Adventure Rock*, Viacom's *Neopets* and Sulake's *Habbo Hotel* are targeted at the over-sixes. Nevertheless the under-sixes are 'immersed' (Rideout et al., 2003: 4) in media practices and new technologies almost from birth. A 2005 British survey revealed that 53 per cent of 0- to 6-year olds used a computer daily (Marsh et al., 2005: 37), and that the most-visited Web sites were television channel (CBeebies, Nick Jr., Disney) or programme-related (*Bob the Builder, Teletubbies, Thomas the Tank Engine*). Only 5 per cent of preschool children accessed a Web site independently, but it was their interests that drove use, usually stimulated by the television programmes they had seen (ibid.). A similar US survey established that 43 per cent of under-sixes had used a computer and 29 per cent had played console games (Rideout and Hamel, 2006: 7), although the percentage of those who watched television on a typical day (75 per cent) far exceeded the percentage of those who used a computer (16 per cent) (p. 7).

However, multiplatform distribution demands different business models, models which few players have yet managed to fathom. So far producer and broadcaster revenues from digital media and video-on-demand have been largely insignificant, with online representing an additional cost for most (C21, 2007; Ofcom, 2007a: 146; Oliver and Ohlbaum, 2007: 33) and a potential threat to other revenue streams such as DVDs (Curtis, 2006b; Steemers, 2010b). Commercially funded broadcasters (but not usually publicly funded broadcasters) and producers with Web sites can generate revenues from advertising, sponsorship, site subscriptions (e.g. *Toggolino* run by SuperRTL in Germany; *MyNOGGIN* in the United States), the sale of merchandise and participation in partner sales, which occur as a result of being redirected from a partner site (Chan-Olmsted and Ha, 2003: 601–2). Rights-owners who license content to third party Web or video-on-demand services can benefit from advertising and/or subscription revenue. For the time being, however, in the preschool sector online revenues are dwarfed by revenues generated from licensed products, DVD sales and even broadcast sales. Furthermore, parents are unlikely to pay extra for preschool content when they can access so much for free either on television or online – including television channel Web sites that offer video clips, games, online activities (printables, music, make and do suggestions), parental advice (Steemers, 2010b) and even complete episodes online – either as a promotional tool (e.g. new episodes of *Roary the Racing Car* on Nick Jr. UK) or on demand (e.g. through the online CBeebies iPlayer, which allows viewers to watch programmes seven days after broadcast transmission).

For the most part, online and multiplatform considerations are growing in importance, but are still secondary in the preschool commissioning process, with television executives, not surprisingly, placing greater priority on the linear stories, scripts and distinctive characters that they think will attract young audiences. As Nick Wilson, Director of Children's Television at Five (2006), remarked,

> I think that anybody who lets their content be dominated by what they're going to put on the web is going to come to a sticky end because I still think content is absolutely king. You've got to get your stories and your scripts and your characters right. It doesn't matter how you deliver them, if they don't work, they won't work.

This does not mean that Web considerations do not play a role. The approach is more stripped down than content aimed at older children, and it is assumed that children are accessing sites together with their parents in a 'lap top' situation, much as it used to be assumed that young children watched television with their mothers (Turner-Laing, 2007). At CBeebies, which together with CBBC had access to a substantial online and interactive content budget of £6.1m in 2007–08 (BBC Trust, 2009: 49), producers are encouraged to think about online offerings and enhanced interactive television as part of a more 'joined-up' commissioning process (Carrington 2007a; also Grant, 2007a). For example, on RDF's live action-animation hybrid *Waybuloo*, it was reported that CBeebies would be investing 'hundreds of thousands of pounds' into the online 'immersive' world of Nara, produced by RDF, which would allow children to interact directly with the animated Pipling characters online (Rushton, 2009b: 14).

However, while older children are migrating to online activities, for younger children, television programmes, DVDs and products (primarily toys), associated with television shows, still constitute the mainstay of their engagement with preschool content and the foundation of the business. For the time being, television remains the quickest and the most effective way of creating awareness among preschool children whose media consumption is still dominated by television (Ofcom, 2007a). Online platforms do offer a complementary, second-level alternative distribution and outlet to broadcasting and a useful way of piloting and promoting new content, but they do not yet provide a funding model to support the production of high quality new programming.

Current developments suggest that television will continue to be the main driver behind the commercial exploitation of preschool television even if it is no longer a key source of funding. Trusted brands (Disney, BBC, Nickelodeon) will continue to function as the dominant players because they have the financial resources, parental trust and know-how to repurpose, distribute and crucially promote content on multiple platforms in support of their wider commercial or public service objectives. In this emerging multiplatform world, there is still plenty of creativity within preschool content creation, but the main issues, as they have always been, are how to make production work as a sustainable business without sacrificing the plurality of supply that underpins the creativity, care and innovation of the best preschool television.

Bibliography

Akbar, A. and M. Carter (2007) 'Dougal, Emu and Mr Strong to the Rescue', *The Independent*, 10 December, p. 11.

Alexander, A. (2001) 'Broadcast Networks and the Children's Television Business', in D. and J. Singer (eds) *Handbook of Children and the Media* (London: Sage), pp. 495–505.

Alexander, A. and J. Owers (2007) 'The Economics of Children's Television', in J. Bryant (ed.) *The Children's Television Community* (Mahwah: Lawrence Erlbaum), pp. 35–56.

Allen, J. (2001) 'The Economic Structure of the Commercial Electronic Children's Media Industries', in D. Singer and J. Singer (eds) *Handbook of Children and the Media* (London: Sage), pp. 477–94.

Alvarado, M. and E. Buscombe (1978) *Hazell: The Making of a Television Series* (London: BFI).

American Academy of Pediatrics Committee on Public Education (1999) 'Media Education', *Pediatrics*, 104 (2), 341–3.

Anderson, D. (2004) 'Watching Children Watch Television and the Creation of Blue's Clues', in H. Hendershot (ed.) *Nickelodeon Nation* (New York/London: New York University Press), pp. 241–68.

Anderson, D. and T. Pempek (2005) 'Television and Very Young Children', *American Behavioral Scientist*, 48 (5), 505–22.

Andrews, S. (2006) ITV Digital Channels Programme Director. Intervention during the BAFTA Children's Committee Public Debate, 13 September.

Ariès, P. (1962) *Centuries of Childhood* (New York: Knopf).

Atkinson, J. (1984) 'Manpower Strategies for Flexible Organisations', *Personnel Management*, August, 18–31.

Atwal, K., A. Millward-Hargrave, et al. (2003) *What Children Watch. An Analysis of Children's Programming Provision between 1997–2001 and Children's Views* (London: Broadcasting Standards Commission/Independent Television Commission).

Banet-Weiser, S. (2007) *Kids Rule! Nickelodeon and Consumer Citizenship* (Durham/London: Duke University Press).

Banham, Annette (2007) (Marketing Director Children's, BBC Worldwide), Interview, London, 14 June.

Barlow, Joanne (2007) (Vice President Marketing and PR, Cartoon Network), Interview, London, 25 June.

Barnatt, C. and K. Starkey (1994) 'The Emergence of Flexible Networks in the UK Television Industry', *British Journal of Management*, 5, 251–60.

Barr, R. (2008) 'Attention and Learning from Media during Infancy and Early Childhood', in S. Calvert, and B. Wilson (eds) *The Handbook of Children, Media, and Development* (Oxford: Blackwell), pp. 143–65.

Bazalgette, C. and D. Buckingham (1995) (eds) *In Front of the Children* (London: BFI).

BBC (2001) *Proposed New Services from the BBC. Annex 2*, <http://www.culture.gov.uk/reference_library/publications/4626.aspx>. Accessed 7 March 2009.

—— (2007) *BBC Response to 'The Future of Children's Television Programming'*, <http://www.ofcom.org.uk/consult/condocs/kidstv/responses/BBC.pdf>. Accessed 1 June 2009.

—— (2008a) *BBC Statements of Programme Policy 2008/2009*, <http://www.bbc.co.uk/info/statements2008/>. Accessed 4 May 2009.

—— (2008b) *BBC Executive Submission to the BBC Trust's Review of Services for Children Aged 12 and under*, <http://www.bbc.co.uk/bbctrust/framework/bbc_service_licences/childrens_evidence.html>. Accessed 9 March 2009.

—— (2009) *TV Show for Toddlers' Emotions*, 19 May, <http://news.bbc.co.uk/1/hi/entertainment/8056824.htm>. Accessed 26 May 2009.

BBC Trust (2008a) *CBeebies Service Licence*, 7 April, <http://www.bbc.co.uk/bbctrust/framework/bbc_service_licences/tv.html>. Accessed 27 February 2009.

—— (2008b) *BBC Response to Ofcom's Second Public Service Broadcasting, Review, Phase 1*, <http://www.ofcom.org.uk/consult/condocs/psb2_1/responses/>. Accessed 1 June 2009.

—— (2009) *Service Review. Review of BBC Children's Services and Content*, <http://www.bbc.co.uk/bbctrust/framework/bbc_service_licences/childrens.html#part-1>. Accessed 4 March 2009.

BBC Worldwide (2002a) *The ITC Review of the Programme Supply Market in British Broadcasting. (Submission to ITC Review)* (London: BBC Worldwide).

—— (2002b) *Annual Review 2001/2002*, <http://www.bbcworldwide.com/annualreviews/review2002/default.htm>. Accessed 5 March 2009.

—— (2003) *"Walking with..." Brand is Monster Hit for BBC Worldwide*, BBC Worldwide Press Release, 15 July, <http://www.bbc.co.uk/pressoffice/bbcworldwide/worldwidestories/pressreleases/2003/07_july/walking_with_brand.shtml>. Accessed 5 March 2009.

—— (2007) *Annual Review 2006/07*, <http://www.bbcworldwide.com/annualreviews/review2007/default.htm>. Accessed 5 March 2009.

—— (2008) *Annual Review 2007/08*, <http://www.bbcworldwide.com/annualreviews/review2008/>. Accessed 5 March 2009.

—— (2009) *BBC Worldwide Limited. Annual Report and Financial Statements for the Year Ended 31 March 2009 (1420028)*. London: BBC Worldwide.

Beatty, Sally (2002) 'Couch Tater Tots. In Battle for Toddlers TV Networks Tout Educational Benefits', *Wall Street Journal*, 1 April, p. A1.

Becker, H. (1982) *Art Worlds* (Berkeley/Los Angeles: University of California Press).

Bennett, J. (2007) *The Future of Children's Media*. Keynote speech by Director BBC Vision to the Showcomotion Children's Media Conference, Sheffield, UK, 5 July.

Berry, G. and J. Asamen (eds) (1993) *Children and Television* (London: Sage).

Bickham, D., J. Wright and A. Huston (2001) 'Attention, Comprehension, and the Educational Influences of Television', in D. Singer and J. Singer (eds) *Handbook of Children and the Media* (London: Sage), pp. 101–20.

Bignell, J. (2005) 'Familiar Aliens: *Teletubbies* and Postmodern Childhood', *Screen*, 46 (3), Autumn, 373–87.

BIS (Department for Business, Innovation and Skills) and DCMS (Department for Culture, Media and Sport) (2009) *Digital Britain – Final Report: Building's Britain Future*, June 2009, <http://www.culture.gov.uk/what_we_do/broadcasting/6216.aspx>. Accessed 29 June 2009.

Blumler, J. (1992) *The Future of Children's Television in Britain*. Research Working Paper VIII (London: Broadcasting Standards Council).

—— (1993) 'Meshing Money with Mission: Purity versus Pragmatism in Public Broadcasting', *European Journal of Communication*, 8 (4), 403–24.

Bourdieu, P. (1993) *The Field of Cultural Production* (Oxford: Polity Press).

Broadcast (1989) 'Children's Programming Lobby Prepares for Battle', 10 March 1989, 2.

—— (2001a) 'Link sold for £15m', 30 March, 3.

—— (2001b) 'Pat has new home', 9 November, 3.

—— (2004a) 'Chorion deal sends Noddy on global mission', 8 October, 10.

—— (2004b) 'Postman Pat teams up with He Man', 26 March, <http://www.broadcastnow.co.uk/news/terrestrial/2004/03/postman_pat_teams_up_with_he_man.html>. Accessed 17 May 2009.

—— (2004c) 'Entertainment Rights buys out Tell-Tale', 17 September, 5.

—— (2009) 'The Annual Survey of the UK's Independent TV Producers', *Broadcast*, Supplement, 20 March.

Brogan, Anne (2007) (Director, Kindle Entertainment), Interview, London, 27 March.

—— (2008) Presentation at the *Making Television for Young Children* Conference, University of Westminster, 12 September.

Brooks, G. (2007) 'Hot Animation makes cuts', *Broadcast*, 14 September, <http://www.broadcastnow.co.uk/news/hot_animation_makes_job_cuts.html>. Accessed 7 April 2008.

Brown, Laura (2007) (Director of Research and Curriculum, Little Airplane Productions), Interview, New York, 2 August.

—— (2008a) Telephone Interview, 21 May.

—— (2009) Email communication, 22 February.

Brown, M. (2009) 'Children's TV Campaigners Attack Ofcom PSB Report', *MediaGuardian*, 21 January, <http://www.guardian.co.uk/media/2009/jan/21/childrens-tv-campaigners-attack-ofcom-psb-report>. Accessed 5 June 2009.

Brown, W. (2002) 'Ethics and the *Business* of Children's Public Television Programming', *Teaching Business Ethics*, 6 (1), 73–81.

Bryant, J.A. (ed.) (2007a) *The Children's Television Community* (Mahwah: Lawrence Erlbaum).

—— (2007b) 'Understanding the Children's Television Community from an Organizational Network Perspective', in J.A. Bryant (ed.) *The Children's Television Community* (Mahwah: Lawrence Erlbaum), pp. 35–55.

Bryant, J. and D. Anderson (eds) (1983) *Children's Understanding of Television* (New York: Academic Press).

BTDA (British Television Distributors Association) (2005) *Rights of Passage: British Television in the Global Market* (London: Television Research Partnership).

Buckingham, D. (1993) *Children Talking Television* (Brighton: The Falmer Press).

—— (1995a) 'On the Impossibility of Children's Television', in C. Bazalgette and D. Buckingham (eds) *In Front of the Children* (London: BFI), pp. 47–61.

—— (1995b) 'The Commercialisation of Childhood? The Place of the Market in Children's Media Culture', *Changing English*, 2 (2), 17–40.

—— (2000) *After the Death of Childhood* (Cambridge: Polity Press).
—— (2002) 'Child-Centred Television? *Teletubbies* and the Educational imperative', in D. Buckingham (ed.) *Small Screens* (Leicester: Leicester University Press), pp. 38–60.
—— (2005) 'A Special Audience? Children and Television', in J. Wasko (ed.) *A Companion to Television* (London: Blackwell), pp. 468–86.
—— (2007a) 'Selling Childhood? Children and Consumer Culture', *Journal of Children and the Media*, 1 (1), 15–24.
—— (2007b) *Beyond Technology. Children's Learning in the Age of Digital Culture* (Cambridge: Polity).
Buckingham, D., H. Davies, K. Jones and P. Kelley (1999), *Children's Television in Britain* (London: BFI).
Burns, M. (2005) 'Animation's Digital Revolution', *Broadcast*, 25 February, 24–5.
—— (2008) 'Animate Innovate', *Broadcast*, 20 March, 26–7.
Buxton M. (2008) 'New Look for Bob the Builder', *C21Media.net*, 9 June, <http://www.c21media.net/news/detail.asp?area=4&article=42275>. Accessed 18 May 2009.
C21 (2007) 'The Pitfalls of Pitching Cross-Platform', *C21 Media.net*, 9 October <http://www.c21media.net/features/detail.asp?area=2&article=37953>. Accessed 29 June 2009.
—— (2008) 'Fifi Creator Sets up Studio', *C21media.net*, 5 June, <http://www.c21media.net/resources/detail.asp?area=79&article=42215>. Accessed 18 May 2009.
Cahn, A., T. Kalagian and C. Lyon (2008) 'Business Models for Children's Media', in S. Calvert and B. Wilson (eds) *The Handbook of Children, Media and Development* (Oxford: Blackwell), pp. 27–48.
Calder, K. (2008a) 'Nighty night! – Kidcasters shaping evening schedules to reflect preschool bedtime rituals', *KidScreen*, 1 April, <http://www.kidscreen.com/articles/magazine/20080401/night.html>. Accessed 6 March 2009.
—— (2008b) 'The Art of Reversioning', *KidScreen*, 1 October, <http://www.kidscreen.com/articles/magazine/20081001/reversioning.html>. Accessed 6 March 2009.
—— (2008c) 'Don't Speak', *KidScreen*, 1 October <http://www.kidscreen.com/articles/magazine/20081001/timmy.html>. Accessed 6 March 2009.
—— (2008d) 'Noddy 60 Years Young', *KidScreen*, 1 September, <http://www.kidscreen.com/articles/magazine/20080901/noddy.html>. Accessed 6 March 2009.
Caldwell, J. (1995) *Televisuality* (New Brunswick: Rutgers University Press).
—— (2004) 'Convergence Television: Aggregating From and Repurposing Content in the Culture of Conglomeration', in L. Spigel and J. Olsson (eds) *Television after TV* (Durham/London: Duke University Press), pp. 41–74.
—— (2008) *Production Culture* (Durham/London: Duke University Press).
Calvert, S. (2008) 'The Children's Television Act', in S. Calvert and B. Wilson (eds) *The Handbook of Children, Media and Development* (London: Blackwell), pp. 455–79.
Caminada, Charles (2001) (Chief Operating Officer, HIT Entertainment), Interview, London, 4 June 2001.
Canadian Heritage (2009) Canadian Audio-Visual Certification Office (CAVCO), <http://www.pch.gc.ca/cavco/>. Accessed 1 March 2009.

Cantor, M. (1975) 'Producing Television for Children', in G. Tuchman (ed.) *The TV Establishment* (Englewood: Prentice-Hall), pp. 103–18.

Cantor, M and J. Cantor (1986) 'American Television in the International Marketplace', *Communication Research*, 13 (3), 509–20.

Cardwell, S. (2006) 'Patterns, Layers and Values: Poliakoff's *The Last Prince*', *Journal of British Cinema and Television*, 3 (1), 134–41.

Carrington, Michael (2007a) (Controller, CBeebies) Interview, London, 6 March.

—— (2007b) 'Thinking BIG for little people', *Televizion*, 20, 48–9.

—— (2009) *CBeebies Rolling Commissioning Move – Q&A with Michael Carrington*, 28 January, <http://www.bbc.co.uk/commissioning/tv/network/genres/cbeebies.shtml>. Accessed 27 February 2009.

Carter, B. (1992) 'Conservatives Call for PBS to go Private or Dark', *New York Times*, 30 April, <http://www.nytimes.com/1992/04/30/news/conservatives-call-for-pbs-to-go-private-or-go-dark.html>. Accessed 5 May 2009.

—— (1994) 'A Cable Challenger for PBS as King of the Preschool Hill', *New York Times*, 21 March, A1, <http://www.nytimes.com/1994/03/21/business/a-cable-challenger-for-pbs-as-king-of-the-preschool-hill.html?scp=1&sq=%22A%20Cable%20Challenger%20for%20PBS%22&st=cse>. Accessed 5 May 2009.

Carter, M. (2004) 'Good deal for good ideas', *Financial Times*, 22 March.

—— (2005) 'Bob the Builder's gaffer prepares to unleash Fifi on world's tots', *The Guardian*, 28 April, 23.

Carugati, A. (2006) 'Sesame Workshop's Knell', January, *WorldScreen*, <http://www.worldscreen.com/archives/register/7564>. Accessed 1 July 2008.

—— (2007) 'Interview with David Weiland', October, *WorldScreen*, <http://www.worldscreen.com/archives/register/14873>. Accessed 1 July 2008.

Casey, B., N. Casey, B. Calvert, L. French, and J. Lewis (2002) *Television Studies. The Key Concepts* (London: Routledge).

Cassy, J. (2000) 'City tunes in to children's TV', *The Guardian*, 5 February, <http://www.guardian.co.uk/business/2000/feb/05/6>. Accessed 16 February 2009.

Castleman, L. (2009a) 'Q&A: Caminada charts startup's next moves', *KidScreen*, 27 March, <http://www.kidscreen.com/articles/magazine/20090327/qa.html>. Accessed 18 May 2009.

—— (2009b) 'Q&A: Murphy touts Corus Kids as global partner', *KidScreen*, 17 February, <http://www.kidscreen.com/articles/magazine/20090217/qa.html>. Accessed 17 March 2009.

Caves, R. (2000) *Creative Industries* (Cambridge, Ma./London: Harvard University Press).

CBeebies (2006) *BBC Children's Webchat for Independent Producers*, 24 May, <http://www.bbc.co.uk/commissioning/tv/network/chat_after.shtml>. Accessed 6 March 2009.

—— (2007) *CBeebies Programme Opportunities*, <http://www.bbc.co.uk/commissioning/tv/network/genres/cbeebies>. Accessed 3 March 2007.

—— (2009) *CBeebies Commissioning Briefs 2009 – Final*, 28 January, <http://www.bbc.co.uk/commissioning/tv/network/genres/cbeebies.shtml>. Accessed 27 February 2009.

Cederborg, Annika (2002) (Acquisitions Executive, Children and Youth, SVT), Interview, Stockholm, 22 April.

Channel 4 (2008a) *Next on 4*, March 2008, <http://www.channel4.com/about4/fullreport.html>. Accessed 3 June 2008.

——— (2008b) *Channel 4's Response to Phase 2 of the Second Ofcom PSB Review*, December, <http://www.ofcom.org.uk/consult/condocs/psb2_phase2/responses/Channel4.pdf>. Accessed 9 June 2009.

Chapman, K. (2006) 'Creating the Perfect Children's Property to Capture a Bigger Audience', Panel Discussion, 21 March 2006, *The Kids' TV Forum Conference*, London.

Chapman K. and G. Lynn (2006) 'Commercial Imperatives', *c21Media.net*, 18 September, <http://www.c21media.net/features/detail.asp?area=2&article=32185>. Accessed 1 June 2009.

Chan-Olmsted, S. and L. Ha (2003) 'Internet Business Models for Broadcasters: How Television Stations Perceive and Integrate the Internet,' *Broadcasting and Electronic Media*, 47 (4), 597–617.

Childs, Greg (2007) (Secretary, Save Kids TV), Interview, London, 14 November.

Chorion PLC (2004) *Annual Report and Accounts* (London: Chorion PLC).

Christakis, D., F. Zimmerman, D. DiGuiseppe and C. McCarty (2004) 'Early Television Exposure and Subsequent Attentional Problems in Children', *Pediatrics*, 113 (4), 708–13.

Christie, J. (2008a) 'Q&A: Jeffrey Dunn plots HIT's course for the next five years', 1 October, <http://www.kidscreen.com/articles/magazine/20081001/qa.html>. Accessed 18 May 2009.

——— (2008b) 'Chorion's renaissance man, Waheed Alli', 1 February, *KidScreen*, <http://www.kidscreen.com/articles/magazine/20080201/chorion2.html>. Accessed 15 March 2009.

Clark, E. (2007) *Inside the Real Toy Story* (London: Black Swan).

Cohen, M. (2001) 'The Role of Research in Educational Television', in D. Singer and J. Singer (eds) *Handbook of Children and the Media* (London: Sage), pp. 571–88.

Cole, A. (2007) 'Distant Neighbours: The New Geography of Animated Film Production in Europe', *Regional Studies*, 42 (6), 891–904.

Cole, C., B. Richman and S. McCann-Brown (2001) 'The World of *Sesame Street* Research', in S. Fisch and R. Truglio (eds) *"G" is for Growing* (Mahwah: Lawrence Erlbaum), pp. 147–80.

Communications Act (2003), Chapter 21, <http://www.legislation.hmso.gov.uk/acts/acts2003/20030021.htm>. Accessed 1 March 2009.

Comstock, G. and E. Scharrer (2007) *Media and the American Child* (Amsterdam: Academic Press).

Contender Entertainment Group (2007) *Directors' Report and Financial Statements*.

Coolman, Victor (2008) (Buyer and Programmer, Nickelodeon, Netherlands), Telephone Interview, 2 June.

Copley, Andi (2007) (Managing Director/Executive Producer, HOT Studios), Interview, Manchester, 9 May.

Corner, J. (1999) *Critical Ideas in Television Studies* (Oxford: Oxford University Press).

——— (2007) 'Television Studies and the Idea of Criticism', *Screen*, 48 (3), 363–9.

Corn-Revere, R. (1997) 'Regulation in Newspeak: The FCC Children's Television Rules', *Cato Policy Analysis*, No. 268, The Cato Institute, 19 February,

<http://www.cato.org/pubs/pas/pa-268es.html>. Accessed 10 December 2008.

Cosgrove Hall (2007) *Directors' Report and Financial Statements for the Year ended 31 December 2007*.

Cottle, S. (1995) 'Producer-Driven Television', *Media, Culture and Society*, 17 (1), 159–66.

—— (1997) *Television and Ethnic Minorities* (Aldershot: Avebury).

—— (2003a) 'Media Organisation and Production: Mapping the Field', in S. Cottle (ed.) *Media Organization and Production* (Sage: London), pp. 3–24.

—— (2003b) 'Producing Nature(s): The Changing Production Ecology of Natural History TV', in S. Cottle (ed.) *Media Organization and Production* (Sage: London), pp. 170–87.

—— (2004) 'Producing Nature(s). On the Changing Production Ecology of Natural History TV', *Media, Culture and Society*, 26 (1), 81–101.

Cowling, J. and K. Lee (2002) 'They Have Been Watching: Children's TV 1952–2002', 30 August 2002, <http://www.ippr.org.uk/uploadedFiles/projects/kidstv.pdf>. Accessed 5 March 2009.

CPBF (The Campaign for Press and Broadcasting Freedom) (2007) *Response to Ofcom's Document 'The Future of Children's Television Programming'*, <http://www.ofcom.org.uk/consult/condocs/kidstv/responses/>. Accessed 1 January 2009.

Crawley, A., D. Anderson, A. Wilder, M. Williams and A. Santomero (1999) 'Effects of Repeated Exposures to a Single Episode of the Television Program *Blue's Clues* on the Viewing Behaviours and Comprehension of Preschool Children', *Journal of Educational Psychology*, 91, 630–7.

Croteau, D. and W. Hoynes (2003) *Media/Society, 3rd edn* (Thousand Oaks/London/New Delhi: Pine Forge Press).

Cunningham, S. and E. Jacka (1996) *Australian Television and International Media-scapes* (Cambridge: Cambridge University Press).

Curtis, J. (2006a) 'Trouble in the Playground', *C21Media.net*, 21 April, <http://www.c21media.net/features/detail.asp?area=2&article=30061>. Accessed 14 May 2009.

—— (2006b) 'Get Shorty,' *C21Media.net*, June 30, <http://www.c21media.net/common/print_detail.asp?article=31096>. Accessed 29 June 2009.

Davenport, Andrew (2008) (Creative Director, Ragdoll Productions), Interview, Stratford-upon-Avon, 14 July.

Davies, H., D. Buckingham and P. Kelley (2004) 'In the Worst Possible Taste. Children, Television and Cultural Value', in R. Allen and A. Hill (eds) *The Television Studies Reader* (London: Routledge), pp. 479–93.

Davies, Phil (2007) (Producer, Astley Baker Davies), Interview, London, 25 October.

Davis, Merion (2008) (Head of Content, S4C), Interview, Cardiff, 26 February.

Davis, H. and R. Scase (2000) *Managing Creativity* (Buckingham/Philadelphia: Open University Press).

DCMS (Department of Culture, Media and Sport) (1999) *The Report of the Creative Industries Task Force Inquiry into UK Television Exports* (London: DCMS).

—— (2001) *BBC New Digital services: Schedule of Decisions: 13 September*, <www.culture.gov.uk/PDF/bbc_digital_schedule.pdf>. Accessed 9 March 2009.

—— (2003) *Code on the Advertising of Food Products to Children*, 1 December, <http://www.culture.gov.uk/images/publications/LettertoDavidCurrie.pdf>. Accessed 1 June 2009.

—— (2004) *Independent Review of the BBC's Digital Television Services*, <http://www.culture.gov.uk/reference_library/publications/4594.aspx>. Accessed 5 March 2009.

Deakin, S. and S. Pratten (2000) 'Quasi Markets, Transaction Costs, and Trust: The Uncertain Effects of Market Reforms in British Television Production', *Television & New Media*, 1 (3): 321–54.

Deans, J. (2006) 'ITV1 Must Keep Kids' Programming', *MediaGuardian*, 25 September, <http://www.guardian.co.uk/media/2006/sep/25/broadcasting. ITV>. Accessed 1 June 2009.

Debertin, Sebastian (2008) (Head of Fiction/Acquisitions and Co-productions, Kinderkanal/Ki.Ka, Germany), Email Communication, 13 June.

Delphis Films (2008) *Pim and Pom Q&A*, <www.delphisfilms.com/images/mail/images/presskit_pim_pom-eng.doc>. Accessed 1 March 2009.

Department of Health (2004) '*Choosing Health:* Making Healthy Choices Easier', CM 6374, 16 November, <http://www.dh.gov.uk/PublicationsAndStatistics/Publications/PublicationsPolicyAndGuidance/PublicationsPolicyAndGuidance Article/fs/en?CONTENT_ID=4094559&chk=H29Li6.>. Accessed 1 June 2009.

Dex, S., J. Willis, R. Paterson, E. Sheppard (2000) 'Freelance Workers and Contract Uncertainty: The Effects of Contractual Changes in the Television Industry', *Work Employment Society*, 14 (2), 283–305.

Dillon, T. (1999) '*Dragon Tales:* The genesis of a make-your-own-instant-franchise formula', October, <http://www.kidscreen.com/articles/magazine/19991001/26892.html>. Accessed 6 June 2008.

Disney (2008) *The Walt Disney Company 2008 Annual Report.*

Dorr, A. (1986) *Television and Children: A Special Medium for a Special Audience* (Beverley Hills: Sage).

Doyle, G. (2002) *Understanding Media Economics* (London: Sage).

Dudko, Mary Ann (2008a) (Director, Mad Duck Consulting, US), Skype Interview, 19 May.

—— (2008b) 'US Perspectives on Educational Content for Children's Programming', Presentation, *Making Television for Young Children Conference*, University of Westminster, 12 September, London.

Dunfield, A. (2000) 'Market aligns for international tot show success', 1 July, *KidScreen*, <http://www.kidscreen.com/articles/magazine/20000701/29474.html>. Accessed 15 March 2009.

Elliot, K. (2001) 'Broadcast millionaires lose £200m in wealth', *Broadcast*, 17 August, 1.

Ellis, J. (2000) *Seeing Things* (London: I.B. Taurus).

Engelhardt, T. (1986) 'Children's Television: The Shortcake Strategy', in T. Gitlin (ed.) *Watching Television* (New York: Pantheon), pp. 68–110.

ER (Entertainment Rights) (2007) *Annual Report and Accounts*, <http://www.entertainmentrights.com/corporate/annualreport/>. Accessed 31 March 2009.

Eryl-Jones, L. (2003) 'Playtime all the time: CBeebies, a case study', *Advertising and Marketing to Children*, July–September, 3–9.

Ettema, J. and C. Whitney (1982) *Individuals in Mass Media Organisations* (London: Sage).

Fanthome, C. (2006) 'The Strategic Development of Children's Programme Provision on Five', *Journal of British Cinema and Television*, 3 (2), 304–17.

Faulkner, S, A. Leaver, F. Vis and K. Williams (2009) 'Art for Art's Sake or Selling Up?', *European Journal of Communication*, 23 (3), 295–317.

FCC (Federal Communications Commission) (1974) 'Children's Television Programs: Report and Policy Statement', *Federal Register*, 39, 39396–409.

—— (1984a) 'Revision of Programming and Commercialization Policies, Ascertainment Requirements, and Program Log Requirements for Commercial Television Stations', *Federal Register*, 49, 23 August, 33588–620.

—— (1984b) 'Children's Television Programming and Advertising Practices: Report and Order', *Federal Register*, 49, 13 January, 1704–27.

—— (1996) 'In the Matter of Policies and Rules concerning Children's Television Programming: Revision of Programming Policies for Television Broadcasters', *Federal Communications Commission Record*, 11, 10660–778.

Fisch, S. (2004) *Children's Learning from Educational Television* (New York/London: Routledge).

—— (2007) 'Peeking Behind the Scene: Varied Approaches to the Production of Educational Television', in J.A. Bryant (ed.) *The Children's Television Community* (Mahwah: Lawrence Erlbaum), pp. 95–110.

Fisch, S. and L. Bernstein (2001) 'Formative Research Revealed: Methodological and Process Issues in Formative Research', in S. Fisch and R. Truglio (eds) *"G" is for Growing* (Mahwah: Lawrence Erlbaum), pp. 39–60.

Fisch, S.and R. Truglio (eds) (2001) *"G" is for Growing: Thirty Years of Research on Children and Sesame Street* (Mahwah: Lawrence Erlbaum).

Five (2008a) *Response of Channel 5 Broadcasting Ltd (Five) to The Digital Opportunity, Phase One of Ofcom's Second Public Service Broadcasting Review*, <http://www.ofcom.org.uk/consult/condocs/psb2_1/responses/>. Accessed 16 March 2009.

—— (2008b) *The Value Generated by Five's Investment in Children's Programming, Five Annex*, Final Report by Perspective, June, <http://www.ofcom.org.uk/consult/condocs/psb2_1/responses/>. Accessed 16 March 2009.

—— (2009) *Children's Programming*, <http://about.five.tv/programme-production/commissioning/commissioning-teams/childrens-programming>. Accessed 29 February.

Fowler, Karen (2007) (Executive Producer, Sesame Workshop), Interview, New York, 1 August.

Franklin, J., L. Rifkin and P. Pascual (2001) 'Serving the Very Young and the Restless: Children's Programming on Public Television', in D. Singer and J. Singer (eds) *Handbook of Children and the Media* (London: Sage), pp. 507–20.

Fry, A. (2002) 'Preschool TV: Underage Achievers', *C21Media.net*, 1 October, <http://www.c21media.net/features/detail.asp?area=2&article=4314>. Accessed 1 December 2003.

—— (2007) 'Licensing Special: Sector Overview – How to Post a profit in Licensing', *Broadcast*, 7 September, 26–9.

Gardner, H. (1993) *Frames of Mind: The Theory of Multiple Intelligences* (New York: Basic Books).

—— (2006) *Multiple Intelligences: New Horizons in Theory and Practice* (New York: Basic Books).

Garrison, M. and D. Christakis (2005) *A Teacher in the Living Room. Educational Media for Babies, Toddlers and Preschoolers* (Menlo Park: Kaiser Family Foundation).

Garside, J. (2008) 'Chorion profits fall to earth with a (Mr) Bump', *The Daily Telegraph*, 17 June, <http://www.telegraph.co.uk/finance/newsbysector/mediatechnologyandtelecoms/2791856/Chorion-profits-fall-to-earth-with-a-Mr-Bump.html>. Accessed 8 August 2008.

Gitlin, T. (2000) *Inside Prime Time*, Rvd edition (Berkeley/Los Angeles/London: University of California Press).

Gladwell, M. (2000) *The Tipping Point* (London: Little, Brown and Company).

Götz, M. (2007a) 'What Constitutes a Good Preschool Programme?', *Televizion*, 20, 18.

—— (2007b) 'Television Viewing from Before Birth up to the Age of 5', *Televizion*, 20, 12–17.

Goldsmiths Media Group (2000) 'Media Organisations in Society: Central Issues', in J. Curran (ed.) *Media Organisations in Society* (London: Arnold).

Gomery, D. (1994) 'Disney's Business History: A Reinterpretation', in E. Smoodin (ed.) *Disney Discourse* (London: BFI), pp. 71–86.

Grant, J. (2005) 'Utley puts Cosgrove back on the map', *C21Media.net*, 12 November, <http://www.c21media.net/features/detail.asp?area=2&article=27531>. Accessed 17 March 2009.

—— (2007a) 'Joined-Up Thinking—Part One', *C21Media.net*, 1 February, <http://www.c21media.net/features/detail.asp?area=2&article=34223>. Accessed 29 June 2009.

—— (2007b) 'Joined-up Thinking—Part Two' *C21Media.net*, 7 February, <http://www.c21media.net/features/detail.asp?area=2&article=34315>. Accessed 29 June 2009.

—— (2008a) 'Is this the end of Saturday mornings?', *C21 Media.net*, 26 November, <http://www.c21media.net/features/detail.asp?area=2&article=46108>. Accessed 9 January 2009.

—— (2008b) 'New Injury for ER', *C21 Media.net*, 4 December, <http://www.c21media.net/resources/detail.asp?area=79&article=46322>. Accessed 1 March 2009.

—— (2008c) 'Peer Group', *C21Media.net*, 22 October, <http://www.c21media.net/features/detail.asp?area=2&article=45338>. Accessed 17 March 2009.

—— (2008d) 'ER has Big Idea about sell-off', *C21Media.net*, 16 June <http://www.c21media.net/news/detail.asp?area=4&article=42422>. Accessed 17 May 2009.

—— (2008e) 'ER chief quits amid takeover talks', *C21Media.net*, 19 March, <http://www.c21media.net/news/detail.asp?area=4&article=40630>. Accessed 31 March 2009.

—— (2008f) 'UK animation studio to cut jobs', *C21Media.net*, 17 June, <http://www.c21media.net/resources/alt_index.asp?article=17299&area=79>. Accessed 15 May 2009.

—— (2008g) 'Cosgrove Hall moves, cuts more jobs', *C21Media.net*, 4 December, <http://www.c21media.net/news/detail.asp?area=4&article=46343>. Accessed 15 May 2009.

—— (2009a) 'California Dreaming', *C21Media.net*, 24 February, <http://www.c21media.net/features/detail.asp?area=2&article=47815>. Accessed 4 March 2009.

—— (2009b) 'Sesame Workshop cuts 20% staff', 12 March, *C21Media.net*, <http://www.c21media.net/news/detail.asp?area=4&article=48186>. Accessed 15 May 2009.

Grimston, J. (2008) 'Eh-Oh Creator of *Teletubbies* has new TV Gold mine', *The Sunday Times*, 10 February, 7.

Hamelink, C. (2002) 'Media Globalisation: Consequences for the Rights of Children', in C. von Feilitzen and U. Carlsson (eds) *Children, Young People and Media Globalisation* (Göteborg: Nordicom), pp. 33–42.

Hastings, G. et al. (2003) *Review of Research on the Effects of Food Promotion to Children*. Final Report. Prepared for the Food Standards Agency (University of Strathclyde Centre for Social Marketing), <www.food.gov.uk/multimedia/pdfs/foodpromotiontochildren1.pdf>. Accessed 1 June 2009.

Havens, T. (2007) 'Universal Childhood: The Global Trade in Children's Television and Changing Ideals of Childhood', *Global Media Journal*, 6 (10), <http://lass.calumet.purdue.edu/cca/gmj/sp07/gmj-sp07-havens.htm>. Accessed 20 May 2009.

Hayes, D. (2008) *Anytime Playdate* (New York: Free Press).

Hendershot, H. (1998) *Saturday Morning Censors* (Durham/London: Duke University Press).

—— (1999) '*Sesame Street*: Cognition and Communications Imperialism', in M. Kinder (ed.) *Kids' Media Culture* (Durham/London: Duke University Press), pp. 139–77.

—— (2002) 'Children and Education (*Sesame Street*)', in T. Miller (ed.) *Television Studies* (London: BFI), pp. 80–4.

—— (2004) (ed.) *Nickelodeon Nation* (New York and London: New York University Press).

Herman, E. and R. McChesney (1997) *The Global Media* (London/Washington: Cassell).

Hesmondhalgh, D. (2007) *The Cultural Industries* (London: Sage).

HIT Entertainment (N.D) *Global Fact Sheet*, <http://www.hitnewsonline.com/press/detail/global_fact_sheet/>. Accessed 31 March 2009.

—— (1996) *Report and Accounts 1996*.

—— (1997) *Report and Accounts 1997*.

—— (1998) *Report and Accounts 1998*.

—— (1999) *Report and Accounts 1999*.

—— (2001) *Annual Report and Accounts 2001*.

—— (2004) *Annual Report and Accounts 2004*.

—— (2007a) 'Hit Entertainment forges strategic alliance with Chapman entertainment for representation rights for new preschool properties in North America and Japan', 18 June <http://www.hitentertainment.com/PRPDFs/HITChapmanPR_Final_6-18-07.pdf>. Accessed 8 July 2008.

—— (2007b) *The Future of Children's Television Programming Discussion Paper*, 20 December, <http://www.ofcom.org.uk/consult/condocs/kidstv/responses/>. Accessed 1 January 2009.

Hofman O. and O. Schmid (2002) 'Wertschöpfungsketter Kinderfernsehen', *Televizion*, 15 February: 1–11, <http://www.br-online.de/jugend/izi/deutsch/publikation/televizion/15_2002_2.htm>. Accessed 4 March 2009.

Holt, J. (2003) 'Vertical Vision: Deregulation, Industrial Economy and Prime-time Design', in M. Jancovich and J. Lyons (eds) *Quality Popular Television* (London: BFI), pp. 12–31.

Home, A. (1993) *Into the Box of Delights* (London: BBC Books).

Home, Anna, (2007) (Chair, Save Kids TV), Interview, London, 14 November.

Hoskins, C., S. McFadyen and A. Finn (1997) *Global Television and Film* (Oxford: Oxford University Press).

Hoskins, C., S. McFadyen, A. Finn and A. Jäckel (1995) 'Film and Television Co-Production. Evidence from Canadian-European Experience', *European Journal of Communication*, 10 (2), 221–43.

Hoskins, C. and R. Mirus (1988) 'Reasons for the US Dominance of the International Trade in Television Programmes', *Media, Culture and Society*, 10 (4), 499–515.

Hoskins, C., R. Mirus and W. Rozeboom (1989) 'US Television Programs in the International Market: Unfair Pricing?', *Journal of Communication*, 39 (2), 55–75.

House of Commons, Culture, Media and Sport Committee (2007) *Public Service Content: First Report* H-C 36-II, <http://www.publications.parliament.uk/pa/cm200708/cmselect/cmcumeds/36/3602.htm>. Accessed 5 June 2009.

Hughes, Estelle (2007) (Former Controller, CiTV), Interview, London 8 March.

Hume, Lenora (2008) Executive Vice President, Production and Programming, HIT Entertainment, Presentation at the *Making Television for Young Children Conference*, University of Westminster, 12 September.

Huston, A., D. Anderson, J. Wright, D. Linebarger, and K. Schmitt (2001) '*Sesame Street* Viewers as Adolescents: The Recontact Study', in S. Fisch and R. Truglio (eds) *"G" is for Growing* (Mahwah: Lawrence Erlbaum), pp. 131–43.

Huston, A. and J. Wright (1983) 'Children's Processing of Television: the Informative Functions of Formal Features', in J. Bryant and D. Anderson (eds) *Children's Understanding of Television* (London: Academic Press), pp. 35–68.

ITC (Independent Television Commission) (1996) *Children's Perceptions of Toy Advertising*, <http://www.aeforum.org/aeforum.nsf/3deac671ffcb0cc780256c5100355eb5/e31aff917d398a36802567a700403c3a/$FILE/aitc0029.pdf>. Accessed 1 June 2009.

—— (2000) *Copycat Kids? The Influence of Television Advertising on Children and Teenagers*, <http://www.ofcom.org.uk/static/archive/itc/research/index.htm>. Accessed 1 June 2009.

—— (2001) *Boxed In: Offence from Negative Stereotyping in TV Advertising*, <http://www.ofcom.org.uk/static/archive/itc/research/index.htm>. Accessed 1 June 2009.

—— (2002) *Annual Report and Accounts for 2001*, <http://www.ofcom.org.uk/static/archive/itc/itc_publications/annual_report/2001/index.asp.html>. Accessed 5 May 2009.

—— (2003a) *ITC Notes: Children's Television*, <http://www.ofcom.org.uk/static/archive/itc/itc_publications/itc_notes/view_note73.html>. Accessed 5 May 2009.

—— (2003b) *Annual Report and Accounts for 2002*, <http://www.ofcom.org.uk/static/archive/itc/itc_publications/annual_report/2002/index.asp.html>. Accessed 5 May 2009.

ITV (2004) *ITV's Response to the Independent Review of the BBC's New Digital Television Services*, <http://www.culture.gov.uk/independent_review/independent_review_bbctv.html>. Accessed 8 March 2009.

——— (2006) *Television Advertising of Food and Drink Products to Children: Options for New Restrictions*, <http://www.ofcom.org.uk/consult/condocs/foodads/responses/im/>. Accessed 1 June 2009.

——— (2007) *ITV1: 2006 Review and 2007 Statement of Programme Policy* (London: ITV).

Jacobs, J. (2001) 'Issues of Judgement and Value in Television Studies', *International Journal of Cultural Studies*, 4 (4), 427–47.

——— (2004) 'Teletubbies', in G. Creeber (ed.) *Fifty Key Television Programmes* (London: Hodder Arnold), pp. 203–7.

Jarvik, L. (1998) *PBS: Behind the Screen* (Rocklin: Prima Publishing).

Jenkins, B. (2005) 'UK kidcasters get into the creative process from the get-go', *KidScreen*, 1 October, <http://www.kidscreen.com/articles/magazine/20051001/uk.html>. Accessed 4 March 2009.

Jenkinson, D. (2005) 'He-man sister act set to push ER into the US', 17 March, *C21Media.net* <http://www.c21media.net/features/detail.asp?area=2&article=23966>. Accessed 17 March 2009.

Jeremy, D. (2002) 'Clash of the Child Titans', *Broadcast International*, 12 April, 24–8.

Johnson, Brown (2001) (President of Nickelodeon Preschool), Interview, New York, 10 September.

Jordan, A. (2000) 'Is the three-hour rule living up to its potential?' Annenburg Public Policy Centre, <http://annenbergpublicpolicycenter.org/05_media_developing_child/childrensprogramming/3hour-rule.pdf>. Accessed 24 December 2008.

——— (2004) 'The Three-Hour Rule and Educational Television for Children', *Popular Communication*, 2 (2), 103–18.

——— (2008) 'Children's Media Policy', *Children and Electronic Media*, 18 (1), 235–53.

Kapur, J. (1999) 'Out of Control Television and the Transformation of Childhood in Late Capitalism', in M. Kinder (ed.) *Kids' Media Culture* (Durham/London: Duke University Press), pp. 122–39.

Keighron, P. (2006) 'Kids TV – Child's Play', *Broadcast*, 17 March, 20.

Kinder, M. (1991) *Playing with Power* (Berkeley/Los Angeles: University of California Press).

Kirkorian, H. and D.Anderson (2008) 'Learning from Educational Media', in S. Calvert and B. Wilson (eds) *The Handbook of Children, Media and Development* (Oxford: Blackwell), pp. 188–213.

Klasen, Frank (2008) (Head of Editorial, Children's Department, SuperRTL, Germany) Interview, London, 16 May.

Klein, R. (1988) 'Is Our Youth Going Down the Tube? Children's TV', *The Sunday Times*, 13 November 1988, p. n/a.

Kline, S. (1993) *Out of the Garden: Toys, TV, and Children's Culture in the Age of Marketing* (London: Verso).

——— (1995) 'The Empire of Play', in C. Bazalgette and D. Buckingham (eds) *In Front of the Children* (London: BFI), pp. 151–65.

Kubey, R. (2004) *Creating Television* (Mahwah: Lawrence Erlbaum).

Kunkel, D. (1998) 'Policy Battles over Defining Children's Educational Television', *The Annals of the American Academy of Political and Social Science*, 557, 39–53.

—— (1999) 'Children's Television Policy in the United States: An Ongoing Legacy of Change', *Media International Australia*, 93, 51–63.

—— (2007) 'Kids' Media Policy Goes Digital: Current Developments in Children's Television Regulation', in J.A. Bryant (ed.) *The Children's Television Community* (Mahwah: Lawrence Erlbaum), pp. 203–28.

Kunkel, D. and B. Watkins (1987) 'Evolution of Children's Television Regulatory Policy', *Journal of Broadcasting & Electronic Media*, 31 (4), 367–89.

Kunkel, D. and B. Wilcox (2001) 'Children and Media Policy', in D. Singer and J. Singer (eds) *Handbook of Children and Media* (London: Sage), pp. 589–604.

Kuzmyk, J. (2005) 'Canada: More money in the Cookie Jar', *C21Media.net*, 17 February, <http://www.c21media.net/features/detail.asp?area=2&article=23585>. Accessed 17 March 2009.

—— (2008) 'Comedy in the Jar', *C21Media.net*, 13 February, <http://www.c21media.net/features/detail.asp?area=2&article=39999>. Accessed 17 March 2009.

Lane, H. (2007) 'Night Fever', *The Observer*, Magazine, 25 November, p. 46ff, <http://www.guardian.co.uk/theobserver/2007/nov/25/features.magazine47>. Accessed 17 June 2009.

Laybourne, G. (1993) 'The Nickelodeon Experience', in G. Berry and J. Asamen (eds) *Children and Television* (London: Sage), pp. 303–7.

Lees, N. (2005a) 'Cresting the wave in a flood of preschool', *Kidscreen*, April, <http://www.kidscreen.com/articles/magazine/20050401/preschool.html?page=2>. Accessed 1 March 2009.

—— (2005b) 'Growing up Preschool: Kidcasters find Fertile Ground with the Four to Seven Demo', *Kidscreen*, September, <http://www.kidscreen.com/articles/magazine/20050901/preschool.html?page=2>. Accessed 1 March 2009.

Lemish, D. (2007) *Children and Television* (Oxford: Blackwell).

—— (2008) 'The Mediated Playground: Media in Early Childhood', in K. Drotner and S. Livingstone (eds) *The International Handbook of Children, Media and Culture* (London: Sage), pp. 152–67.

Lennard, D. (2004) 'United States of Animation', *C21Media.net*, 18 May, <http://www.c21media.net/features/detail.asp?area=2&article=20435>. Accessed 21 June 2009.

Lent, J. (1998) 'The Animation Industry and its Offshore Facilities', in G. Sussmann and J. Lent (eds) *Global Productions* (Cresskil: Hampton Press), pp. 239–54.

—— (2001) 'Overseas Animation Production in Asia', in J. Lent (ed.) *Animation in Asia and the Pacific* (Bloomington/Indianapolis: Indiana University Press), pp. 239–46.

Lesser, G. (1974) *Children and Television: Lessons from Sesame Street* (New York: Random House).

License (2008) 'Top 100 Global Licensors', *Licence!*, April 2008, 2–27.

Lindstrom, M. and P. Seybold (2003) *Brandchild* (London: Kogan Page)

Linebarger D. and D. Walker (2005) 'Infants' and Toddlers' Television Viewing and Language Outcomes', *American Behavioural Scientist*, 48 (5), 624–45.

Linn, S. (2004) *Consuming Kids* (New York: Anchor Books).

Lisosky, J. (2001) 'For all Kids' Sakes: Comparing Children's Television Policy-making in Australia, Canada and the United States', *Media, Culture and Society*, 23 (6), 821–42.

Litton, Howard (2007) (Managing Director, Nickelodeon UK) Interview. London, 6 June.

Livingstone, S. and M. Bober (2005) *UK Children Go Online. Final Report of Key Project Findings* (London: LSE).

Lloyd, Claudia (2007) (Head of Animation and Children's, Tiger Aspect Productions), Interview, London, 20 November.

London, R. (2007) 'Producing Children's Television', in J.A. Bryant (ed.) *The Children's Television Community* (Mahwah: Lawrence Erlbaum), pp. 77–94.

Ludorum (2007) *Annual Report and Accounts for the Year Ended 31 December.*

Luke, C. (1990) *Constructing the Child Viewer* (New York: Praeger).

Lury, K. (2002) 'A Time and Place for Everything: Children's Channels', in D. Buckingham (ed.) *Small Screens* (London/New York: Leicester University Press), pp. 38–60.

—— (2005) *Interpreting Television* (London: Hodder Arnold).

Marcus, D. (2003) 'Public Television and Public Access in the US', in M. Hilmes (ed.) *The Television History Book* (London: BFI), pp. 55–9.

Marsh, J. et al (2005) *Digital Beginnings: Young Children's Use of Popular Culture, Media and New Technologies* (Sheffield: Literacy Research Centre, University of Sheffield).

Mayo, E. and A. Nairn (2009) *Consumer Kids* (Constable: London).

McAlister, M. and M. Giglio (2005) 'The Commodity Flow of US Children's Television', *Critical Studies in Media Communication*, 22 (1), 26–44.

McChesney, R. (2002) 'Children, Globalization, and Media Policy', in C. von Feilitzen and U. Carlsson (eds) *Children, Young People and Media Globalisation* (Göteborg: Nordicom), pp. 23–32.

McCollum, J. and J. Bryant (2003) 'Pacing in Children's Television Programming', *Mass Communications and Society*, 6 (2), 115–36.

McGown, A. (n.d) 'Pre-School Television', *Screenonline*, <http://www.screenonline.org.uk/tv/id/862404/index.html>. Accessed 8 January 2009.

McLaughlin, Lucille (2007) (Executive Producer, BBC Scotland), Interview, Glasgow, 13 December 2007.

McMahon, K. (2008) 'Interview: Emma Tennant', 5 November, <http://www.broadcastnow.co.uk/news/interviews/2008/11/interview_emma_tennant.html>. Accessed 10 May 2009.

Melody, W. (1973) *Children's Television: The Economics of Exploitation* (New Haven/London: Yale University Press).

Messenger Davies, M. (1989) *Television is Good for your Kids* (London: Hilary Shipman).

—— (1995) 'Babes 'N' the Hood: Pre-school Television and its Audiences in the United States and Britain', in C. Bazalgette and D. Buckingham (eds) *In Front of the Children* (London: BFI), pp. 15–33.

—— (2001a) *'Dear BBC': Children, Television Storytelling and the Public Sphere* (Cambridge: Cambridge University Press).

—— (2001b) 'Pre-schoolers: A Special Audience', in G. Creeber (ed.) *The Television Genre Book* (London: BFI), pp. 100–2.

—— (2004) *BBC Digital Review: CBEEBIES and CBBC*, Department of Culture, Media and Sport, <http://www.culture.gov.uk/reference_library/publications/4594.aspx>. Accessed 5 March 2009.

—— (2006) 'Production Studies', *Critical Studies in Television*, 1 (1), 21–30.

—— (2007) *The Future of Children's Television Programming, October 2007: Some Responses from the Academic Community*, <http://www.ofcom.org.uk/consult/condocs/kidstv/responses/>. Accessed 1 January 2009.

Messenger Davies, M. and B. Corbett (1997) *The Provision of Children's Television in Britain: 1992–1996* (London: Broadcasting Standards Commission).

Midgley, C. (2006) 'Can I build it? Yes, again: Interview (Keith Chapman), *The Times*, 2, 8.

Mielke, K. (2001) 'A Review of Research on the Educational and Social Impact of *Sesame Street*', in S. Fisch and R. Truglio (eds) *"G" is for Growing* (Mahwah: Lawrence Erlbaum), pp. 83–95.

Milmo, C. (2005) 'Can we sell it? Yes, we can', *The Independent*, 5 April, 12–13.

Minow, N. and C. Lamay (1995) *Abandoned in the Wasteland* (New York: Hill and Wang).

Mitchison, A. (2004) 'The Mother of all Boohbahs', *The Sunday Telegraph*, 7 March, 4.

Mitroff, D. and R. Herr Stephenson (2007) 'The Television Tug-of-War: A Brief History of Children's Television Programming in the United States', in J.A. Bryant (ed.) *The Children's Television Community* (Mahwah: Lawrence Erlbaum), pp. 3–34.

Mittel, J. (2003) 'The Great Saturday Morning Exile: Scheduling Cartoons on Television's Periphery in the 1960s', in C.A. Stabile and M. Harrison (eds) *Prime time Animation* (New York: Routledge), pp. 33–54.

Molotsky, I. (1997) 'One Tough Bird, After All; How Public Broadcasting Survived the Attacks of Conservatives', *The New York Times*, 27 November, E1, <http://www.nytimes.com/1997/11/27/arts/one-tough-bird-after-all-public-broadcasting-survived-attacks-conservatives.html>. Accessed 5 May 2009.

Montgomery, K. (2007) 'Advocating Children's Television', in J.A. Bryant (ed.) *The Children's Television Community* (Mahwah: Lawrence Erlbaum), pp. 229–57.

Moran, K. (2006) 'The Global Expansion of Children's Television: A Case Study of the Adaptation of *Sesame Street* in Spain', *Learning Media and Technology*, 31 (3), 287–300.

Morrow, R. (2006) *Sesame Street and the Reform of Children's Television* (Baltimore: John Hopkins University Press).

Negus, K. (2006) 'Rethinking Creative Production away from the Cultural Industries', in K. Negus (ed.) *Media and Cultural Theory* (London: Routledge), pp. 197–208.

Newcomb, H. and R. Alley (1983) *The Producer's Medium* (New York: Oxford University Press).

Northam, J. (2005) 'Rehearsals in Citizenship: BBC Stop-Motion Animation Programmes for Young Children', *Journal for Cultural Research*, 9 (3), 245–63.

Ofcom (Office of Communications) (2004a) *Child Obesity: Food Advertising in Context*, 22 July <http://www.ofcom.org.uk/research/tv/reports/food_ads/>. Accessed 1 June 2009.

—— (2004b) *Ofcom Research Sets Food Advertising to Children in Context*, News Release, 22 July, <http://www.ofcom.org.uk/media/news/2004/07/nr_20040722>. Accessed 1 June 2009.

—— (2004c) *Review of Public Service Television Broadcasting – Phase 1: Is Television Special?*, 21 April, <http://www.ofcom.org.uk/consult/condocs/psb/psb/>. Accessed 1 June 2009.

—— (2004d) *Review of Public Service Television Broadcasting – Phase 2: Meeting the Digital Challenge*, 28 September, <http://www.ofcom.org.uk/consult/condocs/psb2/>. Accessed 1 June 2009.

—— (2005) *Ofcom Accepts Commercial Public Service Broadcasters' Proposals on Tier 3 Obligations*, News Release, 25 February, <http://www.ofcom.org.uk/media/news/2005/02/nr_20050225>. Accessed 1 June 2009.

—— (2006a) *The Communications Market 2006*, <http://www.ofcom.org.uk/research/cm/cm06/>. Accessed 5 March 2009.

—— (2006b) *Television Advertising of Food and Drink Products to Children: Options for New Restrictions*, 28 March, <http://www.ofcom.org.uk/consult/condocs/foodads/foodadsprint/>. Accessed 1 June 2009.

—— (2006c) *Draft Annual Plan 2007/8*, 12 December, <http://www.ofcom.org.uk/consult/condocs/annual_plan2007/annual_plan200708/printversions/fullprint.pdf>. Accessed 9 June 2009.

—— (2007a) *The Future of Children's Television Programming*, 3 October, <http://www.ofcom.org.uk/consult/condocs/kidstv/kidstvresearch.pdf>. Accessed 30 October 2007.

—— (2007b) *The International Perspective: The Future of Children's Programming Research Report*, Annex E, 3 October, <http://www.ofcom.org.uk/consult/condocs/kidstv/>. Accessed 24 June 2009.

—— (2007c) *Children's Television Output Analysis, 2003–2006*, Annex C, 3 October, <http://www.ofcom.org.uk/consult/condocs/kidstv/>. Accessed 24 June 2009.

—— (2007d) *Television Advertising of Food and Drink Products to Children: Final Statement*, 22 February, <http://www.ofcom.org.uk/consult/condocs/foodads_new/statement/statement.pdf>. Accessed 1 June 2009.

—— (2007e) *Communications Market Report*, <http://www.ofcom.org.uk/research/cm/cmr07>. Accessed 1 June 2009.

—— (2007f) *Terms of Reference: The Future of Children's Programming*, 13 February, <http://www.ofcom.org.uk/tv/psb_review/childprog/tor/>. Accessed 1 June 2009.

—— (2008a) *Communications Market Report*, <http://www.ofcom.org.uk/research/cm/cmr08/>. Accessed 5 March 2009.

—— (2008b) *Ofcom Statement on Reduction in ITV Children's Programmes*, 18 March, <http://www.ofcom.org.uk/tv/ifi/reduction_itv/>. Accessed 1 June 2009.

—— (2008c) *Ofcom's Second Public Service Broadcasting Review – Phase One: The Digital Opportunity*, 10 April <http://www.ofcom.org.uk/consult/condocs/psb2_1/consultation.pdf>. Accessed 1 June 2009.

—— (2008d) *The Future of Children's Television Programming: Future Delivery of Public Service Content for Children – Annex 10 to Phase One of Ofcom's Second Review of Public Service Broadcasting*, 10 April <http://www.ofcom.org.uk/consult/condocs/kidstv/statement/statement.pdf>. Accessed 1 June 2009.

—— (2009) *Ofcom's Second Public Service Broadcasting Review: Putting Viewers First*, Final Statement, 21 January, <http://www.ofcom.org.uk/consult/condocs/psb2_phase2/>. Accessed 5 June 2009.

Oliver and Ohlbaum Associates (2007) *The UK Children's TV Market*, Annex B, A Report for Ofcom, 11 June, <http://www.ofcom.org.uk/consult/condocs/kidstv/>. Accessed 5 March 2009.

Optima (2004) *The Likely Costs and Benefits of a UK Animation Fund. A Report by Optima for Pact*, 3 February (London: Optima).

Oswell, D. (1995) 'Watching with Mother in the Early 1950s', in C. Bazalgette and D. Buckingham (eds) *In Front of the Children* (London: BFI), pp. 34–46.

—— (2002) *Television, Childhood and the Home* (Oxford: Oxford University Press).

Pact (2006) *Response to Ofcom's Consultation on Television Advertising of Food and Drink Products to Children: Options for New Restrictions*, June, <http://www.ofcom.org.uk/consult/condocs/foodads/responses/nr/pact_nonconf.pdf>. Accessed 1 June 2009.

—— (2007) *Overseas Sales of UK TV Programmes Jump 20%*, Press Release, 18 April, <http://www.pact.co.uk/press/releases/detail.asp?id=5967>. Accessed 19 April 2007.

Palmer, E. (1987) *Children in the Cradle of Television* (Lexington: Lexington Books).

—— (1988) *Television and America's Children* (New York/Oxford: Oxford University Press).

Palmer, E. and S. Fisch (2001) 'The Beginnings of *Sesame Street* Research', in S. Fisch and R. Truglio (eds) *"G" is for Growing* (Mahwah: Lawrence Erlbaum), pp. 3–24.

Patrick A. (2006) 'In Tots' TV Shows, A Booming Market, Toys get Top Billing', *Wall Street Journal*, 27 March, <http://www.commercialexploitation.org/news/totstvtoys.htm>. Accessed 1 June 2009.

PBS (2008) *PBS Consolidated Financial Highlights*, <www.pbs.org/aboutpbs/.../2008PBSConsolidatedFinancialHighlights.pdf>. Accessed 24 June 2009.

Pecora, N. (1998) *The Business of Children's Entertainment* (New York: Guilford Press).

—— (2004) 'Nickelodeon Grows Up. The Economic Evolution of a Network', in H. Hendershot (ed.) *Nickelodeon Nation* (New York/London: New York University Press), pp. 15–44.

—— (2007) 'The Changing Nature of Children's Television: Fifty Years of Research', in N. Pecora, J. Murray and E. Wartella (eds) *Children and Television* (Mahwah: Lawrence Erlbaum), pp. 1–40.

Pecora, N., J. Murray and E. Wartella (eds) (2007) *Children and Television* (Mahwah: Lawrence Erlbaum).

Pennington, A. (2006) 'Regional Focus: Manchester – A Tale of Two Studios', *Broadcast*, 17 November, 27.

Persson, Cecilia (2007) (Vice President Programming, Acquisitions and Presentation, Cartoon Network, UK), Interview, London, 25 June.

Piaget, J. (1969) *The Psychology of the Child* (New York: International University Press).

Pilkington Committee (1962) *Report of the Committee on Broadcasting* (London: HMSO).

Piore, M. and C. Sabel (1984) *The Second Industrial Divide* (New York: Basic Books).

Plummer-Andrews, T. (2006) 'Retrospective! Successfully Reviving Classic Properties', Presentation, 21 March, *The Kids' TV Forum Conference*, London.

Polsky, R. (1974) *Getting to Sesame Street* (New York: Praeger).

Postman, N. (1982) *The Disappearance of Childhood* (New York: Vintage Books).

Poussier, Dominique (2002) (Directrice de Programme Jeunesse, TF1) Interview, Paris, 19 March.

Ragdoll (2007) *The Future of Children's Television Programming. Ragdoll Response to Ofcom Discussion Paper*, 20 December, <http://www.ofcom.org.uk/consult/condocs/kidstv/responses/>. Accessed 24 December 2008.

Raugust, K. (1996) *Merchandise Licensing in the Television Industry* (Boston: Focal Press).

—— (2004a) *The Animation Business Handbook* (New York: St Martin's Press).

—— (2004b) *The Licensing Business Handbook*, 6th edn (New York: EPM Communications).

Reeve-Crook A. (2007a) 'Top kids firms buck market', *C21Media.net*, 23 July, <http://www.c21media.net/news/detail.asp?area=4&article=36777>. Accessed 10 May 2009.

—— (2007b) 'Canadian Buyer for UK's Contender', *C21Media.net*, 14 June, <http://www.c21media.net/news/detail.asp?area=4&article=36252>. Accessed 15 May 2009.

—— (2008) 'Disney up the junction with UK toon house', *C21Media.net*, 1 April, <http://www.c21media.net/news/detail.asp?area=4&article=40814>. Accessed 14 March 2009.

Rideout, V. and E. Hamel (2006) *The Media Family: Electronic Media in the Lives of Infants, Toddlers, Preschoolers and their Parents* (Menlo Park: Kaiser Family Foundation).

Rideout, V., E. Vandewater and E. Wartella (2003) *Zero to Six: Electronic Media in the Lives of Infants, Toddlers and Preschoolers* (Menlo Park: Kaiser Family Foundation).

Roberts, G (2006) 'Fifi gives Bob the Builder's Creator yet another Television Hit', *The Independent*, 3 May, 17.

Robertson, R. (1994) 'Globalisation or Glocalisation?', *The Journal of International Communications*, 1 (1), 33–52.

—— (1995) 'Glocalisation: Time-Space and Homogeneity-Heterogeneity', in M. Featherstone, S. Lash and R. Robertson (eds) *Global Modernities* (London: Sage), pp. 25–44.

Robins, K. and J. Cornford (1992) 'What is "Flexible": about Independent Producers?', *Screen*, 33 (2), 190–200.

Rogers, J. (2007) 'CITV to End Kids Spending Freeze', *Broadcast*, 12 December, 3.

Rosser, M. (2007) 'Dancing to a new toon, *C21Media.net*, 25 January, <http://www.c21media.net/features/detail.asp?area=2&article=34114>. Accessed 17 March 2009.

Runett, R. (2009) 'Wall Street Fallout Hurting … Sesame Street? *The MotleyFool.com*, <http://www.fool.com/investing/general/2009/04/22/wall-street-fallout-hurting-sesame-street.aspx>. Accessed 29 April.

Rusak, G. (2008a) 'US – Dominant preschool players take "if it ain't broke" approach to fall skeds' *KidScreen*, October, <http://www.kidscreen.com/articles/magazine/20081001/falltv3.html>. Accessed 3 March 2009.

—— (2008b) 'A peek inside KidScreen's popular 30 Minutes with…', *KidScreen Daily*, 14 February, <http://www.kidscreen.com/articles/news/20080214/30min.html>. Accessed 3 March 2009.

Rushton, K (2008a) 'CiTV Books First New UK Order in 18 Months', *Broadcast*, 3 July, 3.

—— (2008b) 'Deverell: BBC Children's could learn lessons from Five', *Broadcast*, 4 July, <http://www.broadcastnow.co.uk/news/multi-platform/news/deverell-bbc-childrens-could-learn-lessons-from-five/1686585.article>. Accessed 6 July 2009.

—— (2009a) 'Happy and "hippy" kids telly', *Broadcast*, 8 May, 28–9.

—— (2010b) ' "Immersive" web world for CBeebies' Waybuloo series', *Broadcast*, 17 April, 14.

S4C (2006) *Annual Report*, <http://www.s4c.co.uk/abouts4c/annualreport/e_index2006.shtml>. Accessed 15 May 2009.

—— (2007) *S4C Response to 'The Future of Children's Television Programming'*, 20 December <http://www.ofcom.org.uk/consult/condocs/kidstv/responses/>. Accessed 24 December 2008.

Sandler, K. (2004) ' "A Kid's Gotta Do What a Kid's Gotta Do": Branding the Nickelodeon Experience', in H. Hendershot (ed.) *Nickelodeon Nation* (New York/London: New York University Press), pp. 45–68.

Saundry. R. and P. Nolan (1998) 'Regulatory Change and Performance in TV Production', *Media Culture and Society*, 20 (3), 409–26.

Schiller, H. (1989) *Culture Inc.* (Oxford/New York: Oxford University Press).

Schneider, C. (1987) *Children's Television: The Art, the Business and How it Works* (Lincolnwood: NTC Business Books).

Schor, J. (2004) *Born to Buy: The Commercialized Child and the New Consumer Culture* (New York: Scribner).

Schosser, Suzanne (2002) (Programmdirektor, Super RTL Germany), Interview, Cologne, 21 February.

Schreiber, D. (2006) 'Hit opens doors to producers', *Broadcast*, 10 April, <http://www.broadcastnow.co.uk/news/multi-platform/news/hit-opens-doors-to-producers/157671.article>. Accessed 6 July 2009.

—— (2008) 'Angelina Ballerina goes CGI', 7 April, *Broadcast*, <http://www.broadcastnow.co.uk/news/multi-platform/news/angelina-ballerina-goes-cgi/1077706.article>. Accessed 6 July 2009.

Schwalbe, Doug (2008) (Executive VP Sales and Co-Production, Classic Media, New York), Telephone Interview, 15 May.

Scott, A. (2004) 'The Other Hollywood: The Organizational and Geographic Bases of Television-Program Production', *Media Culture and Society*, 26 (2), 183–205.

Screen Digest (2006) 'Europe's Animation Industry Grows: Television Output Stable while Features Struggle for Distribution', December, 423ff.

—— (2007) *Response from Screen Digest to Ofcom's Consultation on Children's Television*, 19 December, <http://www.ofcom.org.uk/consult/condocs/kidstv/responses/>. Accessed 15 March 2009.

Segal, Rebecca (2002) 'On How the Economic Climate is Persuading US Networks to Keep Production in the Family', *Broadcast*, 18 January, 14.

Seiter, E. (1993) *Sold Separately: Parents and Children in Consumer Culture* (New Brunswick: Rutgers University Press).

Selig, Josh (2007) (Founder and President, Little Airplane Productions), Interview, New York, 2 August.

—— (2008) (Founder and President, Little Airplane Productions), Email Communication, 20 July.

—— (2009) 'Simple is Good: Part Two', *KidScreen*, March, <http://www.kidscreen.com/articles/magazine/20090327/simple.html>. Accessed 5 May 2009.

Selig, J. and L. Brown (2008) *Show & Tell Research*, 5 February, Internal Memo (New York: Little Airplane Productions).

Selig, J. and H. Tilert (2008) Little Airplane Productions, Presentation at the *Making Television for Young Children Conference*, University of Westminster, 12 September.

Sesame Workshop (2007) *Sesame Workshop Annual Report*, <http://www.sesameworkshop.org/inside/annualreport>. Accessed 5 May 2009.

—— (2008) *Sesame Workshop Annual Report*.

Shepherd, R. (2008) 'Ents Rights Boss under Pressure as Bid Fails', *Broadcast*, 23 June, <http://www.broadcastnow.co.uk/finance/news/2008/04/ent_rights_boss_under_pressure_as_bid_fails.html>. Accessed 31 March 2009.

Sheridan, S. (2004) *The A–Z of Classic Children's Television* (London: Reynolds and Hearn).

Sigman, A. (2007) *Remotely Controlled: How Television is Damaging our Lives* (London: Vermilion).

Simensky, L. (2007) 'Programming Children's Television: The PBS Model', in J.A. Bryant (ed.) *The Children's Television Community* (Mahwah: Lawrence Erlbaum), pp. 131–46.

Singer, J. and D. Singer (1998) '*Barney and Friends* as Entertainment and Education. Evaluating the Quality and Effectiveness of a Television Series for Preschool Children', in J. Asamen and G. Berry (eds) *Research Paradigms, Television and Social Behaviour* (Thousand Oaks: Sage), pp. 305–67.

Singleton-Turner, R. (1994) *Television and Children* (Borehamwood: BBC Television Training).

Skala, Christopher (2007) (Senior Vice President Programming and Development, HIT Entertainment) Interview, London, 22 February.

SKTV (Save Kids TV) (2007) *Response to Consultation: The Future of Children's Television Programming*, <http://www.ofcom.org.uk/consult/condocs/kidstv/responses/>. Accessed 24 December 2008.

Sinclair, J., E. Jacka and S. Cunningham (eds) (1996) *New Patterns in Global Television* (Oxford: Oxford University Press).

Snoddy, R. and R. Evans (1988) 'Hurd Unveils Biggest TV Shake-Up for 30 Years', *Financial Times*, 8 November, 1.

—— (1990a) 'Parliament and Politics: Mellor Wants Extension of Quality Obligation', *Financial Times*, 9 February, 10.

—— (1990b) 'Survey of The New Face of British Broadcasting (2): Deregulation: a Typically British Compromise – Outcome of the Biggest TV Shake-up for 30 Years', *Financial Times*, 16 October, p. n/a.

Spencer Simon (2007) (Producer, *Thomas and Friends*, HIT Entertainment), Interview, London, 21 June.

Starkey, K. and C. Barnatt (1997) 'Flexible Specialization and the Reconfiguration of Television Production in the UK', *Technology Analysis & Strategic Management*, 9 (3), 271–85.

Starkey, K., C. Barnatt, and S. Tempest (2000) 'Beyond Networks and Hierarchies: Latent Organizations in the UK Television Industry' *Organization Science*, 11 (3), 299–305.

Steemers, J. (2004) *Selling Television: British Television in the Global Marketplace* (London: BFI).

—— (2005) 'Balancing Culture and Commerce on the Global Stage. BBC Worldwide', in G. Lowe and P. Jauert (eds) *Cultural Dilemmas in Public Service Broadcasting* (Göteborg: Nordicom), 231–50.

—— (2010a) 'The BBC's Role in the Changing Production Ecology of Preschool Television in Britain', *Television and New Media*, 11(1) 37–61.

—— (2010b) 'Little Kids TV: Downloading, Sampling and Multiplatforming the Preschool TV Experiences of the Digital Era', in J. Bennett and N. Strange (eds) *Television as Digital Media* (In Press).

Steinberg, J. (2009) 'Rivals unafraid to borrow, or steal, from each other', *New York Times*, 23 February, <http://www.nytimes.com/2009/02/24/arts/television/24nick.html?_r=1&pagewanted=1&8dpc&_r=1>. Accessed 23 February 2009.

Stevenson, Jocelyn (2007) (Writer/Producer, TT Animation), Interview, London, 31 October.

Stewart, Alison (2007) (Executive Producer, CBeebies) Interview, London, 21 June.

Stipp, Horst (2007) 'The Role of Academic Advisors in Creating Children's Television Programs: The NBC Experience', in J.A Bryant (ed.) *The Children's Television Community* (Mahwah: Lawrence Erlbaum), pp. 111–28.

Stokes, Melanie (2007) (Director, Kindle Entertainment), Interview, London, 27 March.

Sunshine Holdings 3 Limited (2008) *Directors Report and Financial Statements for the Year Ended 31 July 2008*, <http://www.hitentertainment.com/corporate/companymanagement.html>. Accessed 31 March 2009.

Sweney, M. (2007) 'ITV Plan to Cut Kids' Shows Succeeds', *MediaGuardian*, 22 March <http://www.guardian.co.uk/media/2007/mar/22/ITV.broadcasting1>. Accessed 1 June 2007.

—— (2008) 'BBC Worldwide to review children's strategy after £7.2m annual loss', *MediaGuardian*, 8 July, <http://www.guardian.co.uk/media/2008/jul/08/bbc.mediabusiness/print>. Accessed 9 September 2008.

Tashjian, J. and J. Campbell Naidoo (2007) 'Licensing and Merchandising in Children's Television and Media', in J.A. Bryant (ed.) *The Children's Television Community* (Mahwah: Lawrence Erlbaum), pp. 165–87.

TBI (Television Business International) (2003) 'In with the old', *Television Business International (TBI)*, 8, 1 August, 23ff.

—— (2006a) 'Canada: the Next Generation', *TBI*, 8, August, 69ff.

—— (2006b) 'The Kids TV Industry by Numbers', *TBI*, August, 70ff.

—— (2006c) 'Fun and games and kids TV', *TBI*, May, 67ff.

—— (2007a) 'Live and Kicking', *TBI*, 10, October, 77.

—— (2007b) 'Playing with Toys', *TBI*, 1 April.

Teifi, Siân (2008) (Director, Sianco Cyf), Interview, Cardiff, 26 February.

Tenret, Julia (2008) (Buyer, Lagardère, for Tiji and Canal J, France), Telephone Interview, 24 June.

Thickett, J. (2007a) 'Showcomotion – Ofcom's Review of Children's Programming', Project Director, Keynote to Showcomotion Conference, 6 July, <http://www.ofcom.org.uk/media/speeches/2007/07/children>. Accessed 5 May 2009.

Thickett, James (2007b) (Director of Research, Ofcom), Interview, London, 27 November.

—— (2007c) *Ofcom and the Future of Children's Programming*, Voice of the Listener and Viewer Conference on Children's Television, 15 May.

Thomson, C. (2001) *Proposed New Services from the BBC. Letter to Andrew Ramsay, Director Creative Industries, Media and Broadcasting Directorate*, DCMS, 9 January,

<http://www.culture.gov.uk/reference_library/publications/4626.aspx>. Accessed 8 March 2009.

Thompson, J. (2008) 'Woolworths' toy suppliers battle for unpaid millions', *The Independent*, 4 December, 62.

Tracy, D. (2002) *Blue's Clues for Success* (Chicago: Dearborn Publishing).

Tschang, T. and A. Goldstein (2004) 'Production and Political Economy in the Animation Industry. Why Insourcing and Outsourcing Occur', Paper presented at the DRUID Summer Conference, *Industrial Dynamics, Innovation and Development*, Elsinore Denmark, June 14–16.

Tunstall, J. (1993) *Television Producers* (London: Routledge).

Turow, J. (1981) *Entertainment, Education and the Hard Sell* (New York: Praeger Publishing).

—— (1984) *Media Industries* (New York/London: Longman).

Turner-Laing, Laura (2007) (VP Global Digital and Music, Entertainment Rights), Interview, London, 25 September.

Umstead, R.T. (2009) 'N, Noggin to adopt parent net's family name', *Multichannel News*, 28 February, <http://www.multichannel.com/article/189298_Nick_Of_Time_For_Rebrand.php>. Accessed 2 March 2009.

Ursell, G. (1998) 'Labour Flexibility in the UK Commercial Television Sector', *Media, Culture and Society*, 20 (1), 129–54.

USGAO (2007) *Telecommunications: Issues Related to the Structure and Funding of Public Television* (Washington: United States Government Accountability Office).

Van den Berg, Chloe (2006) (Director of International, Entertainment Rights) Interview, London, 16 October.

Van Evra, J. (2004) *Television and Child Development*, 3rd edn (Mahwah: Lawrence Erlbaum).

Van Kollenburg, Jean-Loeck (2008) (Programme Buyer, Z@pp and Z@ppelin, Netherlands Public Broadcasting), Telephone Interview, 21 May.

Viacom (2008) *Annual Report Pursuant to Section 13 or 15 (d) of the Securities Exchange Act of 1934. For the Fiscal Year ended December 31, 2008*.

VLV (Voice of the Listener and Viewer) (2007) *The Future of Children's Television Programming. A Response by the Voice of the Listener and Viewer (VLV) to Ofcom's Consultation*, December, 2007, <http://www.ofcom.org.uk/consult/condocs/kidstv/responses/>. Accessed 1 June 2009.

Vogel, H. (2007) *Entertainment Industry Economics*, 7th Edition (Cambridge: Cambridge University Press)

Wagg, S. (1992) ' "One I Made Earlier": Media, Popular Culture and the Politics of Childhood', in D. Strinati and S. Wagg (eds) *Come on Down? Popular Media Culture in Post-war Britain* (London: Routledge), pp. 150–78.

Wainright, D. (2006) *Ready to Learn: Literature Review. Part 1: Elements of Effective Educational TV*, Annenberg School for Communication, University of Pennsylvania, <http://pbskids.org/read/research/television.html>. Accessed 28 October 2008.

Walker, S. (2002) 'Children's Programming: Back to School', September, *Television Business International*, <http://global.factiva.com/>, no pages given. Accessed 6 July 2009.

Waller, E. (2006) 'Teletubbies firm in JV with BBC Worldwide', *C21Media.net*, 21 September, <http://www.c21media.net/news/detail.asp?area=4&article=32264>. Accessed 31 March 2008.

—— (2007) 'Kabillion-Dollar Business', *C21Media.net*, 16 October, <http://www.c21media.net/common/print_detail.asp?article=38114>. Accessed 29 June 2009.

—— (2008) 'A Demanding Business,' *C21Media.net*, 4 March 2008, <http://www.c21media.net/features/detail.asp?area=2&article=40355>. Accessed 29 June 2009.

—— (2009) 'Kids L&M drives Chorion figures', 16 February, <http://www.c21media.net/news/detail.asp?area=4&article=47642>. Accessed 15 May 2009.

Walters, J. (2006) 'Saving Face: Inflections of Character Role-Play in *Shameless*', *Journal of British Cinema and Television*, 3 (1), 95–106.

Wartella, E. (1994) 'Producing Children's Television Programming', in J. Ettema and D.C. Whitney (eds) *Audiencemaking* (London: Sage), pp. 38–56.

Wasko, J. (2001) *Understanding Disney* (Cambridge: Polity).

Webb, J., T. Schirato, and G. Danaher (2002) *Understanding Bourdieu* (London: Sage).

Webdale, J. (2007) 'Disney enters Bunnytown', *C21Media.net*, 26 October, <http://www.c21media.net/news/detail.asp?area=4&article=38277>. Accessed 10 March 2009.

Wells, P. (2001a) 'Children's Cartoons', in G. Creeber (ed.) *The Television Genre Book* (London: BFI), pp. 105–7.

—— (2001b) 'Moral Panics', in G. Creeber, Toby Miller and John Tulloch (eds) *The Television Genre Book* (London: BFI Publishing), pp. 98–100.

—— (2006) *The Fundamentals of Animation* (Lausanne: AVA Publishing).

—— (2007) *Scriptwriting* (Lausanne: AVA Publishing).

Westcott, T. (2002) 'Globalisation of Children's TV and Strategies of the "Big Three"', in C. von Feilitzen and U. Carlsson (eds) *Children, Young People and Media Globalisation* (Göteborg: Nordicom), pp. 69–76.

Wildman, S. and S. Siwek (1987) 'The Privatization of European Television: Effects on International Markets for Programs', *Columbia Journal of World Business*, Fall, 71–6.

Williams, K. (2003) *Understanding Media Theory* (London: Arnold).

Wilson, Nick (2006) (Director of Children's Programming, Five) Interview, London, 28 November.

Winder, C. and Z. Dowlatabadi (2001) *Producing Animation* (London: Focal Press).

Winn, M. (1977) *The Plug-in Drug* (New York: Penguin).

Wood, A. (1997) 'Sidelines', *Broadcast*, 19 September, 19.

—— (2005) 'Comment- Children lead the way', *Broadcast*, 25 February, 16.

Wood, Anne (Founder) (2008) (Ragdoll Productions), Interview, Stratford-upon-Avon, 14 July.

Wood, Anne and Andrew Davenport (No Date) *Frequently Asked Questions*, <http://www.bbc.co.uk/cbeebies/teletubbies/grownups/faq.shtml>. Accessed 5 November 2008.

Wood, D. (2004) 'Flying the Flag for Animation', *Broadcast*, 15 October, 24–5.

Wood, Chris (2007) (Director of Children's Responses, Ragdoll Productions), Interview, Stratford-upon-Avon, 15 March.

Woolery, G. (1985) *Children's Television. The First Thirty-Five Years, 1946–1981, Part II, Live, Film, and Tape Series* (Metuchen/London: The Scarecrow Press).

Worldscreen (2003) 'Sesame Workshop's Gary E. Knell', *WorldScreen*, 1 April, <http://www.worldscreen.com/archives/register/288>. Accessed July 2008.

Wright, J., A. Huston, R. Scantlin and J. Kotler (2001) 'The Early Window Project: *Sesame Street* Prepares Children for School', in S. Fisch and R. Truglio (eds) *"G" is for Growing* (Mahwah: Lawrence Erlbaum), pp. 83–95.

Zanker, R. (2002) 'Tracking the Global in the Local: On Children's Culture in a Small National Media Market', in C. von Feilitzen and U. Carlsson (eds) *Children, Young People and Media Globalisation* (Göteborg: Nordicom), pp. 77–94.

Index